VALUES AND DEVELOPMENT: APPRAISING ASIAN EXPERIENCE

M.I.T. STUDIES IN COMPARATIVE POLITICS

Under the general editorship of Harold D. Lasswell, Daniel Lerner, and Ithiel de Sola Pool.

The Emerging Elite: A Study of Political Leadership in Ceylon, Marshall R. Singer, 1964.

The Turkish Political Elite, Frederick W. Frey, 1965.

World Revolutionary Elites: Studies in Coercive Ideological Movements, Harold D. Lasswell and Daniel Lerner, editors, 1965.

Language of Politics: Studies in Quantitative Semantics, Harold D. Lasswell, Nathan Leites, and Associates, 1965 (reissue).

The General Inquirer: A Computer Approach to Content Analysis, Philip J. Stone, Dexter C. Dunphy, Marshall S. Smith, and Daniel M. Ogilvie, 1966.

Political Elites: A Select Computerized Bibliography, Carl Beck and J. Thomas McKechnie, 1968.

Force and Folly: Essays on Foreign Affairs and the History of Ideas, Hans Speier, 1969.

Quantitative Ecological Analysis in the Social Sciences, Mattei Dogan and Stein Rokkan, editors, 1969. **Social Ecology** (paperback edition), 1974.

Euratlantica: Changing Perspectives of the European Elites, Daniel Lerner and Morton Gorden, 1969.

Revolution and Political Leadership: Algeria, 1954-1968, William B. Quandt, 1969.

The Prestige Press: A Comparative Study of Political Symbols, Ithiel de Sola Pool, 1970.

The Vanishing Peasant: Innovation and Change in French Agriculture, Henri Mendras, 1971.

Psychological Warfare against Nazi Germany: The Sykewar Campaign, D-Day to VE-Day, Daniel Lerner, 1971 (reissue).

Propaganda Technique in World War I, Harold D. Lasswell, 1971 (reissue).

Leader and Vanguard in Mass Society: A Study of Peronist Argentina, Jeane Kirkpatrick, 1971.

The Changing Party Elite in East Germany, Peter C. Ludz, 1972.

Technology and Civic Life: Making and Implementing Development Decisions, John D. Montgomery, 1974.

Values and Development: Appraising Asian Experience, Harold D. Lasswell, Daniel Lerner, and John D. Montgomery, editors, 1977.

VALUES AND DEVELOPMENT:
APPRAISING ASIAN EXPERIENCE

EDITED BY
HAROLD LASSWELL, DANIEL LERNER, AND
JOHN D. MONTGOMERY

The MIT Press
Cambridge, Massachusetts, and London, England

This book was set in IBM Composer Press Roman by The Blue Ridge Group, Ltd., and printed on R & E Book and bound by The Colonial Press Inc. in the United States of America.

Library of Congress Cataloging in Publication Data

Main entry under title:
Values and development.

    (M.I.T. studies in comparative politics)
    Papers from the 1971-1972 meetings of a continuing seminar sponsored by South East Asia Development Advisory Group.
    Includes index.
    1. Economic development—Congresses.
2. Underdeveloped areas—Urbanization—Congresses.
I. Lasswell, Harold Dwight, 1902- II. Lerner,
Daniel. III. Montgomery, John Dickey, 1920-
IV. Southeast Asia Development Advisory Group.
V. Series: M.I.T. studies in comparative politics
series.
HD82.V26   330.9'172'4   76-47529
ISBN 0-262-12074-7

CONTENTS

INTRODUCTION

This book is the product of a continuing seminar on development administration sponsored by SEADAG (South East Asia Development Advisory Group). During the year 1971-1972 the seminar met four times under the chairmanship of Harold D. Lasswell and produced a valuable set of papers and a sequence of illuminating discussions. To illustrate the benefits of continuing seminars as a mode of intellectual exchange and to preserve the contributions of this particular seminar, chairman Lasswell decided to publish this collection of papers and invited participants Daniel Lerner and John D. Montgomery (founding father of this continuing seminar) to join him as coeditors.

The papers in this book focus on the interaction of value systems with development policy and administration. They articulate and assess the array of problems that becomes salient whenever and wherever traditional values are confronted by demands for modernization. The underlying issues are much the same in all such confrontations, but the contexts in which they occur differ significantly, and the sequences through which they move toward success (or failure) vary greatly. Since most developing countries are making major decisions at the national level, the principal context for analyzing development policy and administration is the government. In most western societies at comparable levels of industrialization, its role as an instrument of modernization is greater today than at any previous time.

In the new nations of Asia, the government is the initiator, executor, and arbiter of virtually all development efforts. It allocates the nation's resources—natural, fiscal, technological, even human—and seeks to augment them by arrangements with richer nations. In the latter, where the private sector is strong, international relations, including development operations, often are conducted by individuals and corporations with or without government intervention. In developing countries, where the private sector typically is weak, the public sector tends to be the leading element and government the principal source of national guidance.

The exploration of development policy and administration in these diverse national contexts has led us toward the Lasswellian paradigm of the social process: Participants → seeking to maximize values → utilize institutions → affecting resources. In most societies participants seek to maximize at least these eight values: power, wealth, skill, enlightenment, well-being, affection, respect, rectitude. Values in this context are neither "attitudes" nor "behaviors" as defined in the conventions of empirical social research. They can be the object of systematic analysis and observation, however, when they are conceived in the Lasswell tradition as "preferred outcomes." Manifestations of such preferences, and of the efforts to advance them, are important as evidence of both individual and social purpose. They also can serve as useful indicators of the sources and consequences of development. Because of their elusive quality, values usually have been either assumed (in the case of "growth," for example) or ignored in the name of scientific neutrality in most of the literature on development. This volume is a tentative venture at remedying this deficiency.

Montgomery's introductory essay explores the possibility of identifying the arenas in which individuals and institutions express preferences that change at different levels and in different sectors of development. He presents a theoretical comparison of modernizing values in traditional, transitional, modern-industrial, and postindustrial societies, as they become manifest in agriculture, industry, education, and public health which provides a series of hypotheses that can be tested by observations of both "macro" and "micro" political behavior. Dominguez has aggregated data to show gross investments and changes in value systems under revolutionary leadership; he has drawn upon experience in China, the Soviet Union, and Cuba for comparative purposes, to demonstrate that changed value priorities can be observed and systematically compared at the macro political level. Maynard's study of value changes at the village level during a period of rapid development makes use of anthropological techniques applicable to the Lasswell paradigm. He then proceeds to test some of the other hypotheses proposed in Montgomery's essay and to draw conclusions that will have special interest for development administrators. Voelkner's data, also village based, define and compare value-related investments which he has identified by means of aerial photography and arranged in scalograms to show the sequence of their appearance. By this ingenious method, he, too, is able to identify dominant values at different stages of development. The Krug-Schwarz-Bhakdi essay reports briefly on six years of research on "investments" made at the village level in response to opportunities for modernization in Thailand. The focus of this study is on the behavioral manifestations of collective commitment. The research demonstrates the feasibility of using value-oriented behavior at the village level as a basis for programming government contributions to developmental goals to maximize the prospects of affirmative public response.

The amenability of values to objective observation and classification is further tested in Braibanti's essay, which retains the strongly theoretical flavor characteristic of his work, while allowing an equally strong practical skepticism about the knowability of values and about their role in institutionalization to surface. After reviewing the setting of values in developmental institutions, he explores empirical and phenomenological approaches to the identification of values in institutional behavior. He concludes that a really satisfactory means of creating and studying social organizations as servants of individual human purposes has yet to emerge. Undaunted by Braibanti's skepticism, Shanmughalingum uses contrasting values among different ethnic groups in Malaysia as a basis for analyzing the intended and real impact of the second development plan in rural sectors. Pyong-choon Hahm identifies changing value orientations in law and religion in Korea, restating the eight-fold classification applied earlier in the volume to such disparate countries as Cuba, China, the Soviet Union, Laos, Thailand, and Malaysia.

The two concluding essays present more general theories about the issues. Garry Brewer's analysis of the use of models provides a guide to further application of formal statements of value schemes and other developmental relationships. Lasswell's concluding essay describes a series of modes of interactions among values which are a continuing concern of policymakers charged with developmental responsibilities.

H.D.L.
D.L.
J.D.M.

VALUES AND DEVELOPMENT: APPRAISING ASIAN EXPERIENCE

1 TOWARD A VALUE THEORY OF MODERNIZATION
JOHN D. MONTGOMERY

Ultimate values are rarely a conscious preoccupation of modern administrators. Indeed, aloofness from such subjective and impalpable phenomena is a source of professional pride. This presumed value-oblivion
permits administrators to relegate overt value choices to philosophers
and politicians and to claim for their own judgments a computer-like
objectivity. In theory, administrative scientists are free to design systems
that will carry out any orders that are legally transmitted from an
authoritative source, however hateful such orders may be. In a democratic state, this professional self-denial is confirmed by a favorite claim
of elected officials that it is their métier to identify and translate collective private values into public laws and policies, leaving to administrators the function of carrying them out. It is a claim not rigorously
enforced by either party, but it serves as an insulator for both.

The mythical quality of this distinction between policy and administration has long been recognized. The actual power of administrators to
sabotage or veto policies they dislike is one of the main complaints of
those who believe that political leaders, speaking for the people, should
have their will executed without mediation. Nor do politicians always
scrupulously refrain from intruding upon the objective standards of
administrators. It could even be argued that legislators are least effective when dealing explicitly with values, and administrators least so
when they ignore them. No element of legislation is as vacuous as the
statements of public good that occur in preambles to legislation and
have no justifiable force; no administrator is as efficient in securing
public commitment to government programs as one who is attuned to
the values of his community.

In spite of the illusory quality of this dichotomy between policy and
administration, the concept itself has helped management science make
important contributions to human knowledge. It has suggested ways of
observing objective administrative behavior without regard to the substantive values of public policies. It has generated specialists in at least

three major classes or dimensions of administrative action: task performance, the development and observance of routines, and the building and preserving of institutions. Specialists in any of these three dimensions can claim to act in a value-free context. Public administration, in the sense of identifying efficient, effective, and equitable means of carrying out public policy, benefits from its studied indifference to conflicting values.

Development administration, however, cannot so easily evade values as relevant, and even central, issues. Oriented toward change, it is concerned in a special way with such managerial goals as efficiency, adequacy, and institutional stability. Its "tasks" include generating certain social responses that are considered essential to the modernizing purposes of a government—scarcely a value-neutral activity. Its "routines" have to encourage participation by citizens and groups whose behavior is to be influenced by programs of modernization. Its "institutionality" must incorporate linkages to a vast range of associations and enterprises that are not ordinarily the concern of public bureaucracies. In short, an important function of development administration is to influence the social behavior of citizens and groups whose active cooperation is a necessary element in modernization. Success in achieving this task is observed easily in the behavioral commitments of client-beneficiaries. For example, modern citizens are expected to build, manage, and operate factories, or to produce more and better food, to attend schools in order to gain and use relevant modern knowledge, or to engage in health practices that will keep their productivity and longevity high. The "modernized" performance of citizens as clients can be used as an indirect indicator of the success of development administration.

Modern behavior requires more than obedience to law. Even in industry, where technology has reduced complex tasks to a series of interrelated but simple chores, managers are not satisfied with workers who perform like zombies. Modernization demands of citizens in all fields the dynamic capacity for generating further changes. It requires active commitment and investment. If government is to take a leading role in modernization, its function must be more than one of securing compliance with new regulations or the acceptance of new, prepackaged technologies. To transcend these relatively passive forms of modern behavior, governments have to generate opportunities for citizens to make investments and take action that will produce benefits both for themselves and for society as a whole. In development administration a major link between individual behavior and public good is the opportunity government can create for citizens to improve their lives.

This point of view is not, of course, traditional in either economics or public administration. Development plans focus on other considerations like foreign exchange requirements, import substitution or export generation, input-output analysis of government programs, and inflation control. None of these elements seem to depend on such details as citizen behavior, values, motivations, or even administrative capacity. Planners may also be concerned with technological problems such as the feasibility of proposed industrial complexes, mineral exploitation schemes, or multipurpose dams. In rare cases national planning may even include some administrative choices, such as preferences for public enterprises over government agencies, or for an optimal location of new developmental ministries in the hierarchy of government. But in dealing with such issues, planners seldom devote very much attention to the behavioral aspects of development administration. How citizens participate in modernization, or the processes by which their acts of commitment are to be elicited, are taken for granted or left to chance. This aspect of the administrative process is the black box of development planners. It is a major source of program failure.

It is true that some forms of development require only elite participation. Large-scale enterprises and massive constructions can be produced by foreign technologies and equipment and still satisfy the criteria of cost-benefit feasibility. But even such projects ultimately depend on affirmative public support. Larger social outcomes like worker productivity, the effective use of new resources, and the application of surplus earnings to developmental investments are the multipliers of a government's initial efforts. These multipliers do not appear at all unless favorable decisions are made by large numbers of citizens who believe that their active commitments to development will serve them individually.

The conjunction between individual values and public purposes can convert a public option into an individual opportunity. From the individual's point of view, opportunity means a chance to act for the enhancement of one's values; from the government's, it means designing and conducting developmental programs so that they can convey valued benefits to large numbers of citizens. These relationships must not be conceived mechanistically because individual values are so differently interpreted and weighted and the opportunities that governments can offer vary so widely in different sectors of development. It is the essential nature of values that their manifestation in human life changes as they enter different spheres of action. As values emerge from the individual's inner consciousness and influence his behavior, they condition his institutions and eventually shape his environment. Indeed, the shaping and sharing of values is one definition of the art of politics. As people try to achieve valued outcomes through institutional processes, they make increasingly specific demands on the available resources, and their efforts shift from symbols and signs to acts, which in turn accumulate in the form of social change. Indicators of the presence and influence of values thus run the spectrum from the psychological evidence of individual change responses to the accumulated social behavior identifiable as the patterns of civic culture.

Governmental development programs influence, rearrange, commit, invest, and respond to values. They are usually conceived in discrete sectoral terms, of which the most important are industry, agriculture, education, and public health. They culminate in the changed institutional practices associated with changed values. In each case, therefore, planners have to use public investment to initiate action with the expectation that thousands or millions of supportive individual decisions will follow. These individual decisions involve many kinds of changes in the standards of productive behavior, the making of additive private investments in public opportunities, and new commitments to the processes and interactions of government. The shape of each decision to "change" depends on individual motives and choices. Collectively, these decisions produce new institutional behavior, but individually they depend on private role perceptions and value preferences. Each developmental sector requires a specific mixture of investments, innovative research and investigation, changes in the performance of routine functions, and broadening relationships to other participants. The incentives that modernizers or agents of change have to provide in order to elicit such behavior obviously vary for each of these roles. The conventional assumption that economic gain alone provides sufficient motives for change fails to accommodate the subtleties of these variations.

One way of exploring the various motivations to change is to examine how an individual may advance his own value position by participating in the modernization of those sectors considered essential to development. The Lasswell classification of values* is suited admirably to this task, because when it is applied to the major sectors of modernization (industry, agriculture, education, and public health), it permits

---

*Often denoted by the acronym PEWBSARD, for Power, Enlightenment, Wealth, well-Being, Skill, Affection, Respect, and rectituDe.

us to examine practically all forms of behavior which are considered modern. In the process, it also suggests new tasks for administrators who are concerned with generating opportunities as a means to modernization.

Industrialization is often taken to be the first step in modernization. But since its impact on human life is so important economically, its relationships to other value systems has often been obscured. Wealth is often thought to be the universal incentive in industrial endeavor, and indeed it is fairly easily converted to other values in the Lasswell inventory. It can buy power and skill. It can supply outward forms of affection and respect, and it seems to render enlightenment and rectitude superfluous. Power is perhaps the next most easily recognized value served by industrialization, since capitalists make such great efforts to control industrial production through conglomerates and mergers, without regard to whether efficiency or profit ensues. This drive for wealth and power is a sign (though not necessarily a socially useful one) of a ripening industrial sector. If these two "heavy" values are considered sordid, it may be comforting to note that the others are also present in modern industry.

Enlightenment motivates those numerous professional managers and industrial analysts for whom corporate behavior becomes a subject of absorbing fascination it itself. Well-being cannot be ignored in an era when plant safety standards are introduced under the pressure of unionism and public law, and when industry has to invest scarce resources in environmental protection. Skill values attract individual workers such as clerks and technicians to pursue exacting standards even in the absence of monetary incentives. Affection in its industrial form is loyalty, a value served in Japanese factories far more than in those of North America, but clearly also visible in early European phases of industrialization when family ("the putting-out system") and village units were used as the basis of production. Respect is involved in equal rights employment standards and in corporate decisions to support local charities, as well as the individual efforts of white-collar workers to climb the career ladder even when the economic rewards are marginal. Rectitude is an important element in corporate responsibility, the stability of contract relationships, and the effort to establish and protect standard brand names. The dominant values required for industrial modernization, however, especially in its early phases, seem to be wealth, power, and skill (WPS, for convenient reference).

A parallel inventory of the values involved in agricultural modernization shows an equally diverse variation in the possible motives for individual decisions. Again, wealth is the most obvious, its universality being reaffirmed even in the case of supposedly apathetic peasants whose orientation to the market economy is weakest. Indeed, much of the technology of the Green Revolution is based on the assumption that increased productivity will produce individual profits and thus supply an incentive for continuing innovation. Power is a less obvious value today in agricultural modernization, since the feudal basis for political dominance is declining as a result of larger social changes under way. Even so, it is noteworthy that the larger and more influential farmers tend to make the most effective use of new organizations and technologies to improve their local and national political positions. Certainly in well advanced agricultural systems, farming reaches a stage of consolidation and corporate organization that serves the same power values as these forms of behavior do in the industrial sector.

Enlightenment motivates those engaged in the scientific research and experimentation that leads to technological change. Well-being is an extremely important factor in the ongoing efforts to improve the quality of rural life in order to curb the rush to the overcrowded cities during the transition to modern society. Skill is a source of great pride among local farmers, variations in whose performance have been observed everywhere in the world, even when the basic technologies used are similar on adjacent farms. Affection in rural communities is often institutionalized about the abstraction of land ownership, the basis for family stability and a powerful incentive which land reform often converts to improved productivity. Respect is evident in every rural organization that uses cooperative activity to improve the condition of individual farms, yet also requires leadership in order to promote adherence to collective goals and standards. Rectitude serves the same contract-stabilizing function in agriculture that it does in industry, especially during periods of increased emphasis on marketing and in the expansion of off-farm supporting services. In sum, the dominant values that serve as incentives to rural modernization seem to be wealth, well-being, and skill (WBS).

Modernization also affects individual decisions in the service sectors of society. In education and health, the values involved appear to be even more broadly distributed along the Lasswell spectrum. In the educational sector, power is displayed in the restrictions imposed as a means of limiting important positions to those with formal schooling, who, in turn, regard education as a passport to the elite ranks. This value also explains efforts to retain the elitist content of education in a society desperately needing widespread technical skills. Enlightenment, sometimes treated as the end of all education, obviously motivates both teachers and students, though not necessarily in comparable degrees. The direct correlation of wealth to education has been observed in every country. Income disparities are directly and positively related to educational disparities, and while the reasons for these relationships are circular, the facts are too obvious to overlook.

Education also serves the value of well-being, for both longevity and the capacity to enjoy the arts are directly associated with learning. Skill, including the conversion of knowledge to social benefit, is surely a supreme task of education, especially in transitional societies. Affection, which Lasswell has interpreted to include the capacity to transcend family and clan relationships in larger loyalties, takes the form of a civic culture or syndrome of social attitudes and political behavior that strongly seems to be conditioned by the educational process. Most societies accord respect to educated persons, and a major function of education during periods of rapid development is to convert a general deference to education into conditions favoring socially useful applications of knowledge. Rectitude is considered a function of education as much in traditional as in modern societies, but its developmental dimension arises from the need for reinforcing the habit of meeting obligations as these multiply into new social roles. Superficially, at least, the values of enlightenment, respect, and skill (ERS) seem dominant in education when it becomes a formal modernizing system.

Biomedical services represent another sector where values are important to development. Well-being is the individual value most clearly served by an effective health system. To practitioners, both wealth and enlightenment are also inducements to participate, and both require some government intervention to integrate private values and social ends. For instance, the private doctor-patient relationship is profitable to the doctor but inefficient in a developing society. Research on cancer and heart disease may be appealing to physicians desiring international recognition but is less likely to serve the underdeveloped world than similar efforts devoted to nutrition. Power obviously induces some to enter medical school because they enjoy the responsibility for making decisions about the essentials of life. It also explains the powerful influence of organized medicine in public affairs and presents challenges to development planners and administrators concerned with linking private values to public policy. One approach is through systematic attention to the development of skills—those of nurses, dressers, and paramedical personnel especially—to provide essential services to the masses not served by physicians in developing countries.

The appeal of values of affection can also challenge the loyalties and humanitarian concerns of medical personnel expected to serve in remote areas. Respect, too, is an important incentive in medical service—the "my-son-the-doctor" syndrome is not exclusively an American phenomenon. And probably no profession is more concerned with rectitude and the ethics of innovation than the biomedical group. The dominant individual values as incentives to modernization in the public health sector seem to be well-being, skill, and affection (BSA).

This somewhat mechanical recital of the value complexes abstractly present in these four developmental sectors is intended to show the range of choices that individuals have in pursuing developmental opportunities. Planners tend to assume that wealth is the sole motivator in industry and agriculture, enlightenment in education, and well-being in public health. Consequently, developmental administrators have not considered systematically either the other value resources available for broadening citizens' motivation to engage in modernization or their implications for the design of new technological systems in these four modernizing sectors.

Economic motivation alone cannot provide the basis for developmental choices when private gain fails to accommodate public benefit. Some manipulation of the market system is possible in the public interest, but the social costs would be prohibitive if the government were to intervene economically in every sphere of human behavior affected by a developmental plan. Governments have to rely on values other than wealth to provide incentives to modernization. Politicians rely on various forms of exhortation, but administrators must be more systematic in relating their programs to the value preferences of the citizens they seek to influence.

For development planners, the most desirable citizen behavior involves various forms of individual investment in opportunities for modernization, although other forms of commitment, both passive and active, are also necessary. Economists define developmental investments as the provision of labor and capital or the forgoing of immediate gains in the interest of future wealth. They are able to measure the degree of effort represented by each such investment entirely in monetary terms, and they can also compute its productive utility. Political scientists have enlarged the perspective by considering the regularity with which wealth can be invested to bring a power return, as when industrialists use their added economic resources to gain political ends.

Sociologists can demonstrate that wealth also brings respect, especially during periods of transition in the aftermath of industrialization. The interrelationships among these three "heavy" values (WPR) constitute a major political issue in industrial societies. In traditional preindustrial societies, on the other hand, a quite different set of relationships can be observed. Here the basic value available to governments for encouraging modernizing investments is respect, which defines the source of both power and wealth among elites and also depends on rectitude for the attitudes of affection (loyalty) upon which the system depends. In such societies, the convertability among respect, rectitude, and affection (RDA) constitutes a major political issue. But transitional, that is, slightly industrialized, societies are characterized by displacements in these very relationships. In these societies, the emergence of new sources of power and wealth, and the reliance on skill as the means of converting enlightenment to wealth are found. Although changes are constantly taking place in the social configuration of value systems, the redefinition of enlightenment, skill, and well-being (ESB) is probably the most important single source of cultural dislocation during periods of rapid development.

Development could be grossly characterized as a successive displacement and reconciliation among heavy value sets, in a sequence of modernization from RDA through ESB, arriving at a moving modern stage in which PWR dominates. Even this stage is not a permanent social order. In the utopian postindustrial society described by many of the present American and European protest movements, the values BAR (well-being, affection, and respect) appear to be on the rise, though this judgment may prove faulty if modern technology fails to solve its most pressing problems.

If it is grossly true that different value clusters are ascendant during different periods in the process of change, it follows that the task of the development administrator in inducing people to take advantage of the opportunities to develop will also change. For despite the fact that all individual values can be found in all societies and that all values serve to motivate performance in each sector, it is also evident that the dominant mixture of values is different both in the different sequences of development and in the different sectors in which modernization takes place. Developmental programs seeking to enlist public commitments must, therefore, differentiate among the values to which they appeal in industry, agriculture, education, and health. They must also respond to different values dominant at the various phases of development. Table 1.1 lists some plausibly dominant values for motivating the forms of mass behavior considered modern in each of these four sectors as development proceeds.

Industry

The industrial worker in a traditional society has to develop a variety of skills to move from family to factory production, and the skills themselves take on their own value subsets in terms of self-discipline and effectiveness independently of the economic motive. In a transitional society, wealth may be a latent value, but power becomes an equally important concern as workers begin to find themselves at a disadvantage in confronting management. The power motive expands to a larger political arena as unions seek to influence elections and lawmaking and at the same time, labor seeks respect and respectability. In

Table 1.1
Value-Related Motivations for Mass Adoption of Modern Practices

Society/Sector	Industry	Agriculture	Education	Health and Biomedical Sciences
	(WPS)	(WBS)	(ERS)	(BSA)
Traditional (RDA)	SW	RS	DR	RA
Transitional (ESB)	WP	WS	SB	BW
Modern (Industrial) (PWR)	PR	EW	EW	BD
Post-Modern (BAR)	BR	EB	BA	RA

The values:
Power, Englightenment, Wealth, well-Being, Skill, Affection, Respect, rectituDe.
The hypotheses:
1. Industry is least compatible with the value structure prevailing in traditional societies and most compatible with those of modern and post-modern societies.
2. The principal motivating values in agriculture are compatible with some dominant values and exist in all societies.
3. Mass-motivating values in education also change over time and are most compatible with dominant values in transitional and post-modern societies.
4. Gaining popular commitment to modern health practices involves identical motives in traditional and post-modern societies although the technologies are different.
5. W is the dominant value in 6 of these 16 situations; B in 6; R in 6; S in 4; A in 3; and P, E, and D in 2.
6. In traditional societies, the search for R is a more powerful motive for mass modernization than that for W or P; in transitional societies, W B or S. In modern societies, W and E are the most general mobilizing values; the utopian post-modern society is expected to restore B A R.
7. No single value appears dominant in any society as a mobilizing factor in all four sectors; nor is any single value dominant in any one sector at all stages of modernization.

the hypothetical post-modern era, when presumably industrial productivity has diminished the urgency of wealth accumulation and a more humane welfare state has succeeded capitalist or socialist polities, the values of well-being and respect supposedly will dominate the motives of industrial workers.

Agriculture

Respect is a dominant value in traditional societies in which farming, private or feudal, is an esteemed calling, and the introduction of modern techniques would presumably draw on skill values and link them together with those symbolized by respect. Skill remains a key value in transitional agriculture, marked by the rise of market activities and the appeal of wealth. Modern agriculture involves greatly increased use of modern science and technology, drawing on the farmers whose enlightenment values can be linked to wealth incentives. In the utopian ecology-minded post-modern phase, enlightenment remains a key value, but the pursuit of wealth is supposedly to be replaced by the more humanitarian concern for general well-being.

Education

This function is strongly associated with conservative values of respect and rectitude in traditional societies. They gradually yield to concerns of skill development (literacy especially) and well-being (improved living conditions) as the young prepare themselves through schooling to take leading roles in the transition to more modern living. In the modern industrialized societies, education is a source of wealth, but an equally important motivating value is the desire for enlightenment, especially in the physical and applied sciences. In our imaginary post-modern age, education is expected to assume a function less change-oriented, and more closely associated with humanitarian values like well-being and affection.

Public Health

Biomedical sciences, an important source of modernization, appeal to respect (for human life and dignity) and affection (in the sense of encouraging individual behavior that will benefit the community) in traditional societies where the most important public health needs are those of sanitation and social hygiene. In transitional societies, when individual lives are subject to the stress of change, health involves a concern for well-being and an important motive to the adoption of modern precautions in the interests of productivity (wealth). In modern societies, well-being, especially through industrial and mine safety programs and their equivalents, remains an important concern, and observance of health standards becomes a matter of moral obligation (rectitude), as manifested by such social concerns as those leading to prohibition, anti-smoking campaigns, quarantine of disease, and the intervention of government in such hitherto private concerns as narcotics use and food and nutritional standards. If a post-modern style of organization ever appears in the biomedical sector, it will presumably appeal to respect values, permitting greater individual freedom in choice of life styles (including the use of drugs), and to those of affection (in which humanitarian loyalty replaces obligation and coercion as incentives to make use of modern medical knowledge).

Placing the sectoral motivations in this time sequence, impressionistic as it is, makes it possible to suggest which sectoral values conform most closely to the dominant values of a given society, and to predict which developmental tasks a government will find easiest to promote through reliance on the social reinforcement of responses to opportunities. Some of the hypotheses suggested by this approach are stated below the matrix in Table 1.1.

Any attempt to convert this matrix to the practical needs of the development administrator will, of course, have to begin with empirical analysis. Some form of empirical verification will always be required to discover, in any given context, which individual values could be used as a basis for generating the developmental opportunities that are likely to elicit mass support.

Empirical verification is not instantly at hand, however. If value-related investments were to be compared on the basis of published data aggregated nationally, the assumed shifts in priority that accompany different stages of development could be tested by making comparative international studies. Unfortunately, only a few of the existing national indicators extend far enough across time to permit us to measure those changes in priorities that actually occurred as development proceeded. Some such data do exist. We can ascertain that societies engaged in increased efforts to promote wealth as they proceeded into modern industrialization. For example, changes in the rate of infrastructure investments such as railroads and roads, and steel and energy production show such efforts. So do rates of change in the proportion of the population earning wages in the industrial sector. Similarly, investments in power could be revealed by statistics on the proportion of the population in military service and on defense expenditures per capita or as a percentage of GNP.

Other data are less satisfactory. Rectitude would be reflected in various measures of the application of legal standards to private transactions, by church memberships or attendance, and by other indicators of the systematic observance of individual rights. Even respect, difficult as it is to observe as a national phenomenon, could be revealed in the relaxation of government restrictions on political activity, the degree of freedom of the press and of the opposition, ethnic (linguistic) equality, and the competitiveness of the political party system—all of which appear in the standard tables of world indicators. Affection, as defined here, could be inferred generally from existing data on the frequency of protest demonstrations and political assassinations (negative indicators) and the absence   of social tension. Well-being and enlightenment indicators are more obvious, and could be found in various records of medical services and nutritional adequacy and standard communications and educational data. Measurements of skill investments would include the degree of improvement in human resources and literacy and the degree of "modern outlook" as reported in the standard abstracts of social indicators.

For the moment, however, the want of adequate longitudinal records of most of these data discourages any major attempt to explore and test the hypotheses above. It would be possible to cluster countries at different supposed stages of development to compare the factors and test the hypothesized priorities among them, but the difficulty of converting the gross national data to comparable form so that they would indicate relative levels of real effort makes this approach unpromising.

A more promising method, still retaining national data as indicators, would be to study situations in which time has been foreshortened: that is, where accurate data exist far enough back in history to permit scholars to make longitudinal surveys of value-related investments. The revolutionary case—China and Cuba, for example—permits us to examine social change from an early transitional period to post-revolutionary times. Some "distortions" doubtless occurred in the assigning of investment priorities in these countries, because the decision-making has been concentrated for so long in the hands of a few traditionalists or ideologues; but the general hypothesis regarding the shifting basis of social commitment to values at different stages of development can be confirmed by such studies as Jorge Dominguez's in this volume.

Shifts in modernizing public investments should be still more evident when observed at local levels, where individual behavior is so closely related to community purposes, and where different units can be directly compared on the basis of raw data because of cultural similarities and opportunities. Paul Maynard's anthropological study of the Mieng Phuong village cluster in Laos precisely fits those specifications. It

applies the three behavior indicators described above (standards acceptance, individual investment, and new commitments to civic processes)
to the Lasswell value categories in order to test the hypothesized relationships. By using aerial photographs and census data, Harold E.
Voelkner has constructed a Guttman scale showing developmental
sequences and also classified observable physical investments and shifting occupational activities according to the proposed value analysis. The
resulting data permit him to offer an imaginative test of the hypothesized changes in value-related activity associated with development.

The intensive studies by Dominguez, Maynard, and Voelkner do provide important insights into the problems of change, but they are
neither recurrent nor easily reproducible. Converting these insights into
instruments of policy is a task political scientists have only begun to
perform. The only systematic effort to develop information relating
administrative "outputs" to social "outcomes" in the form of popular
investments in development is now under way in Thailand. Robert E.
Krug, Paul Schwarz, and Suchitra Bhakdi present evidence showing that
investing behavior in thousands of villages can be observed through
governmental reporting channels. As this book goes to press, a Thai
government agency is preparing to make programing decisions on the
basis of this evidence. Individual behavior aggregated about developmental opportunities is slowly becoming a measurable factor in the
analysis of social change.

The hypothesized relationships are for the most part sustained
empirically by the methods presented in this volume. The actual forms
of investments made by the masses taking advantage of the opportunities for modernization may not be motivated consciously in terms of
values, but in most cases the relationship is clear enough so that it can
be determined from both direct observation and the results of surveys.

A further hypothesis that administrators who structure their
developmental programs in terms of opportunities are more effective in

securing favorable popular responses than those using coercive or other regulatory means is also subject to verification by comparative field studies. It should even be feasible to examine the beliefs of development administrators regarding the reasons for public adoption of desirable practices in order to determine whether those most conscious of the range of values that motivate development are also the most effective in designing their programs to elicit the greatest response.

If this behavioral orientation to development administration were to become a serious dimension of national planning, governmental organization itself would gradually begin to display new properties. Just as organization theory has succeeded in maximizing efficiency in task performance, adequacy in administrative routines, and stability and flexibility in institutions, so we can anticipate that an empirical science could emerge to improve the capacity of public agencies to mobilize popular commitments to development. The general outlines of such an organizational approach can be projected on the basis of experience in participative management.

The proposed approach differs from conventional public administration in that it treats civil servants as sources of reform and as reinforcers of innovation. It would require them to share many of the privileges and responsibilities of developmental decisionmaking with individual citizens or client groups. A new organizational objective would be not merely to encourage citizen participation for its own sake, but to make use of administrative resources to maximize the rational processes of decisionmaking by which individual citizens commit themselves to the opportunities for self-improvement created by a government's programs of modernization. These processes depend on value orientations that cannot be left exclusively to theorists and legislators if governments are to make the most effective use of the most abundant resource potential a developing nation can possess, the affirmative commitment of its own citizens.

2 REVOLUTIONARY VALUES AND DEVELOPMENT PERFORMANCE: CHINA, CUBA, AND THE SOVIET UNION
JORGE I. DOMINGUEZ

Introduction

Are revolutions good? Revolutionary government performance is evaluated on eight basic values of social life and four modes of their enjoyment.[1] *Power* is the participation in decisions about severe sanctions, or the capacity to change outcomes. *Enlightenment* involves knowledge, insight, and access to information. *Skill* is the proficiency in any practice—in arts and crafts, in trades or professions. *Wealth* is income, including both goods and services. *Well-being* includes both health and safety. *Respect* includes status, honor, recognition, prestige, glory, or reputation. *Rectitude* comprises the moral values of virtue, goodness, and righteousness. *Affection* includes love, friendship, and loyalty.

Security is the expectation that this value enjoyment will last. *Liberty* is the ability to act according to one's own personality without an undue effort at self-denial, and without subjection to undue external constraints. *Equality* of both opportunity and result entails the fairly even distribution of both access to, and actual possession of, values among individuals in a social system. *Growth* entails the increase of the current stock of any one value.

The focus of this essay is on three countries which have experienced large-scale turnovers in virtually all spheres of life. Political incumbents have been replaced. Social relations have been altered drastically. New economic systems have been fashioned. New belief systems have given new shape, order, and purpose to these transformations. Several different processes have been involved. The old order has been destroyed and replaced by the new. Elites in the new political system have had to mo-

An earlier version of this essay was the basis for my remarks at the Annual Meeting of the American Society for International Law, Washington, April 1973; they appeared in the *Proceedings*. A revised version of those remarks has been published in *Worldview*, July 1973. I am grateful to Timothy Colton, Lincoln Gordon, Daniel Lerner, Carmelo Mesa Lago, John D. Montgomery, and Lucian Pye for comments on earlier versions.

bilize instruments of support—political, symbolic, economic, coercive— to carry out their policies.[2] The task of this essay is to assess the performance of these political systems in the "early" periods of their rule. No more than their first two decades of rule are covered.

Hypothesis

Revolutionary political systems are consummatory systems. Political cultures can be classified as consummatory or instrumental according to their response to change. Consummatory cultures link most social relationships to rectitude as a value, and ascribe moral meaning to most behavior patterns. Instrumental cultures do not evaluate social conduct in terms of wider, transcendental meanings but only in terms of more narrow and particular ones. All spheres of life—social, political, economic, familial, religious—are linked under a common standard of rectitude in consummatory systems; they tend to be more segregated in instrumental systems. Gratification in daily life in consummatory systems follows from the transcendental values associated with an act; in instrumental systems, gratification in daily life is more likely to follow from the practical ends achieved by the act. In an instrumental system, there may be widespread differentiation and pluralism in the political, social, and economic systems; this is much less likely in consummatory systems. Consummatory systems are found both in traditional and in modernizing revolutionary societies.[3]

Revolutionary governments emphasize goals in four performance areas: power, rectitude, affection, and skill. These are linked and seen as necessary to the system's functioning. The greater the emphasis on the expansion and concentration of power and on modern skills distinguishes revolutionary from traditional consummatory systems, while the stress on a unified, pervasive standard of rectitude distinguishes revolutionary from instrumental modern or modernizing systems.

Revolutionary governments seek to centralize power and rectitude, and private, non-governmental bases of political power are attacked. Churches, sects, and other sources of nongovernmental standards of morality also are attacked. Hence the equality of distribution of resources in power and rectitude is reduced, and affection and rectitude also are deprivatized. Public policy emphasizes the public life and is not embedded in traditional familial relationships. Standards of morality are transferred from the private to the public arenas. The revolutionary system seeks other values, but these four are necessary and decisive.

Revolutionary governments emphasize growth in power and skill. Growth in power becomes the prerequisite for changes in all other value spheres. Political participation, under controlled conditions, is stimulated to provide new power resources which, in turn, challenge the more traditional and established power resources. Political education, propaganda, and internal security are professionalized and increased. Skill is emphasized to provide the means with which to operate the political, economic, and social systems effectively over the long run. Technical training, therefore, receives considerable emphasis.

A revolutionary government will probably emphasize equality above other values in its earliest years, both to seek social justice and as a payoff for the political support which brought it to power, but it need not continue to emphasize this equality, either in the long run or even by the end of the first decade of revolutionary rule. Other tasks may claim its attention and physical resources. Liberty as a mode of enjoyment will probably be sacrificed, because it becomes an obstacle to the achievement of many other goals.

Such a political system seeks and welcomes economic growth. Drastic policies may be implemented to achieve growth and other values may be sacrificed to it. But the system's basic features can survive during the first two decades either in the absence of economic growth, or in the presence of a very erratic growth pattern. Revolutionary governments survive partly because of the power monopoly, partly because of the zeal of public rectitude, and partly because such governments typically spend much time recovering from prerevolutionary economic dislocations and international hostility. They may, therefore, be allowed a "grace period" of limited or erratic economic growth by their peoples. A revolutionary system may also welcome and seek growth and greater equality in enlightenment, respect, and well-being. These are not essential, however, and may be sacrificed. Enlightenment, for example, could cause political difficulties for the regime. Its benefits appear to be derived from an investment in skill, and the system will choose to stress skill more than diffused enlightenment. Respect will be emphasized if it does not threaten the dominant groups. Revolutionary systems are expected to be in nearly constant motion, especially but not only during the early years. Therefore, the pattern of security as a mode of enjoyment is likely to be erratic.

Value Performance in the Soviet Union
and the People's Republic of China

From the earliest years of revolutionary rule, both China and the Soviet Union increased their educational enrollments. The Chinese increase in primary school enrollment was particularly impressive in the first half decade. The number of secondary general schools (including the agricultural middle schools) grew faster than their vocational schools. The growth in the number of agricultural schools explains the difference, and suggests a skill orientation, also important in higher education. The early Soviet stress was on polytechnic studies in primary and secondary education. Academic studies have come to play a more prominent role only since the early 1930s. There has been considerable growth in the educational system at various levels. Urban rural gaps are still significant in both countries, but efforts to spread education in the rural areas also appear to be strong.[4]

The long term pattern of well-being, especially in the Soviet Union, seems quite impressive. However, well-being values have received seconadary or residual priority compared to wealth or power values. Patterns of well-being in China also are reported to be quite favorable. However, some studies have suggested important interruptions in the growth of well-being during the considerable economic and political preoccupations of the 1950s and 1960s.[5]

Growth in respect for women has been an important though qualified outcome of both Chinese and Soviet revolutions. The economic participation rate of Soviet women is high, close to twice the U.S. level. However, most Soviet women are employed in unskilled work. The proportion of women in the higher professional echelons decreases as rank advances, even in fields where women predominate, such as education and health. The Soviet government has allocated considerable resources to the expansion of child-care facilities, but these have not met the demand. The political role of women within the party, or in the Central Committee, has been very marginal. As the importance of political ranks increases, the proportion of women decreases.[6]

Although the data for China are poorer, the trends appear to be similar. The revolutionary government sought to increase the participation of women in the work force, and successfully opened administrative and supervisory positions to women in places of work where both sexes worked together—a sharp break from the traditional pattern. However, women continue to be employed disproportionately in lower ranked jobs. The expansion of child-care services was slow, and the evidence suggests an erratic pattern during the 1950s. Women also were engaged more in politics than before revolutionary rule, but there is once again an inverse relationship between political power rank and the proportion of women at that rank.[7]

Respect for women and affection patterns were changed in other ways. The divorce rate was negligible in traditional China and Tsarist Russia, but increased significantly in both countries during the early years. Over the longer term, however, it has stabilized in the Soviet Union. Women are less embedded in traditional family relationships and more engaged in production. The state emerged as a new focus of loyalty, and affection became deprivatized, despite opposition, as a matter of policy. The efforts to change the fundamental character of the Soviet family have receded since the mid-1930s. It is interesting to note that two-thirds of families responding to a large survey of Soviet refugees in the early 1950s believed that the cohesiveness of their family had been affected by Soviet policies.[8]

Respect for non-Russian ethnic groups has not increased in the Soviet Union since the revolution. Russification, both linguistic and cultural, was most extreme under Stalin, but it both preceded and succeeded him. The trend in the 1920s was toward an increase of political respect for non-Russian nationalities, and the Russian share of party membership declined. These trends, however, stopped by the end of the 1920s, to be resumed after Stalin. The proportion of Russians in the party was the same in 1927 and 1961, and in both years it was greater than would be expected from their share of the population.[9] The term "Han imperialism" in China suggests that many of the same problems exist there. The revolt in Tibet in the 1950s, for example, shows a lot of discontent. The Soviet and Chinese efforts to control the linguistic and cultural minorities stem also from strategic considerations, for these minorities are concentrated overwhelmingly along their borders. Whatever the cause, respect for non-Chinese and non-Russian nationalities has been held in check. One of the effects of the Cultural Revolution was the minorities' further loss of power and cohesiveness.[10]

In both countries, rectitude has been transformed by the curtailment of nongovernmentally controlled religion and the rise of ideological standards of morality under government supervision. The Soviet Union nationalized landed and other Church property and the schools. Anti-religious propaganda developed around 1922, and continued until about World War II, although the attacks on the Russian Orthdox Church as an institution abated first in the late 1920s.[11]

In China, Confucianism had strong secular components and, with but a brief exception before World War I, has not been conceived of as a church. The approximately three million Chinese Christians at the time of the coming to power of the Communists were a small share of the population. Their links with the West were cut off and Christian churches were attacked as institutions. The possibility of founding "national" Christian churches, however, suggests that religion, strictly defined, has been permissible at times. Buddhism did not have an all-China ecclesiastical structure; monasteries tended to be autonomous. Buddhism was not a missionary or evangelizing religion in modern China. The Chinese Buddhist Association, sponsored by the government and party, has established considerable control over the previously dispersed monastic communities. The scope of Buddhist activity has been restricted, and Buddhist doctrine has been reinterpreted to fit the new conditions. The slow disappearance of Buddhism as an autonomous institution and set of beliefs has been the chief trend.[12]

In both China and the Soviet Union, Islamic communities were perceived more as national than as religious entities. In the Soviet Union, therefore, this meant that Islamic peoples and institutions may have suffered less from political attack than Orthodox Christianity in the 1920s. Under Stalin, however, Russification merged with antireligious propaganda to lead to a significant attack on Islamic institutions and communities until World War II and Stalin's death.[13]

A new public morality based on ideology has arisen in both the Soviet Union and China. The official ideology in both countries seeks vigorously to inculcate a homogeneity of beliefs, perspectives, and symbols among the citizenry, and to achieve a "moral unity" of the people.

The authority to interpret this morality falls to the party and its leadership. Rectitude is deprivatized, precisely because a public standard of rectitude, admitting no competition, is now essential. Toward the end of the early revolutionary period, the Soviet Union slid into Stalinism; China, into the Cultural Revolution. Though the responses differ (emphasis on economic growth at the expense of socialist man, or emphasis on such a "new man" at the expense of other values), the crisis of public rectitude is common to both.

By the beginning of the First Five Year Plan in 1928, the Soviet economy had finally reached the pre-World War I total economic output. Impressive though this achievement was, it also suggests no economic growth from the Tsarist government's baseline in the first decade of revolutionary rule. There was no uninterrupted upward trend either. There were gains but also setbacks. The vigorous debate over industrialization in the mid-1920s highlighted the weaknesses and backwardness of the Soviet economy.

If the economic pie had not grown from a Tsarist baseline, the existing wealth may have been more equally distributed. Income inequality in the Soviet Union during the late 1920s was less than in 1914 Tsarist Russia. Inequalities were still less in the late 1920s relative to the early 1920s—a trend which was not interrupted until midway in the First Five Year plan. During the 1930s, income inequalities widened steadily. However, in the early years, the trend was toward an equality of wages within a level of aggregate wealth not yet above prewar levels.[14]

China's net domestic product per capita, in constant prices, was approximately the same in 1952 as in 1933. The country was able to recover quickly from its international and civil wars. There was impressive growth during the First Five Year Plan. The economic effect of the Great Leap Forward, however, was disastrous. Net domestic product in constant prices—without population controls—actually declined to a

1961 trough, to recover gradually thereafter. Thus, China's economy grew during the 1950s, but marked time thereafter. Net domestic product per capita (constant prices) on the eve of the Cultural Revolution was about what it had been on the eve of the Great Leap Forward. It was still below the 1958 peak, though well above the eve of the First Five Year plan. In sum, there was net growth, but the pattern was highly erratic, marked by ups and downs, with the ups outweighing the downs on balance.

Data on income equality are difficult to evaluate, although it seems that rural incomes may have increased relative to urban incomes, and though large differentials continue. Wage differentials within the industrial sector have been less extreme than in the Soviet Union. The 1950-1960 trend has been toward greater wage equalization, even though there were negative aggregate growth rates.[15]

One of the most significant political innovations of this century has been the Leninist party. The political creativity of the Bolshevik revolution included the growth of power at the political center through the organized and controlled expansion of political participation. This method, though different in detail, was replicated in both China and Cuba. Old, often weak power was overthrown; new, stronger and more centralized power appeared. Historical bureaucratic empires centralized power, but could not withstand the expansion of political participation in this scale. Political democratization in Western Europe and the English-speaking British Commonwealth had checked the centralization of power, and dispersed it as mass political participation expanded. The Leninist model, on the other hand, drastically centralized political power while expanding mass participation. The result was not only the growth of power and the loss of equality in power holding, but also the insurance of the long-term holding of power by the new rulers and the loss of liberty for many. These value losses are the costs of a remarkable political achievement, a new way of organizing a political system.[16]

Value Performance in Cuba

Enlightenment and Skill
The revolution in Cuba has expanded its educational scope and domain. More people are now affected by education than ever before. Education is less age-specific than it had been and is now perceived to be relevant to a larger number of issues than before, from the running of the home to the running of the government. In 1961, the government sought to eradicate illiteracy.[17] The gains of that year have been consolidated thereafter. The 1953 census reported that 23.6 percent of the population over ten years old was illiterate (11.6 percent in the cities and 41.7 percent in the countryside). By the end of 1961, the estimate of illiteracy for the adult population was 3.9 percent.[18]

The highest reported primary school enrollment for prerevolutionary Cuba (1958) was 883,884. This figure included public, "superior" public, and private primary school enrollment. Elementary school student enrollment per 1000 population rose from 135 in September, 1958, to 176 in September, 1968 (or a real growth per capita of 30.4 percent for the decade). Primary school enrollment per population had declined from the 1920s to the 1950s. The revolution helped to reverse a process of decay and begin a process of growth. Cuba had approximately 82,500 private and public academic secondary school students in 1958, or 12.6 per 1000 population. This ratio in 1968 was 23.1. Thus the real growth per capita of secondary education was 83.3 percent for the decade.[19] Enrollment in public secondary, technical, and professional schools per 1000 population rose from 2.38 in 1958 to 5.69 in 1968 (or 139.0 percent). Primary and secondary school enrollment growth indicates long-term security, that is, increasing certainty that the literacy campaign was not a passing event but the beginning of a lasting commitment.

There have also been impressive shifts in geographic equality. According to the 1953 census, 43 percent of the population lived in rural areas;

in the 1970 census, it was 39.5 percent. In 1958-1959, only 30.7 percent of the teachers and 30.2 percent of all children enrolled in public primary schools were from rural areas. Because private schools were overwhelmingly urban, these statistics understate inequality. By 1959-1960, these figures were 42.2 percent and 39.4 percent respectively. By 1968-1969, 41.9 percent of all children enrolled in public primary schools were from rural areas. Thus there were more children in primary schools in the rural areas in the late 1960s than would be expected from their share of the population. The key efforts were made early in the revolutionary period, and they have been secured since then.

Class equality has also increased. Adult education schools for workers and peasants enrolled 72,912 in 1959-1960. Since 1961-1962 the minimum enrollment has been 425,000 students. These schools seek to improve the skills of the most previously skill-handicapped. The number of students receiving government scholarships rose from 75,023 in 1962-1963 to 197,623 in 1968-1969, for all levels of schooling from primary to higher education. These increases in numbers were the results of the government's attempt to reduce the economic obstacles to more education.[20]

However, university enrollment per 1000 population fell from 3.9 in 1958, to 3.5 in 1968 (excluding the preparatory schools for workers and peasants, which the Cuban government normally includes in its higher education statistics, but which should be considered as a sign of growth in skill and more equality—not of higher education). At the level of higher education, there is a strong skill orientation. All statistics are for students per 1000 population between 1958-1959 and 1968-1969. Enrollments fell in the humanities (most of which had been in law) from 0.66 to 0.15; and in economics from 0.93 to 0.15. This may help explain Cuban economic problems in the late 1960s. Enrollment in the Teachers' College marked time, from 0.77 to 0.82. In contrast, enrollments rose in the natural sciences from 0.25 to 0.39; in engineering from 0.51 to 0.82; in medicine from 0.60 to 0.90; and in agronomy from 0.18 to 0.27.[21]

Lack of liberty is another problem in the educational domain. Even scholars sympathetic to the Cuban revolution have noted that "the method of instruction could best be described as [a] catechistic-authoritarian, teacher-centered approach characterized by a single teacher talking at a class of passive students." For the population as a whole, the amount and variety of information have declined. In 1956, Cuba's daily newspaper circulation per 1000 population was 129; in 1967 it was 78. In the 1960s, moreover, the government had a monopoly of information. During the 1950s, although there was press censorship, it was weak and porous. Even Castro could publish his attack on Batista in the leading national news magazine![22]

Well-being

The record on well-being is even more complex. The rate of infectious diseases per 100,000 population (gastroenteritis, poliomyelitis, diphtheria, tuberculosis, tetanus, leprosy, measles, typhoid fever, and malaria) has declined from a peak in the first half of the 1960s. However, compared to the prerevolutionary years, leprosy, measles, and tuberculosis showed a rate per 100,000 population in the last reported year of the 1960s which was still higher than in the 1950s. Three other diseases increased during the 1960s and the last reported year showed the highest rates ever for brucellosis, syphilis, and hepatitis.

The mortality rate as a whole was 6.6 per 1000 in 1959. It rose to 7.3 in 1962 and stood at 6.6 again in 1968. The infant mortality rate, however, shows sharp swings. It was 34.5 per 1000 live births in 1959; rose to 39.6 in 1962; fell to 37.6 in 1966; rose again to 40.7 in 1968; and fell to 27.4 in 1973.[23]

The pattern of security is more complicated. The number of hospital beds rose from 36,141 (public and private) to 45,034. The number of beds per 1000 population was stationary: 5.52 in 1958 versus 5.58 in 1968. The number of medical doctors was 6,300 in 1958; close to half of these went into exile. By 1972, the number of medical doctors had reached 7,200. The total number of medical personnel rose from 19,722 in 1963 to 29,969 in 1967. These data argue for modestly increased levels of well-being in the long term, but there have been cutbacks in some health sectors where performance has been at its worst. The number of budgeted hospital beds allocated for the treatment of patients with tuberculosis fell from a high of 4,285 in 1963 to 3,556 in 1968. Those allocated for patients with leprosy fell from a high of 714 (same 1962 through 1965) to 461 in 1968. The rate of infection in these two diseases was worse in the 1960s than in the 1950s.[24]

Security of well-being has increased because of more thorough law enforcement. The murder and robbery rates per 100,000 population fell from 3.37 and 105.93 in 1960 to 1.14 and 93.10 in 1967, respectively. The absolute number of murders fell; the absolute number of robberies remained about the same. Crimes of violence declined both in the early and late 1960s. The decline in the number of crimes against persons was already 10.24 percent between 1958 and 1963.[25]

The pattern of equality is better, though modest. Rural hospitals accounted for 0.3 percent of the budgeted beds in general hospitals in 1958, 8.1 percent in 1962, 8.8 percent in 1966, and 9.5 percent in 1968. Havana province's share of hospital beds in public social assistance institutions for infants and the aged fell from 42.3 percent of real beds in 1965 to 39.6 percent of budgeted beds in 1967. Havana province's share of the population in the 1970 census was 27.3 percent; in 1953, it was 26.4 percent.

The ratio of all public hospital beds per 1000 population declined in Havana province from 14 in 1958 to 12 in 1969. But it rose in Camagüey province from 2.4 to 5.5, and in Oriente province from 1.6 to 3.7. The distribution of medical doctors evened out. From 1899 to

1943, the proportion of medical doctors in the province of Havana had been increasing. By 1955, 62.4 percent of all Cuba's doctors practiced in this province. By 1968, this proportion had fallen to 55 percent, and by 1971, to 42 percent. Thus a trend toward inequality of distribution was stopped and reversed.[27]

Though there has been a trend toward more equality of well-being, the high concentration in urban areas—and especially in Havana—persists. This trend—except for the distribution of medical doctors—was more striking in the earlier 1960s. It appears to have slowed down.

Respect

There was no equality of respect between blacks and whites in prerevolutionary Cuba. However, there was probably less inequality than in the United States, and there was considerable equality of opportunity. Blacks and mulattoes comprised 25.3 percent of the population in 1943 and 26.9 percent in 1953. Among the population aged 20 or older in 1943, blacks accounted for 29.2 percent of the known illiterates. In 1943, on the one hand, 5.8 percent of engineers in Cuba were black, as were 9.5 percent of medical doctors, and 11.9 percent of lawyers and judges. On the other hand, 36.3 percent of unskilled workers, and 55.7 percent of domestic servants were black.

In 1943, among professionals and semiprofessionals, 10.4 percent of the whites, but 19.7 percent of the blacks, earned less than 30 pesos a month; the respective statistics for unskilled workers were 37.3 percent and 50.9 percent; for agricultural workers, 51.7 percent and 62.0 percent.[28] Blacks scored lower in all income categories, controlled for all occupations, in 1943.

In Cuba, the revolutionary government struck down the rather few gains that had been realized, and acted as a deterrent toward greater equality. Most gains in respect (growth and equality) were realized in the early years of its existence, not later.

The revolutionary record is somewhat better on women. The government is committed to a women's "revolution within the revolution." The proportion of women in the economically active population (describing the respondents' principal activity during the prior year) increased from 10.2 percent in 1943, to 17.7 percent in 1969. The proportion of women in the labor force (describing the respondents' principal activity in the prior week) was 17.2 percent in 1953 and 23 percent in 1968.[29] The greater economic incorporation of women in the late 1960s can be explained entirely as a result of modernization. One could not tell a revolution occurred from looking at these statistics.

In a who's who of the Cuban elite at the end of World War I, women accounted for 5 percent of the membership of the Central Committee of the Communist party. Women had accounted for 4 percent of the Party's National Directorate in 1962, 13 percent of the party members in 1963, 7 percent of the delegates to the twelfth labor Congress in 1966, 15.5 percent of all directors and political instructors in party schools in late 1966, and 10 percent of all local government elected officials in 1967. Most women in leadership posts are in "women's jobs" such as Secretary to the Cabinet and Director of Child Care. The only woman in a non-sex-linked leadership position is Nora Frometa, current Minister of Light Industries.[30]

There has been, however, a significant growth in social services. The number of child care centers rose from 37 in 1961 to 332 in 1968. The number of children enrolled in them during this period rose by a factor of 16, from 2,415 to 38,702. Contraceptives are readily available in Cuba, and abortions are legal and performed in state hospitals.[31] In private life, however, relations between men and women, as reported by visitors, do not seem to have changed very much.[32]

Women may expect that the modest trends toward growth and equality in respect may be secure. Their security is also supported by a decline in the rate of rapes per 100,000 population, from 9.93 in 1960 to 5.22 in 1967.[33] There is also likely to be more growth in personal liberty as more women enter the work force, and as more child care, birth control, abortion, and related services become available. For some women, liberty also has increased because divorce has become easier. The rate of divorces per 100 marriages was 8.5 in 1959, 9.7 in 1962, and 18.1 in 1968.[34] These changes did not come about until the mid- and later 1960s. In sum, trends toward growth and equality in respect for women are most marked in the social sphere (though not in personal relations), some in economics, and least in politics. Women also have gained considerably in both security and liberty.

Affection

This discussion of affection is very tentative, because studies for a thorough evaluation of this performance area are lacking. A consequence of a higher divorce rate is that individuals may be less embedded in private relationships of either family or friendship. Indeed, the chief consideration in any discussion of affection in Cuba is the decline of the private affective spheres. Cuban men and women "fly to the assemblies." The assemblies and mass organizations intrude into their private affective lives. The Committees for the Defense of the Revolution have the effect of reducing the scope of the private sphere. Jose Yglesias noted that the members of these committees in a Cuban country town exhibited a "pushiness about people's lives: an insistence that the open life—open to the view of one's neighbors—is the natural life of man."[35]

Affective life also may have become politicized. In 1967, ten carefully selected young people working in an elite youth corps in the Isle of Pines were asked, "What qualities should the person you marry possess?" Five indicated that their spouse must be a revolutionary; two specified no other condition. The marriage rate has responded to politics, too.

The rate of marriages per 1000 population increased from 4.8 in 1959 to 10.7 in 1961 as the result of a vigorous government effort to legalize free unions and to combat illegitimate births. When this campaign abated, the marriage rate returned to 5.9 in 1966. The revolutionary offensive in 1968, however, renewed the zeal to legalize and record all private sex. The marriage rate jumped to 10.5 per 1000.[36] In sum, the divorce rate indicates the secular trend toward more liberty for women. The marriage rate shows the effect of government policies in private affective patterns. Marriage has become more of a political act than before, and non-marital sex has been politicized.

One's life may not be totally one's own. In December, 1964, Augusto Martínez Sánchez, Minister of Labor, attempted to commit suicide. He was officially criticized "because every revolutionary knows that he does not have a right to deprive his cause of a life which does not belong to him, and which can only be legitimately sacrificed facing the enemy."[37] Public affection operates often at the expense of private affection. Loyalty plays a larger role in affection than before. Ernesto (Che) Guevara noted:

Our vanguard revolutionaries must idealize their love for the people . . . They cannot descend with small doses of daily affection to the terrain where ordinary men put their love into practice. The leaders of the revolution have children who do not learn to call their father with their first faltering words; they have wives who must be part of the general sacrifice of their lives to carry the Revolution to its destination; their friends are strictly limited to their comrades in revolution. There is no life outside the Revolution.[38]

Among the effects of the Cuban revolution, therefore, may have been a decline of private affection, a decline in the security that private affection patterns will continue, and a decline in the liberty with which it is exercised.

Rectitude

Standards of rectitude are no longer left to the private sphere. They have been centralized and politicized, away from individuals and churches into the hands of party and government. Moral man in Cuba is judged by ideological standards. The criteria are public, not private, centrally shaped, not dispersed among many religious groups. Centralization and politicization have cut back drastically the degree of equality, security, and liberty available to those who dissent from the single, public, revolutionary standard of rectitude.

The greatest confrontations between the government and most of the churches are now past. The churches have been crippled and constrained. Cuba's institutionalization of rectitude, and the attack on competing standards of rectitude, has been more severe than in other Latin American countries. From 1926 to 1940, when church and state in Mexico were in combat, the number of priests in Mexico fell by 14 percent while the number of inhabitants per priest rose from 3,443 to 5,088. In Cuba, the number of priests dropped by 69 percent from 1960 to 1970, and the number of inhabitants per priest rose from 8,900 to 33,700. A fair proportion of the shift was the result of government-forced deportation.[39] However, antireligious work and propaganda in Cuba seems to have been much less than in other Communist countries. The Roman Catholic Church, the main Protestant churches, and remaining Jewish synagogues and communities in Cuba have become somewhat reconciled to living under the revolution even though nonreligious activities (strictly defined) are prohibited.[40] This does not apply to religious sects which seek to integrate all religious, public, and private life. They have suffered sporadic persecution. These include the Gideonites, Pentecostals, some Afro-Cuban sects, and Jehovah's Witnesses. The last named have suffered unremitting persecution for proselytism.[41] There is no room in Cuba for two consummatory value patterns—according to the revolutionary government, the sects must go.

Government-induced standards of rectitude grow at the expense of all other standards. On balance, because of the relative weakness of prerevolutionary religion, the prevalence of widespread public corruption, and the current power of the government to impose its own standards, the amount of rectitude in the social system may have increased.

Wealth

Real (constant prices) per capita gross national product rose at an annual rate of 1.0 percent during 1950-1958. Real per capita national income declined at an annual rate of -1.0 percent between 1962 and 1966. Because 1962 was a recession year, the drop from prerevolutionary years may have been more severe. Data problems, however, prevent a strict comparison. Nevertheless, the upward trend of the Cuban economy of the 1950s has been stopped and reversed. Gross national product declined from 1968 through 1970 even prior to adjustments for inflation and population growth.[42]

Sugar production is the mainstay of the Cuban economy. It accounts directly for about one-quarter to one-third of the gross national product. It fell from 1961 (one of the highest post-World War II levels) to some of the lowest post-World War II levels in 1962, 1963, and 1964. It rose in 1965, fell in 1966, rose in 1967, and then fell steadily in 1971 and 1972, again to near post-World War II bottom levels.[43] These trends indicate that one dominant feature of the economy has been its erratic pattern, from classic lows to classic highs.

The classic high in sugar production—the 1970 harvest—displaced the rest of the Cuban economy. The diversion of resources to achieve a single task was very costly. This antagonistic relationship between economic sectors has been a second dominant feature of the Cuban economy from the earliest years of the revolution and into the 1970s. Recovery in the nonsugar sectors has taken place since 1970, but not in sugar; it is not yet possible to make reliable comparisons.[44] The performance of the Cuban revolution in economic growth, in sum, has been a failure. Average aggregate annual trends are negative, and from year to year, they have been erratic.

Revolutionary performance has been better in equality and security of wealth. Overt unemployment, including overt seasonal unemployment, has been sharply reduced. The National Council of Economics estimated overt unemployment in 1956-1957 at 16.2 percent of the labor force, varying seasonally with the sugar harvest. In a good year (1958), at harvest peak, it would fall to 7.0 percent. In 1969, unemployment fell to 2.6 percent of the labor force. There is, however, disguised unemployment and underemployment, especially in the service sector, and a general decline in labor productivity. This affects the growth performance of the economy more than the security of those who are unemployed.[45]

Data on prerevolutionary income distribution are inadequate, but there seems to be a greater equality in incomes since 1959. Wage scales set in the mid-1960s range from 64 to 844 pesos per month. During the 1960s, the trend toward wage equalization continued. In 1962, agricultural wages were 61.6 percent of the average. The lowest wage sector of the entire economy in 1962 was for nonsugar crops, at 53.6 percent of the national wage rate; it was still lowest in 1966 but at 56.6 percent of the national wage rate. Its rate of growth during this period was two-and-a-half times the national average. The three highest sectoral wage rates in 1962 were electric power, petroleum and derivatives, and air transport, at 218.3 percent, 193.5 percent, and 190.5 percent of the national wage rate, respectively. The first two had fallen to 183.3 percent and 175.6 percent respectively by 1966; the third, rose to 203.0 percent. The relative levels and trends seem secure. Though there is evidence that Cuba's wage scales have been less egalitarian than the Soviet Union's, it appears that they are more egalitarian than in other Latin American countries.[46]

Small farmers also have benefited. The 1959 Agrarian Reform Law gave the land to those who worked it. Because Cuba's prerevolutionary land tenure laws already gave virtual security to those who cultivated sugar cane, the chief effect of the 1959 law was to eliminate rent payments. Squatters, 8.6 percent of the total number of farmers in the 1946 agricultural census, were given land titles. The land of the small farmers has been guaranteed to them. Farmers also have received other forms of preferential treatment. In short, they have benefited from greater equality and security.[47]

Other policies have a mixed effect on wealth security and equality. The decreased reliance on money and the provision of social services free of charge, have had powerful equalizing effects, because these charges had a greater relative weight on lower incomes. Education, medical care, day care centers, birth, marriage, divorce registries, burials, social security, sports events, public telephone calls and a good deal of housing are free of charge. The rationing of consumer goods, though an indicator of the economy's failure to grow, also has an important equalizing effect.

But privileges are also abundant, and they accrue mostly to bureaucrats, technicians, foreigners, and the formerly rich (whose property had been nationalized but for which they have been compensated, albeit on a low scale). The higher wages of the new upper class, and the rents of old, keep alive luxurious restaurants and similar enterprises, an active black market, and unnecessary imports. Some workers also partake of this luxury, as a result of a decision not to roll back "historical wages" to the new scale. These are the wage levels which some industrial workers acquired in the prerevolutionary period, and which are higher than justified by their productivity.[48]

Security of wealth from crime is more complex. We noted that the robbery rate had fallen. The theft rate per 100,000 population also fell from 379 in 1960 to 235 in 1967. However, the total number of crimes against property was about 37,000 in 1959; it fell steadily to about 10,000 in 1964; and it rose steadily to about 28,000 in 1968.[49] Thus the continuing shortages of consumer goods in the later 1960s may have stimulated crimes against property, and led to a decline in the security of wealth. On balance the thrust toward equality and security of wealth are the dominant themes.

Wealth in Cuba must be enjoyed in a comparative lack of liberty. Workers cannot strike collectively. Their occupational mobility is regulated; their records, with merits and demerits, are kept in a labor file. Workers have complained individually and collectively at various points, but to little avail. Private entrepreneurship (except among peasants) is banned. In the summer, 1970, after working hard and uninterruptedly in the eighteen-month 1970 sugar harvest, on any given day, approximately 400,000 workers—one-fifth of the work force—absented themselves from work.[50] This resulted from the accumulation of relatively spontaneous and uncoordinated decisions by workers. The government also had discouraged the use of institutionalized grievance channels. Setting the number of labor disputes allowed to go to the regional appeal commissions in 1967 at 100, the rate of permissible appeal fell to 80 in 1968 and to 67 in 1969. Setting the number of labor disputes allowed to go to the national appeal commission in 1967 at 100, the rate of permissible appeal fell to 82 in 1968 and to 50 in 1969.[51] Therefore, as labor grievances rose, the government shut off institutionalized channels for the expression of those grievances. The government also neglected the labor unions—yet another possible channel for workers' grievances. Prime Minister Castro has recognized, though belatedly, that the political center was at fault for the neglect of the workers and the workers' movement in the late 1960s.[52]

Peasants, too, enjoy their greater equality and security of wealth with less liberty. Their efforts to resist some government policies, hold on to old private farming practices, and sell in the private markets, have been repressed. Successful repression of a peasant movement occurred, for example, in southern Matanzas province in the early 1960s. Private marketing outlets for farm products were shut off as a result of the nationalization of all private retail trade in 1968.[53]

Power

Four preceding arguments pertain here. The government has invested power to redistribute many values because of its commitment to social justice and because it relies for support and justification on its relationship with the lower class. However, increased equality on power values has not extended to groups previously excluded with regard to respect— blacks and women. The above discussions of affection and rectitude also pointed to the prevalence of a single ideology which, despite contradictions, has the approval of the central governing institutions to govern even the most private aspects of life. Because of the deterioration of the workers' position in the late 1960s, their support of the revolution, greater than that of other social groups in the early 1960s, declined by the late 1960s. The government responded to workers' discontent in the early 1970s with political mobilization, competition, and repression, with mixed effects on liberty and equality.

The law against loafing (March 1971) guarantees the right to a job to all able-bodied citizens, and specifies work as a "social duty." It applies penalties to able-bodied males (but not females) who fail to work, or absent themselves from work. The law may have reduced urban unemployment; rural unemployment still persists.[54]

A systematic effort in the early 1970s to endow labor unions with greater prestige amidst, and usefulness for, workers, was impressive.[55] Competitive elections for local labor union leaders have been held. On the average, 1.8 people were candidates for each post in 1971, and 1.6, in 1972. Though most candidates had prior revolutionary approval, some local labor leaders were elected who were at least lukewarm toward the revolution.[56]

Though there is less equality and liberty in the holding of power, there has been growth in the amount and centralization of power in the economic system. There is now virtually no issue, however private, that is outside the scope of government, and no individual or kind of individual outside its domain. This has been so at least since the 1961 literacy campaign when a systematic effort was made to locate illiterates.[57] The weight of government decisions has increased considerably. Whereas government policy prior to the revolution was important, it now is decisive. The efficacy of government action has increased markedly. Its competence—as the failure of economic growth indicates—is another matter. But it has a decisive impact, benevolent or malevolent, throughout the entire political system. Previous discussions have indicated the increase in the scope, weight, and efficacy of the government. Here it suffices to note the increase of its domain and its centralization.

Membership in government-controlled mass organizations indicates the vast reach of government domain. Approximately 59.5 percent of all adults (aged 15 or above, 1970 census) were members of the Committees for the Defense of the Revolution, and 46 percent of adult women were members of the Women's Federation. All peasants in the private sector belonged to the National Association of Small Peasants, and all industrial and agricultural and many service sector workers, to the Labor Confederation. About 90 percent of all primary school students were in the Pioneers' Union.[58]

The Party in 1970 had at most 1.3 percent of the adult population.[59] Because most decisions were made by party members, this concentrated power in few hands. No new members have entered the Central Committee of the Communist Party since 1965. The common aging of the entire mostly white male leadership blocks possibilities of promotion and centralizes power further. Centralization has also occurred, because the government and party have a power monopoly, and because final, decisive power is further concentrated in Fidel Castro's hands. The tendency to centralize has led to government paralysis. Armando Hart, then the party's national organization secretary, noted in 1970 that "some municipal and regional party cadres have either lost their capacity for leadership or simply lack the necessary capacity to find correct, executive solutions without hesitation or delay."[60] Criticism and competition exist only within clearly defined boundaries. Correction of errors is difficult. Public opposition within the system does not exist. The opposition is outside the system and seeks to overthrow it. The effectiveness of the antisystem opposition has declined drastically from the early 1960s. Even by the most conservative estimates, Cuba's rate of political prisoners (2 per 1000 population) is at least 13 times the rate in Brazil.[61] Power has grown unequally and without liberty. Power holders are more secure in their enjoyment of power than were their prerevolutionary predecessors.

Summary of Cuban Case

Since the revolution, there has been very impressive growth in enlightenment, skill (except for university trained personnel per population), and power. There has been mixed performance in well-being, with growth in some indicators, and decline in others. There has been some very modest growth in respect for blacks, though blacks may have benefited more as part of the lower class, than as blacks. There also has been some improvement in respect toward women which has been most marked in the social, less in the economic, and least in the political sphere. Affection, understood primarily as private social relationships, has declined. Rectitude, defined as the private religious sphere, also has declined. But a civic religion, a government-sponsored ideology, powerful and far-reaching, has appeared. It probably has increased the overall amount of rectitude in the social system. The level of aggregate wealth has declined, or at least stagnated. Economic growth has been the most conspicuous failure of the Cuban revolution.

There have been impressive gains in equality in enlightenment, skill, and wealth, vertically between social classes, and horizontally between urban and rural areas. There also have been gains toward more equality in well-being, though urban-rural, Havana-countryside gaps still remain very high. Findings on growth and equality in respect are the same. For power and rectitude, there has been considerable centralization in few hands, and competing groups are illegitimate. Equality on these two values has declined sharply. The thrust toward equality in enlightenment, skill, well-being, and respect for blacks declined in the latter half of the 1960s. Thus the increase in equality in the late 1960s is limited to greater respect for women in the social sphere, a better (though still very inegalitarian) distribution of medical doctors, and more economic equality. Therefore, by the late 1960s, no new egalitarian gains seemed likely. Egalitarianism itself was denounced by Prime Minister Castro at the Thirteenth Labor Congress in the fall of 1973, auguring perhaps a reversal of the trends of a decade and a half.[62] The net shift toward more equality is accounted for almost entirely by the first half decade of revolutionary rule.

There is a fairly unanimous and positive performance on security, except on affection, and a mixed finding on well-being. The rise in economic crimes in the 1960s may threaten the security of wealth, but increases on other wealth security indicators overcame it. Security of respect for blacks is uncertain. For blacks there was no growth, but an actual decline in wealth, an increase of inequality in power and rectitude, and serious losses of liberty. Such security may be a mixed blessing.

The revolution can be most severely criticized for the loss of personal liberty. Performance is unanimous, but negative. Even in the area of the government's best performances—enlightenment and skill—one of the chief criticisms is stifling uniformity and loss of liberty. If the anti-loafing law institutionalizes security against unemployment, it is also coercive in every other respect. The private spheres in affection and rectitude exist under duress. Economic liberty has been lost, because neither strikes nor private entrepreneurship (except for peasants) is

Table 2.1
The Performance of the Cuban Revolution with Regard to Eight Basic Social Values

	Enlightenment	Skill	Well-being	Respect	Affection	Rectitude	Wealth	Power
Growth	++	++	+/−	+	−	+	−	++
Equality	++	++	+	+	N.R.	−	++	
Liberty	− −	−	N.R.	−	−	−	−	− −
Security	+	+	+/−	+/−	−	−	+	++

allowed. The lack of political competition and criticism is a loss for both liberty and system competence. It atrophies the capacity for expedient and smooth self-correction. Blacks have lost the liberty to be publicly concerned with respect values. Table 2.1 is a "photograph" of the performance of the revolution in the early 1970s compared to the prerevolutionary period. It is a five-point scale, from ++ to −−, where N.R. means "not relevant."

The Cuban revolutionary government has emphasized four values during these past several years. It has expanded and concentrated power and rectitude; it has sought to deprivatize affection; and it has invested heavily in skill for the long-term future of the country. Although enlightenment has also grown, it probably was derived from the investment in skill. The government invested in the growth of wealth, but failed. Of the four modes of value enjoyment, the government has sacrificed liberty. At first, it seemed committed to growth, equality, and security; but the stress on equality has faded. The finding on security was unexpected.

Conclusion

The hypothesis has accounted reasonably for the performance of the three revolutionary political systems in their early periods. The early period encompassed the Cuban revolutionary experience up to the early 1970s, most though not all of China's, and a small fraction of the Soviet experience. These countries established their revolutions with a consummatory political system with a new public morality grounded in a centrally-shaped ideology, directed and implemented by party and government. Political power and participation were expanded, centralized and controlled. A shift in affection patterns aimed toward the revolutionary state was also emphasized. In the educational system, a strong emphasis on skill orientation developed. Private, nongovernmental standards of rectitude came under attack.

None of these systems had an unblemished record of economic growth in the early years. The Soviet Union had barely managed to reach its pre-World War I level. Although recovery was an achievement in itself, the pattern was erratic and underscored serious flaws in the Soviet economic structure. The Cuban performance has been both erratic and, on balance, negative. The Chinese pattern also has been erratic but, on balance, positive. Cuban performance suffers from comparison. Cuba faced the U.S. economic embargo and political hostility, but not world wars. Cuba's losses from civil war pale before the Soviet and Chinese losses. The Cuban economy should have outperformed the others; instead, it was outperformed. All three leaderships stressed economic growth, but they were able to survive without it. Power, rectitude, affection, and skill were stressed even at the risk of economic costs, to be borne by the new ethic of sacrifice. Whereas economic hardships may have toppled the old regime, they served to strengthen the political foundations of the new order. Equality was emphasized on several values, including wealth; but equality of respect, well-being, and enlightenment would be sacrificed if they conflicted with more decisive values. Liberty as a mode of enjoyment was also sacrificed.

Over the longer run, the Soviet Union has changed its policies on many of these values and modes of enjoyment. The Cubans and the Chinese have made some changes, though less drastic. Thus the lack of security of Soviet values may result from the longer history of that political system; the steadier record in China and Cuba could change as their history unfolds.

All three regimes have faced an economic crisis, after prolonged and intricate internal debate, toward the end of the first decade or decade and a half of the revolutionary period. In the Soviet Union, the result was Stalinization with the emphasis on industrialization at great cost to other value and mode of enjoyment policies of the Soviet party and government. In China, the response may have been—at least temporarily— a willingness to sacrifice economic growth for the sake of building a moral socialist man during the Cultural Revolution. Cuba tried a mini-Cultural Revolution—called the Revolutionary Offensive—in the late 1960s, but it got swallowed in the flawed but noble effort to harvest ten million tons of sugar in 1970. The trends since then suggest a renewed stress on economic growth, though not quite on the Stalinist model. If the Cuban revolution could steer, in fact, a middle course between the excesses of single-minded emphasis on either economic growth or rectitude, then perhaps yet another more attractive path in socialist historical development could unfold. This is still, unfortunately, at the level of hope, not fact.

NOTES

1. Harold Lasswell and Abraham Kaplan, *Power and Society* (New Haven: Yale University Press, 1965), pp. 55-56, 74; Karl W. Deutsch, *Politics and Government* (Boston: Houghton Mifflin Co., 1970), pp. 12, 13, 24. For an imaginative empirical application of the Lasswellian approach, see Henry F. Dobyns *et al., Peasants, Power and Applied Social Change: Views on a Model* (Beverly Hills: Sage Publications, 1971).

2. Harold Lasswell and Daniel Lerner, *World Revolutionary Elites* (Cambridge, Mass.: The MIT Press, 1965).

3. David Apter, *The Politics of Modernization* (Chicago: University of Chicago Press, 1965), pp. 83-94; S. N. Eisenstadt, *Modernization: Protest and Change* (Englewood Cliffs, N.J.: Prentice-Hall, Inc., 1966), pp. 2-5, 156-157; and Samuel P. Huntington and Jorge I. Dominguez, "Political Development," in Fred Greenstein and Nelson Polsby, eds., *Handbook of Political Science* (Reading, Mass.: Addison-Wesley Publishing Co.): 5: III.

4. Nicholas DeWitt, *Education and Professional Employment in the U.S.S.R.* (Washington, D.C.: National Science Foundation, 1961); and Leo Orleans, *Professional Manpower and Education in Communist China* (Washington, D.C.: National Science Foundation, 1960); Robert Barendsen, "The Agricultural Middle School in Communist China," *China Quarterly*, no. 8, October-December 1961.

5. Alex Inkeles, *Social Change in Soviet Russia* (Cambridge, Mass.: Harvard University Press, 1968), p. 51; Marie Sieh, "Doctors and Patients," and Robert M. Worth, "Health Trends since the 'Great Leap Forward'," in William T. Liu, ed., *Chinese Society under Communism* (New York: John Wiley and Sons, Inc., 1967); Mark G. Field, "Medical Organization and the Medical Profession," in Cyril E. Black, ed., *The Transformation of Russian Society* (Cambridge, Mass.: Harvard University Press, 1960).

6. Norton Dodge, *Women in the Soviet Economy* (Baltimore: The Johns Hopkins Press, 1966); Barbara W. Jancar, "Women and Soviet Politics," Paper presented at the Annual Meeting of the American Political Science Association, Washington, D.C., 1972; Merle Fainsod, *How Russia is Ruled* (Revised edition; Cambridge, Mass.: Harvard University Press, 1963), pp. 254-255, 265-266, 271, 277-278.

7. C. K. Yang, *The Chinese Family in the Communist Revolution* (Cambridge, Mass.: The MIT Press, 1959), pp. 130-133, 144-154.

8. Ibid., pp. 63-73, 173-182; David and Vera Mace, *The Soviet Family* (Garden City, N.Y.: Dolphin Books, 1964), pp. 216-221, 315-320; Alex Inkeles and Raymond Bauer, *The Soviet Citizen* (Cambridge, Mass.: Harvard University Press, 1959), pp. 189-194, 210-218.

9. Frederick C. Barghoorn, *Politics in the USSR* (Boston: Little, Brown and Co., 1966), pp. 74-83; Fainsod, *How Russia is Ruled,* pp. 254-279; *Problems of Communism,* Vol. 16, no. 5 (September-October, 1967; Special issue).

10. Frank Moraes, *The Revolt in Tibet* (New York: The MacMillan Co., 1960); H.E. Richardson, *Tibet and its History* (London: Oxford University Press, 1962), pp. 169-223; June Dreyer, "Traditional Minorities, Elites, and the CPR Engaged in Minority Nationalities Work," in Robert A. Scalapino, ed., *Elites in the People's Republic of China* (Seattle: University of Washington Press, 1972); and June Dreyer, "China's Minority Nationalities in the Cultural Revolution," *China Quarterly,* no. 33 (January-March 1968). 1

11. John S. Curtiss, "Church and State," in Black, ed., *The Transformation*; Inkeles, *Social Change,* pp. 221-230; Vladimir Gsovski, ed., *Church and State behind the Iron Curtain* (New York: Frederick A. Praeger, Inc., 1955).

12. Holmes Welch, "Buddhism under the Communists," *China Quarterly,* no. 6 (April-June 1961); Joseph R. Levenson, "The Place of Confucius in Communist China," *China Quarterly,* no. 12 (October-November 1962); Roderick MacFarquhar, *The Hundred Flowers and the Chinese Intellectuals* (New York: Frederick A. Praeger, Inc., 1960), pp. 248-257.

13. Alexandre Benningsen and Chantal Lemercier-Quelquejay, *Islam in the Soviet Union* (New York: Frederick A. Praeger, Inc., 1967), pp. 65-161.

14. Abram Bergson, *The Real National Income of Soviet Russia since 1928* (Cambridge, Mass.: Harvard University Press, 1961), chapters 1 and 13; Abram Bergson, *The Structure of Soviet Wages* (Cambridge, Mass.: Harvard University Press, 1944), chapters 5-7; Alexander Erlich, *The Soviet Industrialization Debate, 1924-1928* (Cambridge, Mass.: Harvard University Press, 1967); Maurice Dobb, *Soviet Economic Development since 1917* (New York: International Publishers, 1948), chapters 4-12; E. H. Carr, *The Bolshevik Revolution, 1917-1923* (New York: The MacMillan Co., 1952), Vol. 2.

15. Nai-Ruenn Chen and Walter Galenson, *The Chinese Economy under Communism* (Chicago: Aldine Publishing Co., 1969), chapters 2, 5, and 7; Charles Hoffman, "Work Incentives in Chinese Industry and Agriculture," in Joint Economic Committee of the U.S. Congress, ed., *An Economic Profile of Mainland China* (New York: Frederick A. Praeger, 1968); Ta-Chung Liu and Kung-Chia Yeh, *The Economy of the Chinese Mainland: National Income and Economic Development, 1933-1959* (Princeton: Princeton University Press, 1965), pp. 71-90; Barry M. Richman, *Industrial Society in Communist China* (New York: Random House, 1969), pp. 595-603; 798-817.

16. Fainsod, *How Russia is Ruled*; Barghoorn, *Politics*; Barrington Moore, Jr., *Soviet Politics: The Dilemma of Power* (Cambridge, Mass.: Harvard University Press, 1959); Leonard Schapiro, *The Communist Party of the Soviet Union* (New York: Random House, 1959); T. H. Rigby, *Communist Party Membership in the U.S.S.R., 1917-1967* (Princeton: Princeton University Press, 1968); Richard H. Solomon, *Mao's Revolution and the Chinese Political Culture* (Berkeley: University of California Press, 1971), Parts III and IV; O. Edmund Clubb, *Twentieth Century China* (New York: Columbia University Press, 1964); Benjamin I. Schwartz, *Chinese Communism and the Rise of Mao* (Cambridge, Mass.: Harvard University Press, 1958); James R. Townsend, *Political Participation in Communist China* (Berkeley: University of California Press, 1967); Samuel P. Huntington, *Political Order in Changing Societies* (New Haven: Yale University Press, 1968), chapter 5.

17. For details, Richard R. Fagen, *The Transformation of Political Culture in Cuba* (Stanford: Stanford University Press, 1969), pp. 36-68.

18. Dudley Seers, ed., *Cuba: The Economic and Social Revolution* (Chapel Hill: The University of North Carolina Press, 1964), pp. 196, 204.

19. Computations based on Mercedes García Tudurí, "Resumen de la historia de la educación en Cuba," *Exilio*, Vol. 3, nos. 3-4 and Vol. 4, no. 1, combined (Winter 1969-Spring 1970), pp. 115-116, 120-122, 124-127; Carmelo Mesa-Lago, "Availability and Reliability of Statistics in Socialist Cuba: Part II," *Latin American Research Review*, Vol. 4, no. 1 (Summer 1969), pp. 48, 74; Lowry Nelson, *Cuba: The Measure of a Revolution* (Minneapolis: The University of Minnesota Press, 1972), p. 144; International Bank for Reconstruction and Development, *Report on Cuba* (Washington: IBRD, 1951), pp. 403-414; and Junta Central de Planificación, *Compendio estadístico de Cuba* (La Habana: JUCEPLAN, 1968), pp. 3, 33 (hereafter: Junta, *Compendio*).

20. Junta, *Compendio*, pp. 30-33, 38; *Granma Weekly Review*, January 10, 1971, p. 9; Wyatt MacGaffey and Clifford R. Barnett, *Twentieth Century Cuba* (New York: Anchor Books, 1962), p. 47.

21. Computed from Junta, *Compendio*, pp. 3, 34-35.

22. Samuel Bowles, "Cuban Education and the Revolutionary Ideology," *Harvard Educational Review*, Vol. 41, no. 4 (November 1971), p. 497; Hugh Thomas, *Cuba: The Pursuit of Freedom* (New York: Harper and Row, 1971), pp. 863, 881, 887, 912, 978, 1136-1137; Bruce Russett, *et al., World Handbook of Political and Social Indicators* (New Haven: Yale University Press, 1964), p. 108; and computations from Junta, *Compendio*, p. 3, and *Granma Weekly Review*, June 4, 1967, p. 11.

23. Junta, *Compendio*, pp. 6, 46-47; Mesa-Lago, *Availability*, p. 70; and *Granma Weekly Review*, March 18, 1973, p. 6.

24. Taken and/or computed from Junta, *Compendio*, pp. 3, 43-44; Vicente Navarro, "Health Services in Cuba," *The New England Journal of Medicine*, Vol. 287, no. 10 (November 9, 1972), pp. 957-958; and Roberto Hernández, "La atención médica en Cuba hasta 1958," *Journal of Inter-American Studies*, Vol. XI, no. 4 (October 1969), p. 553. Navarro's estimate of 41,027 "hospital beds existent in 1969" (p. 955) is far lower than the one used in the text; if true, the rate of hospital beds per 1000 population declined during the 1960s. See also Ricardo Leyva, "Health and Revolution in Cuba," in Rolando Bonachea and Nelson Valdes, *Cuba in Revolution* (Garden City, N.Y.: Anchor Books, 1972), p. 480. Leyva's estimates for the 1960s are consistently higher than those of the Cuban government's own statistical publications; his estimate for 1958 apparently left out the private sector. I am grateful to Dr. Jaime Arias for bringing Navarro's essay to my attention.

25. *Granma Weekly Review*, May 11, 1969, pp. 7-9; Santiago Cuba, "La lucha contra la delincuencia," *Cuba socialista*, Vol. 4, no. 40 (December 1964): 28.

26. Computed from Junta, *Compendio*, pp. 44-45; Oficina Nacional de los Censos Demografico y Electoral, *Censos de población, vivienda y electoral: Informe general (enero 28 de 1953)* (La Habana: P. Fernández y Cia., 1955), pp. 49-50, hereafter *1953 Census*; and *Granma Weekly Review*, January 10, 1971, p. 9.

27. Navarro, "Health Services," p. 956; and Hernández, "La atención médica," pp. 550-551.

28. Computed from República de Cuba, *Informe general del censo de 1943* (La Habana: P. Fernández y Cia., 1945), pp. 930-931, 1112-1114, 1203-1205, hereafter *1943 Census*.

29. Computed from *1943 Census*, and *1953 Census*, pp. 167-168; and taken from Jose A. Moreno, "From Traditional to Modern Values," in Carmelo Mesa-Lago, ed., *Revolutionary Change in Cuba* (Pittsburgh: University of Pittsburgh Press, 1971), pp. 479-480; and from Ana Ramos, "La mujer y la revolución en Cuba," *Casa de la Américas*, Vol. XI, nos. 65-66 (March-June 1971), p. 68.

30. Computed from William B. Parker, *Cubans of Today* (New York: G. P. Putnam's Sons, Inc., 1919); from a biographical file on the Central Committee of the Communist party kept by the author; and from Hernán Barrera, "Building the United Party of the Socialist Revolution in Cuba," *World Marxist Review*, Vol. 6, no. 12 (December 1963), pp. 56-58; Miguel Martin, "Informe al Congreso," *Cuba socialista*, no. 62 (October 1966), p. 108; *Granma Weekly Review*, August 28, 1966, p. 3, and October 8, 1967, p. 3; and Fagen, *Transformation*, p. 134.

31. Junta, *Compendio,* p. 49; and *Granma Weekly Review,* July 9, 1967, p. 11.

32. Jose Yglesias, *In the Fist of the Revolution: Life in a Cuban Country Town* (New York: Vintage Books, 1968), chs. 6 and 9; Elizabeth Sutherland, *The Youngest Revolution: A Personal Report on Cuba* (New York: Dial Press, 1969), pp. 169-190.

33. *Granma Weekly Review,* May 11, 1969, p. 9.

34. Junta, *Compendio,* p. 6.

35. Yglesias, *In the Fist,* p. 307.

36. Junta, *Compendio,* p. 6; for a description of the government's "Marriage Palaces," see Sutherland, *Youngest Revolution,* pp. 176-178.

37. *Revolución,* December 9, 1964, p. 1.

38. Ernesto (Che) Guevara, "Man and Socialism in Cuba," in Bertram Silverman, ed., *Man and Socialism in Cuba* (New York: Atheneum, 1971), p. 352.

39. Jorge I. Domínguez, "Cuban Catholics and Castro," *Worldview,* Vol. 15, no. 2 (February 1972), p. 26.

40. For relevant statements by Cuba's Roman Catholic Bishops and various Protestant and Jewish groups and individuals, see Alice L. Hageman and Philip E. Wheaton, *Religion in Cuba Today* (New York: Association Press, 1971), pp. 47-92, 191-269, 279-308.

41. Fidel Castro, "A combatir al enemigo en todos los frentes," *Cuba socialista,* Vol. 3, no. 20 (April 1963), pp. 5, 7-11; Blas Roca, "La lucha ideológica contra las sectas religiosas," *Cuba socialista,* Vol. 3, no. 22 (June 1963); Carlos Moore, "Cuba: The Untold Story," *Présence Africaine,* no. 24 (English edition, 1964), pp. 185, 199-223; Howard I. Blutstein, *et al., Area Handbook for Cuba* (Washington: Government Printing Office, 1971), pp. 177-178, 186-187.

42. Carmelo Mesa-Lago, "Economic Policies and Growth," in Mesa-Lago, ed., *Revolutionary Change,* pp. 330-331; Mesa-Lago, *Availability,* p. 51. Junta, *Compendio,* p. 8, presents data in current prices. The differences between these and Mesa-Lago's statistics is that the former include inflation, the latter are deflated. I am grateful to Carmelo Mesa-Lago for his comments on this section. See also Osvaldo Dorticós, "Análisis y perspectivas del desarrollo de la economía cubana," *Economía y desarrollo,* no. 12 (July-August 1972), pp. 32-38.

43. Thomas, *Cuba,* pp. 1560-1564; *New York Times,* January 28, 1973, p. 55.

44. Jorge I. Domínguez, "Sectoral Clashes in Cuban Politics and Development," *Latin American Research Review,* Vol. 6, no. 3 (Fall 1971); *New York Times,* February 4, 1973, p. 90.

45. International Labor Office, *Yearbook of Labor Statistics, 1959* (Geneva: ILO, 1959): 186; Mesa-Lago, *Availability*, pp. 63-68; Carmelo Mesa-Lago, "The Labor Force, Employment, Unemployment and Underemployment in Cuba, 1899-1970," *Sage Professional Papers in International Studies*, Vol. 1, no. 9 (1972), pp. 40, 43.

46. Roberto E. Hernández and Carmelo Mesa-Lago, "Labor Organization and Wages," in Mesa-Lago, ed., *Revolutionary Change*, pp. 224-235; see also Bertram Silverman, "The War on Poverty: Cuban Style," paper presented at the Annual Meeting of the American Political Science Association, Chicago, September 1971.

47. For the texts of the agrarian laws, see Ovidio Garcia Regueiro, *Cuba: Raíces y frutos de una revolución* (Madrid: IEPAL, 1970); see also Domínguez, "Sectoral Clashes," pp. 73, 78-79; and Ministerio de Agricultura, *Memoria del censo agrícola nacional, 1946* (La Habana: P. Fernández y Cia., 1951), p. 387.

48. Sutherland, *Youngest Revolution*, pp. 16-20; Hernández and Mesa-Lago, "Labor Organization," pp. 229-231, 234-235; K. S. Karol, *Guerrillas in Power* (New York: Hill and Wang, 1970), pp. 429-436; Maurice Zeitlin, *Revolutionary Politics and the Cuban Working Class* (New York: Harper Torchbooks, 1970), pp. xix-xxii; and Reckford, *Does Fidel*, p. 26.

49. *Granma Weekly Review*, May 11, 1969, pp. 7-8.

50. Nelson P. Valdés, "Cuba: ¿Socialismo democrático o burocritismo colectivista?" *Aportes*, no. 23 (January 1971), p. 42.

51. *Granma Weekly Review*, August 17, 1969, p. 2.

52. Ibid., October 4, 1970, p. 2.

53. Nivaldo Herrera, "La ofensiva política en las zonas campesinas de Matanzas," *Cuba socialista*, Vol. 4, no. 39 (November 1963); *Verde Olivo*, Vol. 9, no. 12 (March 24, 1968), and no. 13 (March 31, 1968).

54. *Granma Weekly Review*, March 28, 1971, pp. 1-2; Dorticós, "Analisis," p. 52.

55. For a summary of this activity, *Granma Weekly Review*, August 1, 1971.

56. Ibid., and *Granma Weekly Review*, October 24, 1971, p. 4; and May 7, 1971, p. 2.

57. Seers, ed., *Cuba*, chapter 6.

58. Computed from *Granma Weekly Review*, January 10, 1971, p. 9; October 4, 1970, p. 2; February 28, 1971, p. 2; and August 29, 1971, p. 8.

59. Computed from *Granma Weekly Review*, January 10, 1971, p. 9; and Blutstein *et al.*, *Area Handbook*, p. 220.

60. *Granma Weekly Review*, Febrary 1, 1970, p. 4.

61. Domínguez, "Sectoral Clashes," p. 66; Domínguez, "Cuban Catholics," pp. 26-27.

62. *Granma Weekly Review*, November 25, 1973.

3 VALUE CHANGES IN A "DEVELOPMENT CLUSTER" OF VILLAGES IN LAOS

P. J. MAYNARD

Introduction

A detailed evaluation study of a regional program in Laos disclosed the hitherto unrecognized importance of value changes and conflict in that program. They are discussed in this paper because they are believed to be especially susceptible to further examination through the policy science approach to the analysis of values.

The participants in the planning process of this American-funded project were American and Filipino foreign aid professionals, American foreign aid volunteers, and officials of the Lao central government. Implementation of the program involved individuals from each of the above groups, plus Lao local officials, Lao lowland villagers, and Meo tribespeople transplanted from the mountains. The mixture was further complicated by the occasional participation of proponents of the American counterculture. Each of these groups had its own cultural background and set of values. The same project objectives and operations were regarded, in effect, by the various participants through lenses of different colors and degrees of magnification, thereby raising the possibilities for confusion, conflict, and misinterpretation of the actions and attitudes of one's collaborators or coadministrators.

Moreover, each participant in the planning process was victimized by a form of "tunnel vision," a lack of perception of the "side effects" that aid activities can have upon those sectors of the society which were not the ostensible targets of the given development projects or programs. For example, the construction of a diversion dam, canals, and water flow controls is usually a simple technological task. Its stated objective is to regulate the flow of water so as to increase agricultural production, which, in turns, calls for new agricultural practices by the farmer participants. Often unrecognized, however, are the concomitant changes in the local power structure, and in the attitudes toward, and the institutions related to, the family, accumulation of personal wealth, sanitation, religion, other communities or groups, and education. Acceptance or rejection of these collateral changes, or accommodation to them, will vary among the participants in the project and can affect its outcome significantly.

Some of these changes may have such a positive effect on development that, whether or not the stated objectives were achieved, significant development gains would have been made. An example of such a gain is the implanting of some of the preconditions to development that seem to be essential to the accomplishment of development projects. Montgomery has identified three of these behavioral preconditions: willingness to accept new standards, willingness to invest one's own resources, and willingness to accept civil processes for the resolution of disputes arising out of development change.[1] Insofar as the implementation of an aid project has elicited acceptance within the society of these preconditions of development, positive overall progress will have been made, and the next projects will have a better chance for success.

These behavioral manifestations can be viewed in terms of the Lasswell classification of values that are applicable to all cultures but are manifested in different ways in each cultural context. It is hypothesized further that changes in one value will result in changes in one or more of the others.

The Muong Phieng Evaluation Study

Since 1964, the U.S. Agency for International Development Mission in Laos had been operating a complex of assistance projects in a small valley in Sayaboury Province in the northwest. The valley, which contained about twenty villages with a 1969 population of about 9000 people, lies midway between the Mekong River twenty-five miles to the east, and the Thai border to the west. Prior to 1964, the start of this program, the valley and its population formed an isolated enclave that had little contact with surrounding areas.

It was in this area that one of the first USAID "cluster" programs was started. These programs consisted of a number of development assistance activities performed relatively simultaneously for a group of geographically related villages. The specific mix of activities at any time varied in accordance with the level of development, the economic potential of the area, and the desires of the people. The cluster at which this study was performed, the Muong Phieng Cluster, was one of the smallest. Others ranged in size up to one hundred villages.

The general objective of this approach was to get the maximum benefit from foreign aid by developing the total economic and social environment of the area sufficiently so that it could effectively absorb and employ each aid input. The implicit assumption was that there are interlocking or mutually supporting relationships among the different kinds of aid projects.

By early 1969 it became possible to assess the cultural impact of the Muong Phieng cluster program. The area had had minimum disruption by security factors and offered acceptable conditions for an external evaluation which was subsequently performed by the Stanford Research Institute. The five-year period encompassed by the study saw substantial changes to the physical and social infrastructures. Roads had been virtually non-existent in 1964, when it took the average villager at least two days of walking to make the round trip to either Sayaboury, the capital of the province, or to Muong Nan, a market center in Thailand. By 1969, there were 43 kilometers of all-weather road. Any villager could travel to Sayaboury in about an hour, at the cost of approximately sixty cents. A journey from any part of the cluster to the main town in the cluster, Muong Phieng, or to any other part of the cluster cost only twenty cents by taxi. Taxis made approximately thirty trips a day between Muong Phieng and Sayaboury.

In 1963, there were eleven primary schools (grades one through three) and one "Groupe Scolaire" (grades one through six) with a total of sixteen rooms and seventeen teachers. By 1969, there were fifteen primary and two Groupe Scolaire schools with thirty-nine rooms and thirty-nine teachers. Previously, thirty-two percent of all school age children attended the first three grades, and two percent attended the fourth to sixth grades. By 1969, forty-two percent of all school-age children were in the first three grades and twenty-one percent were in the last three grades of primary school.

Medical facilities increased from two to six fairly well-stocked dispensaries. In 1963, only the two villages that had the dispensaries could use them during the rainy season. By 1969, all villagers could reach the facilities at any time of the year. In 1968, approximately 19,000 cases were handled by them.

There were no rice mills in 1963; in 1969 there were eight. Retail stores increased in number from seven to thirty-three (plus five more just south of the cluster in a group of refugee villages). Cloth, soap, monosodium glutamate, canned milk, aspirin, matches, candles, fish sauce, candy, dry-cell batteries, salt, and ballpoint pens were among the most widely sold items.

Land under irrigation increased from 200 hectares (one dam had been installed by USAID in 1959) to over 600 hectares. Two irrigation projects started during the cluster period were expected to increase this total to well over 3,000 in a few years and were the key elements in the cluster development. The raising of pigs and ducks had greatly increased. Horses, which had been used in all villages for transport, were replaced by motor vehicles. The growing of vegetables also increased, although no quantitative comparison was made.

Religious activities also changed their character. Although there were approximately the same number of *wats* (17 in 1964, and 18 in 1969), the number of monks who resided in them declined from eighteen to eleven. However, many more people were participating in the religious festivals, or *bouns,* held at the *wats.* These *bouns* were held to gain money for the use of the *wats*. Previously, they had been small, very solemn, and attended only by members of the village where the *wat* was located. By 1969, *bouns* could be attended by persons from any village in the cluster. They were also more lively, with generators and sound and movie equipment borrowed from the management of the cluster. *Mohlam* teams (folk singers) were supplied by USIS. Subsequently, the *bouns* became much more profitable.

Another significant change during this period was in the use of money. Prior to the cluster program, the area operated on a subsistence basis. Since then, monetization has become much more important. Starting in 1967, increasing amounts of fertilizer, insecticides, water pumps, buffaloes, and farm tools were bought with credit extended by an aid-sponsored farm credit organization (ADO). These loans were repaid through the sale of rice surpluses at guaranteed prices. Livestock sales also increased, because traders and trucks could now get to the villages at any season.

A marked change in the ethnic composition of the cluster area had begun just before 1964, and, in fact, was instrumental in the selection of Muong Phieng as a cluster site. Some 1,500 Meo hill tribe refugees had been moved in during 1962-1963, adding to the then 5000 population of the area. They adapted extremely well to wet rice cultivation on the irrigated land created by the cluster. As a group they gave the impression of being more energetic than the local Lao and therefore evoked signs of resentment from some of the Lao villagers. Their birth rate was much higher than the Lao's, and their numbers were soon reinforced by an additional 1800 migrants who were resettled immediately adjacent to the southern end of the cluster.

These changes could be observed and measured. When the villagers were asked to cite what they considered the most significant changes during this period, they mentioned the roads first. Second, they cited the reduction in quarreling and theft, and the increase in friendliness and tolerance within the village and between villages.[2] Next, in approximate order of significance (both positive and negative) were the more enjoyable *bouns,* better health, fewer fish and game due to deforestation and damming of the streams, changes from homespun to store-bought clothing, the addition of fish sauce and monosodium glutamate to the diet, the replacement of torches for lighting by pressure lamps, the fewer fruit trees because of the widening of the village roads, the loss of toilet facilities with the removal of the forests, the introduction of Taiwan ducks, the institution of a cluster monthly newspaper, the better water supply. They also mentioned the "Village Development Committees," an institution introduced by the cluster which at that time was too new to be evaluated.

The Contextual Map

The eight values categorized in the Lasswellian system have been given the acronym PEWBSARD (Power, Enlightenment, Wealth, well-Being, Skill, Affection, Respect, and rectituDe). On the basis of this classification, a "contextual map" will be attempted in terms of: (1) conditions existing when the Muong Phieng program started; (2) those at the time of the evaluation study in 1969; (3) the most important net changes; and (4) linkages and interdependencies between the changes. The objective of this exercise is to demonstrate the utility of devising a contextual map in planning developmental activities for any geographic and cultural area.

Power

The 1964 society of the village cluster operated with a minimum need for the overt application of power. Traditional lawful power relationships were well understood by all participants, who fulfilled their roles with little or no question. Official contacts outside the valley were infrequent. Local authority was adequately expressed by an elected village leader (*Nai Ban*) who could call on the next, and highest, level of elected official (*Tasseng*) to resolve difficult problems. The ultimate power was vested in the hereditary royalty, who were shown great deference on the very few occasions that they came in contact with local people.

The principal exercise of power was for the control of water. Rainfall in the area was not abundant; the average was barely enough to support the subsistence cultivation of rice. Diversion of river flow was the only way to maximize the available water. The most powerful family group in the valley was the one whose lands were located in the most favorable location for capturing diverted water. These same people held the positions for the lawful expression of power. They held the only land in the valley that was assured a reasonably good water supply each year. As a result, they were able to establish a dominant economic and power position in the valley before the cluster period.

The village of Muong Phieng, the commercial and administrative center of the valley, became the cluster headquarters. This choice was made in spite of the fact that a preliminary survey of the valley had determined that there was so much internal conflict in this village that the villagers probably could not be induced to build a house for the cluster personnel. This early hostility, which had been reported by USAID personnel (and misinterpreted by them throughout the operation of the cluster), was expressed primarily by the village authorities, who were the only persons with whom the aid personnel dealt during the initial stages of the program. The hostility reflected the leaders' fear that development activities could result in a wider distribution of the limited amount of water and threaten their dominant position. This factor was recognized by the Lao province-level agricultural officer, who often communicated directly with the villagers of Muong Phieng, rather than through the village officials.

The advent of the cluster confirmed the fears of the traditional leaders. The USAID personnel and their Filipino, Thai, and Lao employees brought in, used, and dispensed a wide range of resources and skills. Although the Lao did not aggressively seek a share of many of these resources (in fact, some of the projects were promoted only with difficulty), the aid group's possession of vehicles and fuel, two-way radios, electric power and appliances, and medical supplies, as well as the cooperation and sometimes deference shown to them by Lao officials, gave them an unusual status. Later, as the construction of roads began to markedly improve the environment, the irrigation projects to take shape, and as new land was actually created and awarded, the aid group became—at least in the minds of some government officials—active competitors for power.

An attempt was made by the cluster to introduce a village-level democratic institution to assist in development planning—the Village Development Committees. These committees, one elected in each village, were to assist the village chief (*Nai Ban*) in determining the desires of the villagers regarding development needs. The project was started in 1968; so that by 1969, only preliminary estimates could be made of its success. By this time, however, divergent uses of the committees were being made by the various village chiefs. Some regarded the committees as competitors for power and tried to ignore them. Others used the committees to enlist their villagers in self-help projects—a sometimes onerous task for the village chief. The committees' decisions were also used as excuses to shield the village chief from responsibility for village positions which might be displeasing to his superiors. At least one village chief used the committee to adjudicate internal disputes that previously had been decided by him. The Village Development Committee project thus introduced into village life a scope for political manipulation and a sense of political participation that had not previously existed.

Enlightenment

Before 1964, there was little contact with people and ideas from outside the valley. Occasionally, cattle and buffalo traders starting from south of the valley drove their herds through it. Their destination was Luang Prabang. Villagers trekked for two days to get to either the province capital, Sayaboury, or to a province capital in Thailand, Muong Nan. An occasional trader came from Sayaboury to barter commodities for poultry, hogs, and paddy rice (in good years). Young men conscripted for military service were said never to return, closing out that possibility for enlightenment from outside the valley. There were few radios, and virtually no printed materials. Government agricultural or health officials rarely visited the valley. Filipino doctors and nurses from the hospital in Sayaboury made one or two trips a year during the dry season.

The cluster introduced an explosion of communication devices and media. Direct single-side-band radio contact was immediately established with the USAID headquarters in Vientiane. Problems involving the approval of higher authorities or the ordering of resources could be handled expeditiously, literally while the incredulous villager watched. Many of the jeeps which carried personnel throughout the valley on the various projects had two-way communication with the local headquarters, thereby bringing this aspect of the communication explosion into every village. After two years, a surplus military telephone system was installed, connecting the chiefs of most of the villages with the police station and cluster headquarters in Muong Phieng. Some of the villagers stated that the most important use of this system was to call the veterinarian stationed at Muong Phieng in case of accident or sickness of the farm animals.

A library was established at the headquarters, and a mobile unit started serving all villages on a periodic basis. A monthly cluster newspaper apprised the villages about what was going on in the program. The village development committee in one of two villages that had received little aid, complained that all the aid it got was the newspaper, which described the aid that other villages had received. The expansion of monetization also made it possible for the villagers to buy small radio receivers.

A significant broadening of the villager's knowledge of the political and social life of his country came from his participation in the local *bouns,* Buddhist religious ceremonies. Prior to the establishment of the cluster the *bouns* had been quiet, contemplative, serious affairs involving only the persons of one village. With the opening of the roads between villages, each *boun* became a large, somewhat boisterous event, with sound and movie equipment loaned by the cluster management. Most importantly, from the enlightenment standpoint, USIS supplied *mohlam* teams. These were itinerant singers whose irreverent, ribald and humorous songs were the Lao equivalent of our Buchwald-Mauldin-Jack Anderson commentaries on political figures, current social, political, and economic concerns, and the world in general. They brought to the villages a degree of involvement with Lao political life outside the valley.

Net changes in the values and institutions associated with enlightenment created new expectations regarding the role of the local and national government in the villages. The cluster villager was converted from a self-centered, family- and village-oriented person to one who learned to mix, with some assurance, with persons from other villages as well as with officials, technicians, and other extra-cluster persons. The villagers gained a better understanding of their rights as citizens and increased confidence in undertaking measures to advance them further.

Wealth

The Muong Phieng valley received an average annual amount of rainfall that barely supported a subsistence level of rice production. Villagers whose lowland rice fields did not benefit from the overflow from the valley rivers and streams had to stake out "hai" fields for dry rice in the adjacent mountains. This involved a walk of from two to five kilometers each way. The wealthy villagers were those who had large lowland fields, well located for irrigation, that produced enough rice to eat plus a surplus to sell to less fortunate villagers. These farmers were principally located in the villages of Muong Phieng and Na Tane. Before the establishment of the Cluster, total production permitted only a little bartering of rice to itinerant vendors of small household commodities.

Another indicator of wealth was the ownership of elephants, horses, and buffaloes. Elephants were ideal prime movers in the roadless environment of the valley, and were rented at fixed rates for various kinds of haulage. Buffaloes were, and still are, essential for lowland rice growing. They are also rented. Payment was in paddy rice and amounted to ten to twenty percent of the renting farmer's rice crop.

A principal objective of the aid programs was to install dams and canals to distribute the maximum proportion of the river flow onto the rice fields in a regulated manner. The only place where these irrigation programs met insurmountable resistance was in the village of Muong Phieng, where they threatened the status of the wealthy and politically powerful.

In 1964, the wealth outcome considered most desirable by the great majority of the population in the valley was having enough food to eat each year. The new roads permitted traders to bring trucks to the valley to stimulate the growing of hogs and rice. The aid programs devoted much time and energy to teaching better agricultural practices, including the introduction of better rice strains, better animal and poultry stock, and the use of fertilizers and insecticides.

By 1969, almost all of the horses and elephants had been sold to villagers from the surrounding mountains, since all transport was now carried on by taxi or truck. Possession of buffaloes was still necessary and prestigious, but ownership was more widely distributed; fewer were rented out. In the smaller of the two new irrigation projects, rice production rose as new land was put into crop. A visible sign of new affluence was the presence of thirty-three retail stores (there were seven before 1964). Virtually all of these stores operated on a cash basis.

Tangible evidence of increased rice production was the introduction of eight rice mills where previously there had been none. Almost all of the rice processed by the commercial millers was now sent outside the valley for sale in other towns. Much of the rice bran was recovered, and its use as feed contributed to the increased production of livestock.

One of the sharpest conflicts between the Lao shapers of local power and the American cluster personnel arose over the manner of allocating the right to ownership of land in the large new irrigation area, Nam Tan. The local Lao officialdom wanted the rights to be apportioned to local inhabitants who had the means to work the land. Since the principle of having the new owners actually work on the total project in order to establish their rights (self-help) had been accepted, the local officials wanted to permit the new owners to hire others to perform their required stint of a given number of days of work on the project. The Americans felt that this put a monetary value on the land and would result in all of the land ultimately going to those who were already well off.

The matter was ultimately resolved at the national level in Vientiane. Maximum holdings of any one family was set at three hectares and priority was given first to refugees, second to present owners of land in the irrigated areas who do not hold three hectares (they are given enough to fill out their three hectare allotment), and lastly to persons from the area who do not own land. All self-help had to be performed by the family of the allottee. The Provincial Land Council, which included an American member, adjudicated these tenure problems.

Changes in the values and institutions relating to wealth resulted from the greater availability of material resources and, because of carefully prescribed and invoked procedures, reasonably equitable distribution of these resources. The program allowed for greater scope for personal decisions regarding the use of resources. This, in turn, weakened the position of the former shapers of power, while at the same time giving the villagers a better sense of economic security and a more relaxed view of themselves and their neighbors.

Well-being

The pre-1964 Lao in Muong Phieng valley had literally no medical care in the case of accident or disease. The area had a very high incidence of rabies, cerebral malaria, and intestinal diseases. Among school children examined at the start of the cluster period, some 70 percent were infested with worms. A medical team from the OB hospital in Sayaboury (30 kilometers north) made a tour of the accessible villages once or twice a year during the dry season. Patients could reach the hospital only by walking or by horseback. All other care was supplied by village herbalists and witches.

Physical security, in terms of the threat of attack by countergovernmental forces or by bandits, was never a serious problem before 1964, although isolated incidents had been reported. A local security guard force had been created some years ago but was disbanded for lack of work.

During the cluster development period, the lives of the villagers became less secure in the military sense,[3] though their health improved.

Clinics for dispensing simple drugs and remedies were placed in six of the villages, and the local telecommunication services (jeeps with radios and the telephone system) were available in case of need. The roads made it possible for a patient to be sent to the hospital at Sayaboury within an hour, and air transport from there brought him to facilities in Vientiane, or even Bangkok. Maternal and child care were also available at the clinics. The villagers' changes in expectations regarding health have been as great as those regarding communication. Results in terms of the numbers of children surviving their early years (and possibly also the rate of child birth) were impressive. Whereas children under ten years of age were 32.8 percent of the population in 1964, the figure had risen to 38.1 percent by 1969. More mothers were said to be surviving childbirth. Villagers began to lose their fear of modern medication and to believe that injections were more effective than oral medications. Pursuit of the wealth value so changed the environment that habits essential to well-being had to be reevaluated.

Skill

The level of skills in the villages before 1964 was extremely low. Few children attained the fourth grade, and none left the valley to attend secondary schools. Farming and house building were the only applied skills—and these were primitive. No attempt had been made by the government to offer training of any kind.

These expectations changed during the cluster period. A main development tool of the cluster managers was training, some of which occurred in almost all projects. Training opportunities burst forth upon the villagers in such profusion that it was difficult for them to comprehend or evaluate the benefits to be gained.

Training was offered in several areas: raising vegetables for home use and for market, hygiene and sanitation, maternal and child care, home economics including sewing, rice growing, village leadership, fish production, raising of pigs and ducks, digging wells, and development planning. Most of the training was tied to the care or propagation of resources given to the villagers, such as pure-bred hogs, a new breed of ducks, seeds, water-seal toilets, and fingerling fish. The training effort probably suffered from its own diversity as well as from competition with other elements of the cluster program which also demanded the villagers' time and attention.

In any event, the villagers became aware of alternative ways to accomplish tasks and discovered that formal learning does not necessarily stop after the fourth grade. In some cases the participation of the villagers may have been clouded by strong pressures to join the training classes. In any case, the availability of the many courses created a pervasive atmosphere of change as well as an awareness of certain positive values in change which slowly broadened the villagers' intellectual scope. Specific new skills increased the villagers' wealth, well-being, and participation in the sharing of power. Some skills reduced his dependence on ritualized decisions (selection of the auspiciously correct time to start planting rice, as determined by the *bonzes*) and changed his values concerning religion and rectitude.

Affection

Before 1964, the affective life of the villagers seems to have been limited to positive feelings for family and fellow villagers, along with feelings of fear or distrust for persons of other villages. The extent to which the villagers felt themselves a part of a Lao national community is unclear. This area had at one time belonged to Thailand, and trading relationships still persisted. Some villagers were said to have pictures of the Thai King in their homes.

The complex of Cluster activities produced an unexpected sense of community among the villagers, especially in their feeling toward other valley villages. This attitude was accompanied by a greater feeling of affection and tolerance for neighbors who previously had been feared and distrusted. Villagers sometimes said, "Now we like each other better." One villager noted that before the cluster period each man wore a knife if he ventured outside his village area. This practice had been since abandoned.

This new sense of community included the other Lao villages in the valley, but not the Meo refugee villages. The presence of these settlers introduced new dimensions of competition and fear in the Lao villagers. The Meo were feared because they always carried rifles and grenades (many of the men were active members of the military forces fighting on the Plain of Jars). They hunted in the surrounding area and killed fish by detonating grenades in the rivers. In addition, they were proving to be industrious and effective lowland farmers. Their achievements in getting new land into production put some of the Lao farmers to shame.

Apart from the potential ethnic conflicts, inter-Lao conflicts in the valley changed from physical violence to legal battles. This was both a function of reduced interpersonal hostilities and of the fact that property, with the construction of irrigation facilities, had become worth fighting for.

The depth of the changes in personal attitudes as well as a portent for the future were illustrated by the children's attitudes toward strangers. Where children used to hide when strangers or officials appeared, they no longer showed any fear, and even tried to sell things to visitors.

Respect

In Muong Phieng valley, a society with few material resources, respect was the main currency of social intercourse. Each person knew and accepted his place in the social hierarchy. It was customary for persons of rank to wear a knife, the handle of which was banded in silver. The number of bands indicated the villager's rank.

The gross characteristics of the class structure were simple. The top political stratum consisted of the local representatives of the central government, the Chao Muong and the *Nai Ban*, plus the school teachers. Next were the locally elected authorities, the *Tassengs* (elected from their own group by all of the village chiefs) and the village chiefs (*Nai Bans*). The remainder of the population were agriculturists of varying degrees of wealth and prestige.

The cluster period introduced a middle class of merchants into the community. As owners and dispensers of desirable and readily available consumer goods, they contributed to raising the general economic level. Some store owners operated one or two taxis, thereby subsidizing their trips to Sayaboury for supplies while offering cheap transportation to customers from villages which did not have retail stores.

The cluster also subjected the existing hierarchy of village chiefs to unusual pressures. The villagers began to evaluate their chief's performance in terms of the assistance they were able to secure from the cluster management. Grumbling about "backward" *Nai Bans* was heard, but whether this resulted in removal from office is uncertain. New *Nai Bans* were elected in half of the valley villages during the five years of cluster activity under review.

Two Meo resettlement villages were built in this hitherto wholly Lao valley. They often worked together harmoniously (some of the Meo women had had to hire Lao men to work their rice fields when their men were fighting on the Plain of Jars), but there remained latent antagonism between the Lao and the Meo. The Meo did not comprise a given stratum in valley society; they duplicated the Lao strata except for the top levels, which were held by the Lao. Because of the close contiguity required for the operation of irrigation systems, there was hope that the latent antagonism could be converted into mutual respect, an outcome which, however, had not yet been fulfilled.

A net outcome of the cluster activities was the conversion of the expectation of receiving respect and granting respect from an automatic and nonvolitional mode to a more critical and functional one. Respect now had to be merited in terms of the new power, wealth, and other values before it was granted.

Rectitude

Prior to the cluster era, all village inhabitants followed Buddhism, the national religion. Except for one or two small satellites, every village had a *wat* and a monk in attendance, plus numerous novitiates. Religious festivals (*bouns*) were held regularly in each *wat*, with attendance usually limited (but not restricted) to the *wat's* villagers. Monetary and in-kind contributions to the *wat*—a primary objective of the festivals—were small. The *wat* buildings were very plain, with little of the ornamentation normally characteristic of Buddhist *wats*.

Significant changes were introduced by the cluster. One of the earliest successes reported by the first cluster agriculturist was the elimination of a religious ceremony as the means for selecting the date to start planting rice each season. The date traditionally chosen was too late for this region and increased the possibility of crop failures. He convinced the farmers that an earlier start should be made and thus started a process of secularizing certain local religious practices. As a result, the religious festivals gained in entertainment value.

The improved roads permitted people from many villages to attend, receipts rose, and the villagers began to look forward to a new form of organized entertainment. The village of Na Tane, which was second only to Muong Phieng in wealth and prestige, even purchased its own generator and sound equipment so that it could continue this new kind of *boun* independent of foreign assistance.

Another change came with the introduction of the Meo, most of whom were animists. There was also a large sprinkling of Christians among them, and the first movement of Meo into the valley was assisted by a Protestant missionary group. The village of Nam Hia, had a well-attended Christian church led by a Meo minister. Later a group of catholic Meo arrived and built their church. They were led by an Italian priest. This group developed an economic unity through their cooperative purchase and use of a tractor and other modern farm equipment.

At the same time the monks perceived a secularization of their ceremonies. The number of monks permanently stationed at the *wats* dropped from eighteen to eleven over the cluster period, and the *bouns* became more directly the concern of the *salawat,* the lay chairman of each village *wat* committee.

It is too early to evaluate the consequences or extent of the secularization of Buddhism in the valley. There were difficulties in persuading the farmers to use fertilizer and insecticides. It seems possible that if, at the time of reducing the influence of the clergy on setting the time for rice planting, discussions had been held with the Buddhist monks to apprise them of the proposed change, they might have helped to promote other aspects of the program. Such an approach might have saved face for the clergy and enlisted them on the side of development.

An Application of the Value Map

Operations at Muong Phieng would have been improved had planners tried to elicit the response of the local population to the three categories of behavior Montgomery has postulated as prerequisite to any substantial developmental advance, namely, acceptance of the need to adopt new standards, investment of one's own substance in one's future, and acceptance of institutionalized arbitration and judicial procedures for resolving conflicts arising out of the processes of development.

The following brief classification of changes demonstrates the utility of the policy science approach in testing hypotheses relating to developmental change.

Power

1. *Standards.* Before the project there were prevailing standards of command and obedience relationships; there was little contact with officials. After the project began, new standards emerged, providing new symbols and resources, and giving status to technical change agents.

2. *Investments.* Land and control of water were the sources of the wealthy farmers' (who were also the local officials) power over the villagers (clients) before modernization began. During the cluster period, the villagers, who had been automatically excluded from that source of power, began to find other sources by joining committees to plan development projects and receiving support from the superimposed cluster officials. At the same time, the Royal governor invested his prestige in support of modernization and thus reduced the degree of haggling.

3. *Citizenship and Conflict Mediation.* Before the project, there was no cooperative means for reconciling internal conflict, and the elite resented modernization because it threatened their source of power. Afterward, a Lao cluster employee became accepted as an advisor and mediator of interest conflicts; however, some conflicts between local officials and foreign aid officials remained unresolved. Anticipated ethnic conflict over water rights still posed a problem. On the other hand, the villagers used an innovative (for this area) method for appealing from provincial land councils decisions. Possibly as the power relationships became more diffused, the role of law and administration was increased.

Enlightenment

1. *Standards.* Before the project the village was a "little culture" with few external contacts, and only limited expectations of visits from outside officials. Afterward, villagers began to use radio communications

to summon the government's veterinary services; they made use of library and newspaper facilities; and in general they had developed new expectations for governmental roles.

2. *Investments.* Before the project, villagers had to undergo a two-day trek to central towns for their contact with the larger culture. They had relied on a barter system of exchange for the economic sources of innovation. The youth could invest in modernization only by migrating out of the village. Afterward, villagers could and did purchase radio receivers. They up-graded the Buddhist festivals as a means of enlightenment and socializing.

3. *Citizenship and Conflict Resolution.* Before the project, there was little indication that enlightenment issues created conflict; there was no consciousness of rights, for example. After the project, however, this consciousness increased, and the villagers were faced with the need to adhere to water use regulations.

Wealth

1. *Standards.* Originally, horses, elephants, and buffaloes were an important source of wealth for the elite classes; the poor leased them as needed. Savings had had to be hoarded for years of poor harvest. Afterward, buffaloes and irrigated land became a source of wealth, and new standards of agricultural technology (including new rice strains, the cash economy, the introduction of hogs and ducks, and the use of rice bran for feed) became possible.

2. *Investments.* Originally, poor farmers had to walk two to five kilometers to their fields, while the wealthy owned the fields nearby. Afterward, more poor people began to own buffaloes and hogs and were willing to invest their labor in double-cropping. Eight new rice mills, over twenty retail stores, and a number of taxis and trucks were introduced.

3. *Citizenship and Conflict Mediation.* Before the project, the more wealthy villagers resisted such challenges as the irrigation system and its

regulations; but afterwards, they had to accept land reform and the jurisdiction of the Land Council.

Well-being

1. *Standards.* Before the project there was a high disease rate and a prevalence of witch doctors. Afterward, there were much higher expectations of medical service and a greater acceptance of various facilities for social enjoyment with new standards for the religious festivals.

2. *Investments.* Before the project, the only villager investment in health was in walking to hospitals or waiting for the biennial visit of the mobile medical team. After development of the cluster project they could go to local clinics or ride to the hospital some thirty kilometers away. Although they had made little investment in social organizations for pleasure (except for the religious festivals), they were prepared to invest in sanitary facilities as their utility became increasingly evident.

3. *Citizenship and Conflict Resolution.* Before the project, there was a high crime rate for petty thievery, although the area did not engage the attention of organized banditry—perhaps because there was little valuable property. Afterward, as the population received better care, the Pathet Lao considered the area a threat to their objectives, and made and threatened attack, thereby slowing progress and inhibiting participation by foreign technicians and investors.

Skills

1. *Standards.* Originally the buildings of the villages were primitive. Even after the project, however, the villagers had little perception of the new standards that were about to appear and were so careless in their handling of mechanical equipment that they were unable to keep water pumps and other equipment in repair. This conforms to what Montgomery would call the "crisis of apathy": standards did not change despite government inputs.

2. *Investments.* Before the project, none left the area for training; after it, there was the expectation of emergent new investments in training.
3. *Citizenship-Conflict.* There was no interest in skills, and hence no skill-related conflict before the project. Afterward, the villagers sometimes resisted the new opportunities because the traditional skills were in conflict with government objectives, a condition which might have been improved by a more rational recognition of conflicting preferences;

Affection
1. *Standards.* Before the project, loyalty was limited to the family; there was a distrust of villagers from other villages. After the project, the village became more tolerant of neighbors, and the children less intimidated by visitors.
2. *Investments.* The limited scope of affective relationships created a risk of a fight whenever one ventured outside the small group; the villagers had to protect themselves by wearing knives. After the project had changed these affective relationships, the risks were reduced, the villagers began to travel without wearing knives, and even engaged in joint training with the previously disliked Meo.
3. *Citizenship-Conflict.* Before the project, there were few conflicts except for inter-village jealousies and suspicions. Afterward, this potential for conflict was reduced, because all parties accepted certain joint functions, such as road construction, and made use of legal rather than violent means of reconciling communal conflicts.

Respect
1. *Standards.* Respect relationships before the project existed along hierarchical and status lines; afterward, there were new standards appropriate to middle-class service to the community. New standards also applied to leaders, who were expected to earn the positions they occupied.

2. *Investments.* Before the project, respect investments by villagers included universally observed symbols of rank, such as the silver bands on their knives; afterward, crosscutting projects created conditions of mutuality, involving respect. They also introduced cooperative relationships in organizational activities.

3. *Citizenship-Conflict Resolution.* Before the project, class rivalry was not resolved, but was suppressed, by the rigid structure of relationships. Afterward, there was an acceptance of elections. This reduced somewhat the class-based claim to leadership of the traditional elders.

Rectitude

1. *Standards.* Before the project, the entire village was Buddhist. Afterward, it not only included Christian and animist members, but also introduced some secularization in the old religious festivals, such as that involved in the setting of dates for agricultural activities.

3. *Investments.* There was little investment in the *wat* or the *bouns* before the project. Afterward, there was both larger attendance at the *bouns* and more receipts. One village even purchased an electric generator for its *bouns,* and another built two Christian churches.

3. *Citizenship-Conflict.* Before the project, there had been no religious conflict. Afterward, there was still no provision for the disinvestment in religion that took place as the monks moved out, (although the number of novitiates is said to have increased) and as the status of the clergy seemed to be downgraded. This conceivably might cause some difficulty in the future.

It is now possible to summarize these behavioral indicators (see Table 3.1) in order to explore the nature of the value shifts as the society moved toward modernization. It will be noted that the so-called "soft" values may be declining, while the "hard" values (power, enlightenment, and wealth) are becoming more important. Whether this trend should be encouraged, whether it is inherent in the development process,

Table 3.1
Value Shifts during Modernization Process

Value	Scope of Change	Effect of Technology	Salience
Power	New sources	Reduced elite dependence on land, but other groups permitted to rise. But national policy introduced competitive group	Not major in "before" situation, possibly rising in "after" situation
Enlighten-ment	Broader range	Communications weaken grip of old basis of knowledge and wisdom	Becomes an important source of change
Wealth	More forms	Trucks, farming technology increase opportunity	Possibly a major element in community life
Well-being	Emergent new expectations	Greatly improved services, not yet fully perceived	Potential major source of change
Skill	Not yet affected	Village smothered with opportunity, but not yet responsive	Potential unrealized. A later form of change?
Affection	Broader but thinner links	Technology contributes broadening scope of community affective life	Direction questionable
Respect	Traditional claims weakening	Requires new basis for community leadership	Declining
RectituDe	Secularization, pluralization	Requires new decision-making processes, weakens sanctity of tradition	Declining

or whether effort should be made to stop or lessen the decline of the soft values—or even to strengthen them—is a fundamental question for development policy makers. A more practical problem is whether development administrators can devise programs that will accomplish the goals that are selected.

Conclusion

This analysis of the Muong Phieng Cluster data in terms of the Lasswellian value system has demonstrated that awareness of, or sensitivity to, the value categorization of developmental behavior is an effective means for estimating and predicting the culture-wide influences of developmental, change-oriented activities. As a practitioner in the field of development administration, I believe that a course of instruction such as a one-week seminar of carefully prepared indoctrinational material on the value system for development planners and administrators would immediately sharpen the effectiveness of aid programs. Simultaneously, a limited system of research could start deriving generalizations and principles for use in the field, and test some of the hypotheses suggested here. It would also be possible to explore the broader application of the policy science approach, including the decision processes and policy implementation procedures.

NOTES

1. John D. Montgomery, *Technology and Civic Life. Making and Implementing Development Decisions* (Cambridge, Mass.: The MIT Press, 1974), Chapter 3.

2. Not mentioned in this context, but apparent in comments made in other discussions, was resentment of the recently installed Meo population.

3. Starting in March 1969, the Pathet Lao made attacks and otherwise exerted military pressure on this area.

4 DEVELOPMENT SEQUENCE AND DOMINANT VALUE SHIFTS IN COMMUNITIES OF NORTHEAST THAILAND

HAROLD E. VOELKNER

Introduction

Most programs of modernization aim to influence the behavior of the recipient population regarding the utilization and multiplication of the investment made. As suggested by Montgomery elsewhere in this volume, the success and increased productivity of such programs are enhanced if they can be designed to utilize existing dominant values and the predictable changes which modernization almost inevitably will bring about. These changes are often triggered by new opportunities. Implementation of this proposition depends on two factors. First, it has to be shown that the proposed dominant value categories actually shift with the major phases of the modernization process. Second, identification of these phases through consistent and valid measurement must be made. This paper presents evidence and methodology on how the requirements of both factors can be met.

First, the results of a study[1] will be presented which demonstrate methodological techniques for measuring the major phases as well as the sequence of the modernization process. The methodology uses qualitative institutional and technological attributes as development indicators at the village level. Next, it will be shown that the two dominant Laswellian values associated with the investment of each indicator can be identified by deduction. A simple cross tabulation showing the highest percent present as the dominant value in each major development phase indicates that the predicted shifts from one phase to the other indeed do occur.

Methodology

The technique used to measure development sequence and phases is the scalogram analysis of the cumulative or Guttman scale. The scale is used here to measure the institutional and technological complexity of communities in Loei province in northeast Thailand. Observable qualitative attributes of a physical or social nature were used as indicators. Three of the data sets or sources used are most relevant for this paper: (1) detailed village maps from the Accelerated Rural Development (ARD) Program in northeast Thailand, (2) 1967 aerial photography produced for the Pa Mong Dam Project, and (3) 1970 Thai census data aggregated for each village. The results of these three sets of data show that any one comprehensive data set can be used to measure the degree of complexity (differentiation) in communities.

The special use of the scale technique and the analysis are based on a model of structural development, the Structural Complexity Growth Model (SCG model).[2] A brief sketch of the model is essential in order to follow the interpretations and conclusions made in this paper. The major premise of the SCG model is that societal complexity (differentiation) grows in systematic patterns in time and space. The basic element in the model is human knowledge and the utility-producing structures which process knowledge into some kind of use to a society.

The SCG model functions with only four abstract variables. The first variable is the diversification or the growth of knowledge and its processing structures by a process of differentiation. Growth of knowledge-processing and utility-producing structures takes place in increments of a fairly definite sequence. It results in systems of communication channels for distributing utilities of processed knowledge either in physical forms (such as products and materials), or in the form of energy (such as gas, oil, or electricity), or in the form of ideas (such as news, books, laws, or public opinion and values).

The second variable concerns the relative access of social units (such as villages or individuals or countries) to the communication systems structure, which may be seen as the relative access each unit has to the distribution system. The structural system is all-inclusive in communicating products of human knowledge which range from the most mundane physical to the most esoteric abstract. Access to this system, in general, depends on position in the social hierarchy of a society as well as location in geographic space.

The third variable appears as a direct consequence of an imbalance between variables in both their differentiation and in their position in or access to the distribution system. It is caused by a recognition of new knowledge and potential benefits, coupled with a lack of access to their processed utility. New knowledge without utilization produces stress until the utility is realized through special effort (investment). Because knowledge utility can be obtained only through specific structures, access to such structures must be achieved by investments to build such structures, or to obtain access to existing structures (land, tax, or social reform).

The degree of the third variable, that is, the size of the investment necessary to reduce the imbalance between variables, is amplified by a fourth variable, the rigidity or elasticity of a society in permitting aspired changes to occur. Rigidity can be social or physical. Social rigidity ranges from the extremes of an open, pluralistic society to those of an inflexible caste-ridden society. Physical rigidity is determined by the availability of physical resources, which often depends on the state of technology in a society.

The measurement of development content and sequence involves primarily the first and second variables, the identification of the structural systems of processing and distributing human knowledge. Many parts of this structure are readily recognizable either physically or abstractly and may be seen as indicators (social symbols) of the structure. All expressions of human activity—sounds, behavior patterns, artifacts, thus become symbols of the structure of which they are part. The measurement of the fundamental dimension of societal structure at the village level, its institutional and technological complexity, may begin by identifying different institutional establishments in the village, and other community level artifacts which can also be seen on aerial photography or on detailed maps. A valid alternative set of indicators would be census data on education, occupations, and industries present in each village. Any kind of comprehensive data which adequately represent the complexity (differentiation) of existing structures can be used for measurement. This theoretical assumption makes it possible to test whether scales of occupational complexity based on census data and scales of aerial photography or map data which identify institutional and technological complexity are valid alternatives in measuring levels of societal development.

Measuring Development Sequence and Phases

For this study several measurements were made of the degree of structural complexity in various village communities in the Pa Mong reservoir area in northeast Thailand. Their institutional and technological complexity and thus the relative levels of development in these communities were identified. The technique used was cumulative Guttman scaling, which converts the presence or absence of qualitative indicators of either institutions or technology into a quantitative measure. It converts a list of dichotomous data (attributes) into a single yardstick for measuring social complexity. From that point forward, standard statistics can be used, and correlations with all other types of available data, qualitative and quantitative, can be made.

Cumulative scaling produces an array of cases in hierarchical order showing the accumulative items for each. In this study the cases are villages and the items are the structural attributes of these villages. Data from the maps of the Accelerated Rural Development (ARD) Program in Thailand were used in the first approximation of the relative levels of development of villages. The presence of public structures (school, well, temple, and so forth) in each village was identified from maps and coded as items per village for computer processing into maximal scales.[3]

The diversity of structural attributes of each village is measured by its scale score. For instance, in Figure 4.1, the map scale, village 42 has a scale score of 16 while village 1 has a scale score of 2. This means that village 1 has two items of structural attributes, wells and dirt streets, while village 42 has these two attributes plus others, such as temples, schools, rice mill, market building, and power station. Assuming that the more diversified structurally a village is, the more developed it is, the relative levels of development of villages can be depicted by the array of scale scores.

Most of the items contained in the map scale in Figure 4.1 can also be identified on good aerial photography. (Most recent maps are actually based on aerial photography.) But aerial photography contains much more information which is useful in the analysis of structural complexities, such as distinct attributes in residential construction, agricultural technology, and community patterns.

The villages analyzed on aerial photography for the study ranged from the rather sophisticated district town of Loei to the small remote settlements among the mountains some thirty kilometers west of Loei. Differences in qualitative levels of attributes between these two extremes are readily recognized on the aerial photos, but one can also identify many small differences in housing technology and agriculture between the small mountain villages. Scalogram analysis makes these differences measurable objectively and consistently.

On the 1967 aerial photography, 142 attribute indicators of community or individual investments could be identified in the whole area. Of these items, 95 scaled (Figure 4.2). The items represent any discernible detail of qualitative variation in village patterns, agriculture, dwellings, institutions, and transport access. Some redundancy present in the scale has been removed. The scale on Figure 4.2 shows that the identified

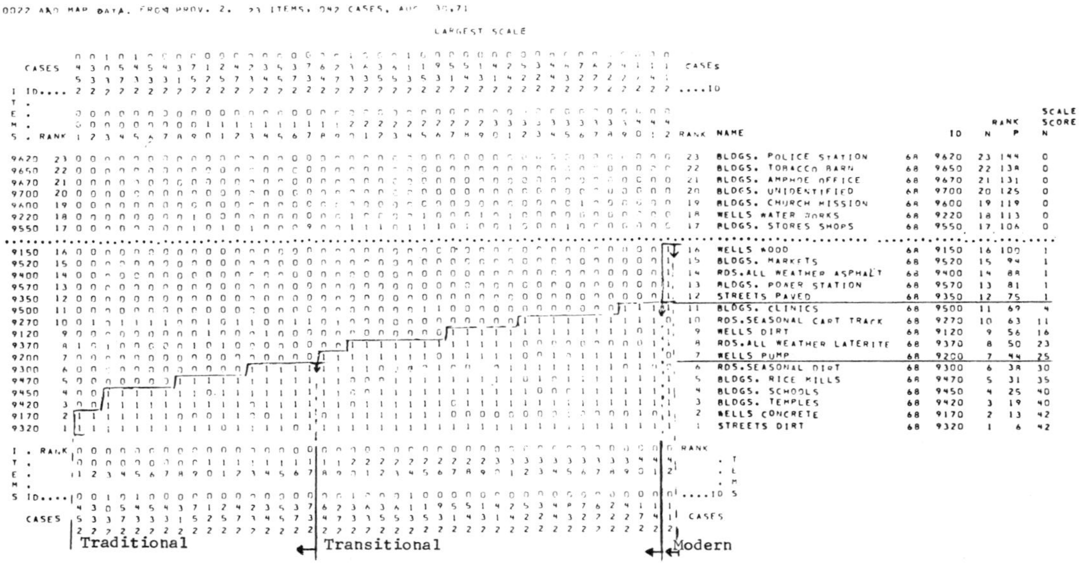

Figure 4.1
Scalogram of Structural Attributes of Forty-seven Thai Villages

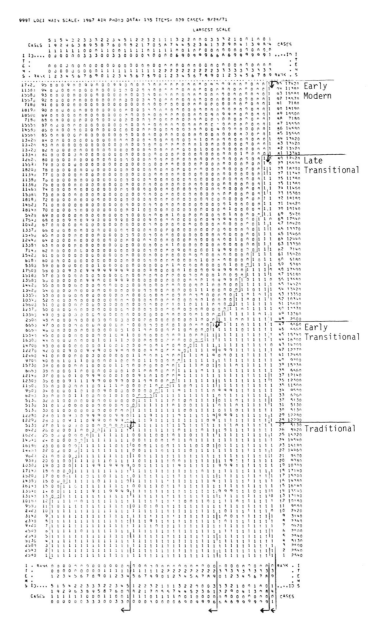

Figure 4.2
Scalogram of Development Investments of Thirty-nine Thai Villages

indicators of village investments are accumulated in a fairly orderly sequence. At the same time, the villages become ordered into a hierarchy of increasing complexity and diversity. Though the same in principle as the scale in Figure 4.1, this much larger scale demonstrates the power of the methodology to show minute details of the development process.[4]

According to the SCG model, the growth of structural complexity is a unidimensional process in societal development. In practice this means that different data sets from different categories of knowledge-processing structure should merely be alternatives in measuring complexity. The aerial photo scale (Figure 4.2) also verifies this major premise of the SCG model, namely that structural differentiation is indeed a unidimensional process. The economic development concepts which conceive of agriculture, residential living levels, transportation, and public or private service institutions as belonging to different sectors, being more or less distinct and independent or at best only correlated in the development process, are contradicted here. The nearly uniform interspersing of items from all these categories in the scale shows that the interdependency between them is much stronger than has previously been possible to determine by sector analyses.

The significance of this finding is that with caution it is only necessary to measure the increasing complexity of any one sector or data category to identify the relevant relative development levels (investment complexity). One can then assess the development state of other sectors in specific villages if the total investment content at each level has otherwise been determined.

For a detailed analysis of the scale one could proceed either by analyzing the development of "sectors" such as dwelling construction, agriculture, or institutions, or by analyzing groups of villages and indicators, as they may represent the major phases of development commonly labeled traditional, early transitional, late transitional, and early modern. Sector content is best analyzed by sector subscales which there was no time to produce, but the following is a brief demonstration of the second type of analysis. Villages 1 to 14 (by rank number), representing the traditional phase, are remote and not even accessible by all-weather dirt roads. They have a scattered or simple line village pattern, but most have at least a temple and a school. Some complex dwellings and temple structures begin to appear. All are growing rice but not much else.

The next group of villages (15 to 29) in the early transitional phase shows some increasing sophistication in village pattern (crossroads or organic) and in agriculture (fruits and vegetables). Institutions are becoming more conspicuous with the addition of Buddhist chapels, flag poles, and entrance structures.

The last group of villages (30 to 38) reflects a growing modernization and commercialization of the late transitional phase: population density and land utilization is high; forest areas between villages have disappeared; commercial agriculture in vegetables and fruits is present as is irrigation and double cropping; some dwellings and institutional structures are built of brick or concrete; and institutional complexes are large with many buildings arranged in patterns. Some industrial and commercial structures are present in subcommunities of the largest villages near the town of Loei, where modern public services in the form of water tanks and paved roads and streets also have appeared.

The last settlement, number 39, is the town of Loei. It represents the early modern phase, indicating its provincial town status by having electric power, an airfield, a market hall, institutional recreation facilities, and several different patterns in larger institutional compounds. If one compares the complexity of this town and the most developed six villages in the late transitional phase with the two least developed villages (rank 1 and 2), the tremendous difference in investment structures becomes apparent. They seem worlds apart in terms of utilization of knowledge. One has to keep in mind, however, that many structures which make some villages higher in development (central villages), provide services (processed knowledge) to the surrounding villages in their microregion, so that these other villages have more utilities available than are indicated on the scale. This is a most important aspect of the central village-microregional pattern for development planning.

The interdependent relationship between the growth of complexity (development) and the economies of scale provided by higher population density, which, in turn, is dependent on land and other resources (physical rigidity) is evident in a few of the correlations presented in Table 4.1. Some quantitative variables were collected from the aerial photography and correlated with the AP Scale scores as part of the factor analysis program. Table 4.1 present the most relevant correlation coefficients produced by the program.

To show that aerial photography data can measure the same structural development pattern of settlements as do much more expensively collected ground data, a comparison was necessary. The most fitting set of data for this purpose were the 1970 Census data for the Loei district. The data were compiled per village by the Thai National Statistic Office (NSO) for this project.

The census data cover occupations and accompanying industries and the levels of education of various age groups in each settlement. This is more specialized information than that of the air photo data, but it is representative of a central and major part of the investment structure in communities.

Structural investment differentiation is related to population size in contiguous settlements. Thus specific structural attributes that are present in different subcommunities are serving the larger settlement as a whole. For structural investment analysis, it is essential to combine subcommunities into functional settlement areas and measure the total structural content as one unit. For Loei, which contains at least eight

Table 4.1
Correlation Coefficients for Village Development Variables

A. Loei AP Scale Scores Corrlated with Variables Collected per Village from Aerial Photography

	Correlation Coefficient
Number of dwellings	.66
Km^2 paddy land	.64
Lack of forest area between next village code	.69
Ha. village area	.63
Number of paved roads	.67
Number of roads with new dwellings	.70
Number of new dwellings	.79
Number of commercial subcommunities	.61
Number of industrial subcommunities	.64
Number of institutions (temples, schools, shops, etc.)	.67
Number of institutional buildings	.60
Size of largest institution building	.75
Largest number of wings on institution building	.67
Institutional boundary code (fences, hedges, walls, etc.)	.60
Institutional tree growth	.65
Number of school rooms estimated	.77

B. Correlations between AP Scale Scores and Selected Census Variables

(per Village)	Correlation Coefficient
Census scale score	.72
Population	.65
Population in agriculture	.63
Number of people literate	.65
Percent males illiterate	-.54
Number of people with secondary education	.65
Number of people with vocational education	.61
Number of people working in electric and water services	.65
Number of people working in construction and repair	.55
Number of people working in manufacturing	.55

C. Census Village Population Correlation with Variables Collected by Aerial Photography

	Correlation Coefficient
Number of dwellings/village from aerial photography	.98
Number of institutions/village from aerial photography	.97
Number of paved roads/village from aerial photography	.80
Number of temples/village from aerial photography	.64
The percentile census scale score	.75
The percentile AP scale score	.64

Means and Correlations were computed by the BMD Factor Analysis Program at the Bureau of Standards Computer Center at Gaithersburg, Maryland.

subcommunities, this aggregation was made in the town area identified as a special subdivision in the district. The importance of this fact for scalogram analysis of communities must be emphasized. Only the sum total of the structural content of groups of subcommunities is usable in scalogram analysis.

Keeping these limitations in mind, the following cursory interpretation of the Loei Census Scale (Figure 4.3) can be made.[5] (Since the census data are for the whole Loei district the scale contains eighty-five villages.) As in the AP scale, the villages appear to be grouped into four major development levels. The traditional phase group (rank numbers 1 to 39) contains predominantly farming and service occupations. Elementary education of people over sixty years of age goes only to the fourth grade. (The elementary education of other age groups is present everywhere and has not been put into the scale.) In the second group of villages, the early transitional phase (rank 40 to 72), commercial and home craft industry occupations appear. The highest education of old people is still only the elementary fourth grade. In the third group (rank 73 to 81), representing the late transitional phase, service, commercial, and manufacturing occupations have been added for the old and young. Education for the old goes beyond the elementary fourth grade to the seventh grade. For the early modern phase (rank 81 to 85), modern public services in the form of water and electricity appear only in Loei town at the top of the scale. Secondary education, both general and vocational, had become available for those over sixty. So has the modern occupation of "administrative executive."

The comparison of the aerial photo data and 1970 census data and scales was made quantitatively by correlation and factor analysis and qualitatively by scalogram analysis on maps. The comparison maps of the air photo and census scales show that in general the microregion and central village locations are almost the same. This is taken as evidence that the air photo data are a valid and highly useful alternative to

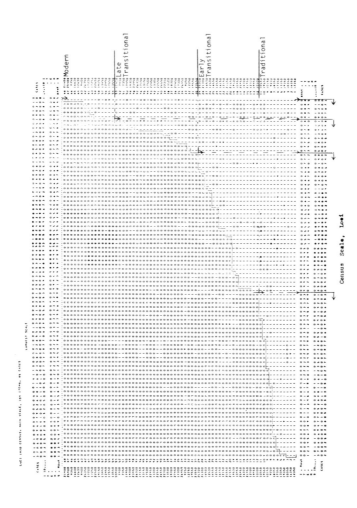

Figure 4.3
Scalogram Interpretation of Loei District Census of Eighty-five Thai Villages

even very intensively collected data on the ground. The major impli-cation is that air photo data can be used anywhere to measure devel-opment levels of microregions, but are especially useful in areas that are either very remote or otherwise have limited access for data surveys on the ground. They also are most applicable for any region where the col-lection of data from aerial photography is less expensive than ground surveys. This is especially the case when aerial photography already has been taken and paid for by other purposes.

Factor analysis was used not only to check on the results of scalogram analysis but also to process the considerable amounts of quantitative data collected from aerial photography and contained in the census data. We also were anxious to see how the factor scores per village produced by factor analysis would compare with the scale scores in the identification of the same village hierarchies. We discovered that the relationship between factor scores and scale scores becomes very close if the scores of certain factors are added before they are compared with the scale scores. The close relationship comes about if only the first two factors (out of 10) are added from a factor-analysis of 75 variables from ground and air photo data sets. The relationship becomes almost a forty-five-degree line, which to us means that the scores can be perfect alternatives in measuring development differences between villages. To test this we plotted the factor scores on a map to see if the same central villages would be identified. Almost exactly the same villages were iden-tified as central villages in the sample area as were identified by aerial photo or map data. In only one case did the neighboring village become the central village, village AP-9 for village AP-8, and here the two villages are contiguous and should be taken as one unit.

We also tried to explain why certain factor scores have to be added before they correlate highly with scale scores. Examining the factors which are correlating with the scale scores, one notices that the variables contained in these factors also represent qualitative differentiation. In other words, they can be reduced to represent the presence or absence of a quality, for instance, industries and educational levels present in the ground data scale, and the number of institutional buildings, school rooms, types of road, temples, estimated hectares of gardens, paddy fields, and hill rice fields in the air data scale.

Factor analysis identifies qualitative specializations from quantitative variance. It does so by grouping villages which are stronger quantitatively in certain qualities, such as high education and larger numbers of non-agricultural population (one factor) versus larger areas of paddy fields, higher percentages and numbers of population in agriculture, and higher uniformity of village dwellings and village patterns (another factor). Those factors which are additive in terms of measuring levels of total development usually can be recognized by entering the scale scores for factor analysis. It appears the addition of these variables does not significantly alter the factors in the factor matrix, but invariably the scale scores load in several factors. We have found scale scores to load in those factors which if added present the closest correlation with the scale scores.

The comparison of ground and air data in both qualitative and quantitative data to us means that: (1) the two methodologies can be valid alternatives in measuring relative development levels of villages; and (2) that they process and measure two different kinds of information in data, each one presenting valuable information for development analysis; (3) however, since one needs the scale scores to identify the factors to be added for development contours, factor analysis alone does not appear to be a useful method for structural development mapping.

The scale methodology through the scale and the scale scores identifies very detailed differences in quality between villages and micro-regions. Factor analysis in the factor scores measures the quantitative difference between villages but it does not identify, except very roughly, the qualitative difference between villages on which the quantities are based. In practice the two methodologies can usefully complement each other. Since both air photo and ground data always contain both qualitative and quantitative information, processing the data by both methods produces more insights into the development structure than if only one or the other methodology is used alone.

We are also interested in a more general conclusion: the qualitative presence of an attribute in a unit can be assumed to increase quantitatively (as an aggregate variable) as the unit adds further attributes, that is, as it rises in the scale. The two types of data, qualitative and quantitative, can serve as substitutes for each other as the availability of reliable data and processing facilities favor one or the other.[6]

Findings: Development Phases and Value Shifts

Cumulative scales which measure the details of the development sequence also can identify the major overlapping phases of development referred to earlier as traditional, transitional, modern, and postmodern. However, the institutions and technologies of each phase do not appear to be exclusive in time and space. Rather, the phases superimpose one on top of the other, as can be seen in the scales. Old institutions and technologies do die out, but at a much slower rate than new institutions and technologies develop on top of them. Thus, all development phases usually are represented by some indicators in the most highly developed communities. If motivational values shift with each phase of the development process, the important implication is that communities do not shift values as a whole but rather, certain layers in the community represent present value shifts. In fact, individual persons may continue to have several sets of values depending on whether their specific investments and activities belong to either the traditional, transitional, or modern phase. Only where a coexistence of values, institutions, and technologies of the different phases is not possible or is not tolerated must elimination take place.

Table 4.2
Primary Social Values at Major Development Levels

Development Level		Values							
		P	E	W	B	S	A	R	D
A. Number and percent each value per development level in Chapter 1, Table 1.1[1]									
Post Modern	%	–	7	–	36	–	29	29	–
	#	–	1	–	5	–	4	4	–
Modern	%	21	14	29	7	–	–	21	7
	#	3	2	4	1	–	–	.3	1
Transitional	%	7	14	21	29	29	–	–	–
	#	1	2	3	4	4	–	–	–
Traditional	%	–	–	7	–	14	21	36	21
	#	–	–	1	–	2	3	5	3
B. Number and percent each value per development level in Air Photo Scale[2]									
Early Modern	%	14	4	32	11	7	4	18	11
	#	4	1	9	3	2	1	5	3
Late Transitional	%	8	2	27	10	23	7	10	13
	#	5	2	16	6	14	4	6	8
Early Transitional	%	–	3	18	24	24	15	9	9
	#	–	1	6	8	8	5	3	3
C. Number and percent each value per development level in Census Scale[3]									
Early Modern	%	13	6	25	19	19	–	6	13
	#	2	1	4	3	3	–	1	2
Late Transitional	%	–	9	33	17	22	11	–	9
	#	–	4	15	5	10	5	–	4
Early Transitional	%	–	7	32	18	32	4	7	–
	#	–	2	9	5	9	1	2	–
Traditional	%	–	–	–	–	18	23	36	23
	#	–	–	–	–	4	5	8	5

1. For each level Σ 2× society values plus 1× sector values.
2. For each level Σ two values per item in air photo scale; see Figure 4.2.
3. For each level Σ two values per item in census scale; see Figure 4.3.

To test the proposition that dominant values are shifting with different phases of development, the two dominant values were deduced which were most likely associated with the investment of each of the items in the scale. In Table 4.2, the two dominant values per item were added in the Item Statistics tables. The contextuality of the phase, which in the item is found in the scale, was considered in assigning which two values were probably dominant.[7]

A simple test of the hypothesis of shifting values required its conversion into quantities per phase. The percent frequency of each value per development phase was computed first for the matrix proposed by Montgomery in Table 1.1. Values with highest percentage presence in each phase are considered dominant and circled by solid lines. The next highest are circled by broken lines. Shifts of dominant values from phase to phase are indicated by arrows. The results are presented in Table 4.2.A.

The same computation and cross tabulation was done for each of the scales. The percentage presence of each value in each of the phases was determined and presented in the same fashion as the hypothetical process proposed by Montgomery. The only difference between the hypothesized relationships and the scale matrices is that the hypothetical pattern includes the postmodern development phase while the scale patterns only reach the early modern phases. At the same time, the traditional phase has been divided into early and late transitional.

The close correlation between the shifting patterns of the hypothesized matrix and the scale matrices is striking. Although these must be considered cursory trial results, they do indicate empirical verification of the validity of the Montgomery hypothesis. Equally important is the demonstration that the two methodologies, scalogram analysis and value analysis, as well as their theoretical models can be combined for development measurement, analysis, and evaluation. The combination can become a most powerful tool for development analysis, if it is further refined and validated through repeated studies and applications.

The chicken-or-egg question of whether values change first and then technology and institutions, or vice versa, is not answered in favor of one or the other. The actual process, as stipulated in the SCG model, is reciprocal. New technology provides new opportunities which, if recognized, change values which, in turn, invite further technology or new institutions. Once started, it is hoped that this spiraling roller coaster will go up without too many downs. It is the role of development administration to speed up the former and reduce the latter. This task becomes easier as the process is better understood and measured.

Summary of Conclusions

1. The scalogram analysis of technological and institutional investments with their deduced dominant motivational values appears to be a feasible empirical method for improving the capacity of public (and private) agencies to mobilize popular commitments to, and investments in, modernization. The methodology presented in this paper may be used to ascertain dominant values in a population for generating real investment opportunities for popular recognition and support.

2. Government agencies, with the help of the demonstrated techniques, can plan to invest in technologies and institutions which offer real opportunities to communities. They can be fitted to the reality of their existing and potential capacities at their stage in the development sequence. Real opportunity must be both perceived by the respondent and supported by a complex system of institutional and technical inputs. Both factors depend strictly on the development stage (sequence) of the development process at any particular time and place. Scalogram analysis is effective in measuring the level of development and the complex content of the support for further possible steps. Identification of dominant motivational values for each investment, in the context of the

relevant development phase, makes the prediction of existing and potentially eminent value categories possible as well.

3. In terms of the Structural Complexity Growth (SCG) model, perceived opportunity is seen as resulting from the advance of the differentiation variable, new knowledge, which causes investment motivation for building the structures necessary for obtaining the benefits from such new knowledge. The methodology with the demonstrated techniques and the briefly mentioned models provide an important tool for generating investment motivation for modernization by identifying which technologies and institutions are specifically within the range of general recognition. Opportunities can be provided by government and/or private "seed investments" which will be multiplied by feasible response investments by people and communities.

NOTES

1. The research for this study was started in December 1970 for the Agency for International Development, under contract to conduct a study of social factors of the Pa Mong area in the Mekong Basin. The results were reported in H. E. Voelkner et al., "Social Factors in Reservoir Settlements Relocation: An Adaptation of Scalogram Analysis Using Aerial Photography and Ground Survey Data Applied to the Mekong Basin Pa Mong Project," Agency for International Development, U.S. Department of State, 1972.

2. Frank W. and Ruth Young, of Cornell University, have been major proponents of and contributors to the structural-complexity growth model. A book giving a more detailed explication of the model is forthcoming.

3. A special computer program was developed for the project. The program is described in Barton Sensenig, III, and Harold E. Voelkner, "Scale I: Maximal Guttman Scaling with Scale Statistics," October 1971. Copies can be obtained from The Comparative Modernization Research Project, Center for International Studies, Cornell University, Ithaca, New York, 14850.

To produce a maximal scale, the scaling program rearranges alternately the binary data of cases (presented vertically) and items (presented horizontally) at the same time that it maximizes a separation of "1's" and "0's" into opposite corners of the matrix. Zeros interspersed among the "1's" and "1's" interspersed among the "0's" are identified as scale deviations. The primary aim of the scaling process is to reduce such deviations by removing a few items at a time which contain the largest number of deviations and reordering cases and items each time this process occurs, until an acceptable scale is produced.

The acceptability of a scale is determined by the coefficient of scalability which is based on the amount of deviation present within a scale. The coefficient measures the percent perfection of a scale. A 100 percent, or perfect, scale is one without any deviations, that is, without any "0's" among the "1's" and vice versa. Such a scale would have a coefficient of 1.00. The generally acceptable limit of scale imperfection is 35 percent. This means that a 65 percent perfect scale or a scalability coefficient of 0.65 has to be attained for a scale to be acceptable.

Only items (attributes) are removed to improve a scale. Items which do not fit into the systematic accumulation, that do not scale sufficiently, are removed by placing them on top of the scale above the dotted scale line (as illustrated in Scale 1). The removed items may form what is called a "shadow scale" which contains unacceptable amounts of deviation but which, nevertheless, contrast the "1's" and "0's" roughly in the same parts of the matrix as the actual scale does below. Such a shadow scale is not present in the ARD map scale (Scale 1) for Province 2, but it is very large and distinct in the air photo and census scales shown later in the text. Shadow scales are significant in time-change analysis.

There are indications from a limited number of time series scales that such items, over time, fill in their zero deviations and scale at a later period.

See also Louis Guttman: "Cornell Technique for Scale Construction" in R. W. O. O'Brian et al. *Readings in General Sociology* (Houghton Mifflin Co., Cambridge, 1951) and several other papers by the author on the subject. The best description of the method, however, can be found in textbooks on statistical methods for social science such as M. J. Hagood and D. O. Price, *Statistics for Sociologists* (New York: Henry Holt Co., 1952).

More recently a possibly improved method of development scaling which permits atrophy of attributes has been suggested by R. K. Leik and M. Matthew, "A Scale for Developmental Processes" in *American Sociological Review* 33 (1968): 62-75.

4. Because this project demonstrates the applicability of scalogram analysis within the parameters of structural-symbolic theory, it may be concluded that the technique used and the theory are fundamentally dependent on each other. This is not the case. Guttman scaling is merely a method of systematically rearranging data according to certain rules to bring out a pattern. A Guttman scale can be interpreted by other theories or without using any theoretical frame of reference.

5. The census scales represent only a first rough processing step to identify the village hierarchy of development in the two districts, and be sufficient for a comparison with the AP scales. For a detailed, careful analysis of "processed knowledge content" considerable refinement through rescaling would be necessary and beyond the scope of this project.

6. The close relationship between quality and quantity can be hypothesized by the following three postulates.

1. Any quantity is generated by a structure which is qualitative, or conversely, the functioning of structure must generate and/or use quantity.

2. Qualitative differences in structure in most cases generate different quantities, or conversely, different quantities have, in most cases, been generated by different qualities.

3. One can measure quantity by qualitative data of structure, or conversely, any quantity contains qualitative data to measure structure.

7. The minor problem in these scales was presented by the few items which may not be at the most stable position in the scale. Items entering or moving out of the system, for instance, technology newly appearing in an area, or old technology slowly disappearing, may not appear in the scale in their proper phase level. New items generally enter at the top of the scale and shift downward until their stable position is reached. Disappearing items eventually move up in the scale and disappear, at last, in the most highly developed communities. Other studies using time series data have indicated this phenomenon.

5 MEASURING VILLAGE COMMITMENT TO DEVELOPMENT

ROBERT E. KRUG, PAUL A. SCHWARZ, AND SUCHITRA BHAKDI

The rationale or logic of the typical development project envisions a chain reaction of outcomes. The intended sequence begins with the immediate project achievements, such as the production of more rice per acre, the introduction of a handicraft industry, or the development of a cadre of highly trained public officials. It continues through a number of intermediate effects, such as higher disposable income or more efficient public administration. It ends with a contribution to the ultimate societal goal of improving the "quality of life" or overall well-being of the beneficiary group. The flow is from narrow, specific outputs that are closely linked to the nature of the project activities through increasingly broad, remote outcomes that are the common objectives of a large number of entirely different types of development programs.

The preparation of detailed, written rationales has proved generally useful for both evaluation and planning.[1] They can be generated by "forward" or "backward" analyses of the pertinent cause-effect links. That is, one can begin with a specified project activity and reason forward, to deduce the first-, second-, and higher-order consequences that are likely to flow from this type of intervention. Or, one can begin with a desired outcome and reason backward, to deduce the antecedent conditions that will have to be created, and therefore the types of interventions that are needed to set the process in motion. The former approach produces hypotheses about *what may happen* (of a negative as well as positive nature), and is the more useful for project evaluation. The latter suggests *what should be done,* and is the method of choice for development planning.

In practice, few rationales span more than the earliest steps of the sequence. The chain of presumed cause-effect links is elaborated in fair detail up to the attainment of one early, intermediate outcome; the remaining links are indicated sketchily, or essentially taken for granted. Evaluations that go beyond crop yields to more ultimate, nonagricultural criteria or beyond the acquisition of skills to more ultimate, noneducational criteria are the exception. Planning exercises that begin with more ultimate, suprasectoral goals and deduce their implications for the various sectors are typically limited to the development of broad strategy guidelines; the planning of specific projects almost always begins with a set of narrower, sector-specific objectives.

There are both bureaucratic and technical reasons for this. The bureaucratic reasons are the simpler. The affairs of government are divided among a number of action agencies, and most planning occurs within the confines of their respective charters. Agricultural agencies plan agricultural programs; eductors plan educational programs; local government agencies plan programs of rural administration. Where there is overlap, there tends also to be keen competition. Strong, suprasectoral planning mechanisms seldom exist.

The technical reasons derive from the extreme conceptual and methodological difficulties which encumber analyses that extend to the more ultimate societal goals. There are no entirely acceptable definitions of life-quality, no suitable measures or scales, no known way of accommodating the large individual differences in needs and values in priority judgments. Nor is it possible to unravel, at the present state of the art, the multitude of cause-effect sequences that jointly impinge on each of the more ultimate goals. The evaluator cannot confidently attribute an observed change to the effects of one specified intervention when dozens of other factors are also at work and offer equally plausible explanations. The planner cannot confidently trace a desired outcome to the single intervention that is the uniquely suitable step to take when dozens of alternative paths exist and offer equally logical promise. Each link of the chain beyond the immediate project outcomes entails additional, increasingly tenuous assumptions. Were the barrier of bureaucratic rivalries to be successfully hurdled, the technical, methodological limitations of the present state of the art would remain as an even more formidable obstacle to effective suprasectoral planning.

These difficulties are further compounded, moreover, by the heterogeneity that is characteristic of the regions within a developing country, of the locales within each region, of the communities within each locale. Resources, progress, needs, constraints can and do vary widely. Different locations (though they may share the same ultimate goals) start with different givens; and action rationales, which try to trace the steps from the present to the desired, clearly must reflect these. But as little is known about the characteristics of the community which determine the efficacy of different projects as about the characteristics of the more ultimate end-states toward which these projects should be directed. The frustrating task of the planner of community development programs has been to chart the shortest course between an unspecified start-point and an ill-defined outcome.

In 1968, the American Institutes for Research began a program of research addressed to these issues, in the context of rural development planning in Thailand. Two factors made Thailand an attractive venue for such research. The first was the existence of a large, growing development program, spurred by the specter of Vietnam, and the even more visible threat of local separatist stirrings. The rapid development of areas long neglected was regarded as both important and urgent. The second was the establishment of mechanisms, in the Royal Thai Government and in the U.S. assistance program, for planning and coordinating the overall effort. There seemed to be an opportunity not only to develop, but also to use and test, new methodologies for suprasectoral planning.

A five-year research program was planned.[2] The central objectives were

1. To develop a criterion of development impact more ultimate than those normally applied to the evaluation and planning of action projects, and sufficiently broad to encompass projects in all of the major sectors;

2. To devise reliable, practical techniques for assessing the status of a specified group or location with respect to this criterion; and
3. To design procedures for using the results of such assessments in the evaluation or planning of development projects.
Essentially, we hoped to extend the effective span of intervention rationales to reach beyond early outcomes to more ultimate goals, and to develop a systematic, data-based procedure for applying these expanded rationales to specific programming decisions.

The Specific Problem of Resource Allocation

The operational problem that raised these issues most clearly (and that served as the primary vehicle for the research) was that of distributing the various types of available development projects among the candidate villages in a given district or province. On the basis of need, a dozen or more different projects could generally be justified at each location. Within the limits of the annual budget, a relatively small percentage of the villages could be selected to receive any assistance whatever. What should be done, and where, to make optimum use of the available resources?

The projects that comprised the rural development program in Thailand encompassed a wide range of activities. (We once tabulated more than thirty different types of interventions.) The following four broad program objectives fairly reflect the main thrust of these diverse operations:
1. Development of infrastructure: Projects such as the construction of rural roads and bridges; water resource development; land development and allocation.
2. Provision of local amenities: Projects such as the construction and staffing of health centers; the introduction of mobile medical services; the construction and staffing of schools; the building of community

centers and other physical improvements such as intravillage roads; the development and support of women and youth groups.

3. Agricultural and occupational development: Projects such as the provision of commodities or credit, and the dissemination of modern agricultural practices; promotion of new crops; training in agricultural and nonagricultural occupations; development of cooperatives and other agribusiness groups; construction and improvements in irrigation systems.

4. Improvement in rural administration: Projects such as the training of district and subdistrict officials; decentralization of funding and project planning; training of village leaders; public information programs.

These projects (and the rationales on which they are based) differ on many dimensions. One of the specific objectives of the research, for purposes of resource allocation, was to identify the dimensions that determine their respective goodness-of-fit to different locations, from the point of view of leverage on local development progress.

The apparent, readily visible differences among even neighboring villages were also large. These included differences on such hard, easily quantifiable dimensions as size, amount of arable land, yield per rai (four-tenths of an acre), distance from all-weather roads, and nonagricultural employment. They also included differences on many soft dimensions that are more difficult to define, but seemed equally relevant to the quality-of-life that is the ultimate societal goal. In a dissertation that built on and expanded the Thailand research, one of our colleagues described these differences as follows:

Thai villages indeed differ, as any villager will confirm. Some are tranquil; some have a history of feuds. Some are pious and sober; others have a jug of moonshine under every porch and card games every night. Some villages are proud of themselves, and proclaim that they grow the sweetest tamarind or the biggest durian or the most beautiful women in the country. Other villages are a collection of houses with only a name for a common bond, and no pride at all.

Some villages are interminably curious. If a stranger strolls through them, he will be asked at every second house to stop and chat. In another village just down the road, he can walk for an hour with hardly a greeting. If he stays for a few days, some villages will prove to be ceremonious in their treatment of him, others relaxed and unbuttoned, still others suspicious and aloof.

Some villages are clean, others are dirty. Some are spread out over several kilometers, each house hidden from its neighbors. In others, the houses will be crammed together until their porches touch.

Villages are unpredictable. In one village located a few minutes away from a large town, the visitor still has to explain that the world is round; in another, hours from anywhere, the headman will let him listen to a recording of a Mozart quintet, played on a wind-up Victrola.

But most importantly, some villages seem able to solve their problems while others cannot. Some villages are victimized by conmen, their daughters seduced by recruiters from the city's brothels, plagued by police looking for a rake-off, unable to stop the river from flooding the fields every year—while other villages ignore the conmen, keep out the recruiters, get the district office to rein in the police, and build an earthen dam to hold back the river.

All of these are everyday aspects of life, and together they shape the quality of life in the village. There are limits, of course. An impoverished village living on the edge of starvation is an unpleasant place to live regardless of any other conditions. But given a typical (for Thailand) level of natural resources, the nature of the village—its gestalt, if you will—is a crucial factor in determining whether its inhabitants' daily existence is generally pleasant or generally unpleasant.

It is perhaps the most commonly overlooked fact of life in developing countries.[3]

Capturing the intervention-relevant essence of these differences, the hard and the soft, and relating it to resource allocation decisions was another of the major research objectives. In all of our studies, we used the village as the unit of analysis, so as to focus the data on the same unit that the program administrators were using as the basis for allocation decisions.

The Investment Hypothesis

The first step was to define the phenomenon or state of affairs that we would adopt as an overall criterion of progress toward the more ultimate societal goals: as the crucial, suprasectoral outcome to which all development projects should be directed. Given the fragmentary nature of the available models of the process of development, there seemed to be no systematic, rigorous procedure for formulating this criterion; and systematic deduction was not attempted. But we did establish three conditions that an acceptable criterion would have to satisfy, and used these three specifications to focus and guide the analytic procedure.

The first was that the criterion would have to reflect progress toward the economic and social development of the village, in the accepted sense of productive modernization. Though traditional life has certain undeniable charms, we had to assume that life-quality would be improved by the amenities that are normally regarded as indicative of a higher standard of living. Any criterion intended for use in the planning of development programs, which are committed to modernization, would have to be firmly grounded in this explicit, overriding objective.

The second was that this criterion also would have to reflect progress toward the related goal of nation-building, in the sense of political stability. In Thailand, and especially in the late 1960s, this outcome was considered especially important. We had rejected the concept of "counterinsurgency" on the grounds that any goal expressed as the countering of a specified negative (rather than the creation of a specified positive) is likely to produce sterile, generally ineffectual programming guidelines. But we did agree that integration is an essential component of development, and established evidence of progress toward "surgency" or "polity strength" as a second specification an adequate criterion must meet.[4]

The third was that this criterion further would have to reflect gains in the quality of life of the villagers, in the sense of their own perceptions. In the current terminology, we wanted the criterion also to serve as a "social indicator" of the village as a good place to live.

The criterion that we eventually adopted was based on the level of village *investment behavior,* which we defined as the degree to which the inhabitants of a village are investing their own resources of time, energy, and funds in the lawful opportunities for economic, social, and political improvements that are available to them. Creating the conditions that foster and sustain high levels of voluntary village investments was the common, suprasectoral goal of development projects that we proposed to use as the basis for resource allocation.

Certain aspects of this proposition should be noted. One is that we used the term "investment" in an entirely general sense, to encompass any and all efforts toward improvement. Listening regularly to a Farmer's Friend radio broadcast to learn about better methods, taking a petition to the district office, leaving the village to take employment elsewhere were all considered to be exemplary investments. Any use made of the opportunities the society affords for gain or advancement was included in this definition.[5]

Similarly, we also included all of the available opportunities within the scope of this definition, whether they are offered by the government or private sources, or generated by the village itself. A privately operated vocational school in the district town would be regarded as an available opportunity, for example; so would a tractor which is available for rent to farmers.

The level of investment activity observed in a given village was to be judged as high or low in accordance with the opportunities available to it, not on an absolute scale. The key question was: How fully is this particular community taking advantage of the available opportunities for improvement, given its present status, needs, and resources? All types of villages, rich or poor, more or less highly developed, were to be assessed on the basis of what each could be doing.

Conceptually, this formulation appeared to be fully congruent with the three specifications we had set out to meet. The logical links that could be posited between increments in the level of village investment and corresponding increments in modernization, polity strength, and life-quality seemed to us highly persuasive.

From the point of view of modernization, an analogous relationship had already been demonstrated in studies of the industrial revolution of the past century.[6] Government initiatives and public funds could stimulate the process but not sustain it. It was not until private citizens began to participate in significant numbers (i.e., to make modernizing investments themselves) that appreciable advances occurred.

From the point of view of nation-building it was clear that the dearth of constructive, mutually rewarding transactions between the village and the institutions of government was one of the main obstacles that had to be overcome. Modernizing investments, by their very nature, create additional needs and a consequent increase in the extravillage linkages that must be established to meet them. Markets, supplies, technical specialists, adjudication mechanisms become increasingly important; as investments expand, so should the network of interdependencies that undergird societal integration.

From the point of view of life-quality, the behavioral statement that an active investment posture implies seemed to represent a far more convincing social indicator than the surveys of grievances or satisfactions that were then being introduced in Thailand. Grievance-reduction is a never-ending process; the solution of one problem inevitably leads to its replacement by another which is often more complex and difficult to solve than its predecessor. Satisfactions are relative also. If a village were truly satisfied, the process of modernization would stop. In reality, as a community begins to develop, dissatisfaction almost certainly increases; the phenomenon of rising aspirations is not only real, but a necessary condition for continued development. A pattern of continuing, increasing investment would seem to be the most constructive adjustment to the development process.[7]

On all counts, the criterion of investment in self-improvement seemed to afford a promising focus for suprasectoral development planning.

The next step was to devise reliable yet practical techniques for assessing this state of affairs in the villages of rural Thailand.

Development of the Investment Index

The development of suitable measurement techniques required: (1) the cataloging of investment opportunities, (2) the identification of valid data sources, and (3) the construction of operational data collection procedures. We shall summarize these steps briefly.[8]

Investment Opportunities

The objective of devising measurement techniques suitable for routine, operational use dominated all aspects of the developmental research. An approach that would require an exhaustive inventory of the investments a given village is making would have been unrealistic. The need was for a sampling procedure, based on a fairly small number of standard indicators on which data could be collected quickly and cheaply.

We began by compiling a list of the kinds of investments that Thai villagers can and do make in opportunities for improvement. From a review of the descriptive literature on rural Thailand and from interviews with knowledgeable observers, some 250 "critical incidents" or factual accounts of discrete villager investments were assembled. These spanned a wide range of investment behaviors, as reflected in the following examples:

1. One farmer put some of his earnings into the bank, having been encouraged to do so by a Chinese middleman. His experience led others to do the same.

2. The villagers spend most of their free time in the dry season weaving bamboo walls, which they sell to merchants.

3. In the hope that their (very large) village might someday become the center of a new district, villagers donated land for the future district offices.

4. One villager bought a Singer sewing machine and sent his wife to the three-month sewing course. When she returned, he put her to work making blouses and shirts.

5. Tobacco was raised by the students under the guidance of the school-teacher on the land where the new school was to be built. The money from the sale of the crop went into the school fund.

Some of the incidents (such as those that described assorted entrepreneurial ventures) seemed to represent sufficiently widespread opportunities to provide a basis for generally serviceable indicators. Other incidents (such as the donation of land) seemed too idiosyncratic for use.

From the master list, we developed a trial set of thirty-one indicators, and assembled data on these from a sample of forty-nine community development workers. First, we asked each worker to consider all of the ten to twenty villages for which he or she was responsible, and to identify the three highest, the three lowest, and the two most nearly in the middle for their enterprise and energy in development efforts. Since the primary task of community development workers is to stimulate development projects, we judged them to be especially good sources for these global assessments. Then, each worker was asked to report on one of these eight villages (selected randomly) in detail, using a questionnaire based on the thirty-one trial indicators. The coefficient of correlation between each indicator and the global village assessments provided a preliminary index of its potential for cross-village, comparative studies.

Subsequently, we repeated this exercise with a second sample of seventy-one community development workers, reporting on a different set of villages. From the combined data, we selected a pool of twenty to twenty-five indicators to constitute the items of an investment index,

Table 5.1
Indicators for an Index of Village Investment

Economic
Number of buses passing through village daily
Number of buses owned by villagers
Number of households using fertilizer*
Number of households using insecticide*
Number of households using improved seed*
Number of shops in village*
Number of rice mills in village
Number of occupations other than rice culture
Number of village members of an agrieconomic group*
Ratio of number seeking seasonal employment to number of subsistence families

Social
Number of monks and novices in village temple
Rating of temple condition
Rating of village school condition
Number of students studying beyond grade four*
Average rating of village houses
Number of village members of a social group*

Political
Ratio of number of merchant leaders to number of leaders
Number of requests to district during past six months
Number of petitions to RTG agencies during past two years
Frequency of villager visits to district town
Frequency of Village Development Committee meetings
Total number of village groups
Number of village meetings last year

*Expressed as percent of households.

which we used throughout the research, with periodic, minor modifications. The items of one form of this index are shown on Table 5.1.

As indicated in Table 5.1, we included social and political investments as well as economic investments in the overall index, in accordance with the central hypothesis, which is based on the concept of investment posture as a general village characteristic. Statistically, the intercorrelations among these three components of the total index were consistently in the vicinity of 0.50, for all subsequent studies. This result was supportive of the view of investment as a unitary construct.

Data Sources

As a basis for the identification of suitable data sources, we had earlier considered fourteen types of data that are commonly used in social research, and ordered them from most to least desirable for field use. This ordering is shown in Table 5.2. The criteria for these rankings were largely judgmental: administrative ease, cost, obtrusiveness, and reactivity (possible effects on the respondents) were the major factors considered. Given adequate validity and a choice of approaches, we planned to select the one ranked highest in Table 5.2.

During the course of the research, we experimented with six of these approaches. Our current choice, for operational use, is a combination of two of these procedures.

Level A: Archives. Our experience with the use of official government records confirmed the negative findings of earlier studies in Thailand. The records in Bangkok and in the provincial offices were mainly sterile. The district offices did have access to directly relevant data, but were a cumbersome source, for two major reasons. The first was that much of this information had been neither published nor tabulated, and had to be extracted and processed on an ad hoc basis, with the help of the responsible district officials. The petitions sent to the district had to be located in the files, for example, then sorted and counted. The second was that there were gaps in village identification. Thus, the district education office would have enrollment records of all classes in all schools, but no record of the home villages of the students. This information had to be obtained from the schools or the villages directly.

Gross discriminations could be made with fair accuracy on the basis of district records, and these might be adequate for certain applications. For the purposes of our study, we decided to focus on village-level data sources.

Level C: Information Collected but Not Reported. This was essentially the technique used in the initial studies with community development workers described above. The assumption was that this group, as a result of their extensive work in the villages, would have made the requisite observations, and be able to report these if asked. The (split-half) reliability of this procedure was 0.89 for the sample of 120 villages. It proved to be an effective, highly economical method for gathering a large amount of village-level data for purposes of the research.

For operational applications, techniques that rely on the recall of the observers have limited use. If the observations are to be made regularly, the next approach of incorporating them in the established reporting mechanisms is the indicated procedure.

Level D: Modification of Information System. The advantage of expanding the established reporting requirements formally is that the field personnel will (presumably) make the requisite observations systematically, following explicit training. In the Community Development Department, the above procedure gave way to a departmental questionnaire, which the field workers were to complete on the basis of site visits made for this express purpose.

Level G: Observation by Outsider Passing Through. An agency that does not have large numbers of field personnel working in villages on a continuing basis cannot establish a routine feedback system. Data must be assembled on an ad hoc basis by teams sent to the villages for that

Table 5.2
An Ordering of Approaches to the Assessment of Population Responses

Level	Data Source	General Characteristics
I	Data presently available from: A. Routine reports, archives, records B. The content of newspapers, radio broadcasts, and so forth	Nothing new is introduced into the data collection system. Evaluations are based entirely on existing data which may be selected, combined, and analyzed in new ways.
II	Data potentially available from: C. Information collected but not routinely reported D. Modification of present data collection system	The present system has to be expanded to provide additional data, but no new techniques and no new data collectors are required. Evaluations are based on data available from the expanded system.
III	Data collected through special directed observations: E. By telemonitoring procedures F. By a villager G. By a passer-through H. By an outsider-in-residence	The present system is augmented by additional observers. Evaluations are based on more detailed descriptions of day-to-day behavior than can be provided by the existing system.
IV	J. Data collected through observation of responses to artificially-created situations	Special stimuli are introduced, and the villagers' reaction is observed by a passive observer (III E, F, G). Evaluations are based on data generated in situations produced deliberately by evaluator.
V	Data collected through active observer-villager interaction in the form of: K. Questionnaires and interviews, factual, nonthreatening content L. Objective tests of aptitude, ability, knowledge M. Questionnaires, interviews, tests of opinion and attitude N. Projective tests, depth interviews O. Manipulative field experiments	Special stimuli are introduced, and the villagers' reactions are evaluated by a skilled observer interacting directly with the villager in face-to-face situations. Evaluations are based on data generated in situations where both stimulus and response are under some degree of evaluator control.

Examples

Tax records
Land sales
Vehicle registrations
Letters to editor

Information which appears only in summary form in reports

Information that CD Workers are not
now asked to include in reports

Number of dwellings being improved
Gambling—magnitude of stakes
Topics of day-to-day conversation
Leisure-time activities
Condition of school

Response to special appeal on radio
Voluntary contributions to staged
campaign
Disposition of "lost" items
Disposition of printed materials sent to
a village

Thai interviewer, demographic ques-
tionnaires
Objective test: Information on Thailand
Disguised test of attitudes toward
officials
Incomplete Sentences Test
Recruiting drive, experimental and
control villages

purpose. This is more costly, but manageable, since frequent updates of the data are not required. (Replication studies yielded a correlation of 0.70 between the investment measures obtained for a sample of ninety-three villages in visits one year apart, and of 0.79 for a second sample of 101 villages in visits eighteen months apart.)

Only one study based on the use of observational data exclusively was attempted. This was carried out by members of the research team on a sample of fifty villages, to determine the potential and limits of this mode of data collection. A reliability of 0.91 was obtained for the average of the estimates made by two independent observers. This suggested that useful, pertinent data can be assembled without any direct, subjective inputs from the villagers whatever. But certain indicators (for example, number of petitions) clearly cannot be obtained through short-term observation, and a combination of this technique and Level K factual interviews would seem to be the indicated approach for on-site data collection.

One low-cost application of this combined approach was introduced in the Accelerated Rural Development Office (ARD). As part of its routine activities, ARD regularly sent staff of its Spot-Check Section to project sites for purposes of inspection. The notion of "piggy-backing" the collection of investment data on this operation was appealing, and suitable forms and training were provided to Spot-Check personnel. **Level H: Observation by Outsiders-in-Residence.** This is unquestionably the most accurate of the approaches, but also the most costly. Except for agencies that maintain a large complement of resident field workers in any event, such as the Community Development Department, it is likely to prove far too time-consuming and expensive for operational use. Its chief applications are for in-depth research.

The study that provided the data for the dissertation earlier referenced used this approach. A team of trained data collectors made visits to a sample of forty-one villages on a rotational basis, such that at least one member of the team lived in each of these villages for a period of approximately six days. Within this time frame, observations could be made that were clearly impossible in the more typical village visit of several hours. As a basis for scoring the indicators related to housing, for example, 5198 of the 5954 houses in the sample villages (87.3 percent) were visited and inspected personally by the researcher.

The results justified the effort. The reliability of the six-item Investment Index that was used in this study was 0.69, quite remarkable for so small a number of indicators. A substantial amount of additional data was also assembled during these extended village visits.

Another characteristic of this study was the use of highly structured observational checklists. In the survey of houses, the quality of construction was scored on the following nine-point scale:

1. leaf walls, thatch roof
2. leaf walls, tin or tile roof; or mat walls, thatch roof
3. mat walls, tin or tile roof
4. some wood used in the walls, tin or tile roof; or solid wood with thatch roof
5. solid wood, tin or tile roof
6. same as "5", with evidence of skilled carpentry and fittings
7. a cabinet house: skilled carpentry throughout
8. same as "7," plus a substantial expense (for example, lower walls made of masonry)
9. an all masonry house.[9]

The utility of such tightly structured checklists is by no means limited to resident studies. The technique can readily be adapted to brief visits, if coupled with a systematic sampling procedure.

Level K: Factual Interviews. Among the village respondents, the headmen proved to be by far the best source of pertinent data. They were also one of the most efficient data sources. Headmen reported to the district at least once a month to collect their salaries, and large numbers could be interviewed in a short time, with a single trip to the district center. In one set of studies, we interviewed as many as 181 headmen in one day with a team of fifteen interviewers. Reliabilities of 0.81, 0.90, and 0.90 were obtained in the three districts surveyed with this concentrated procedure.

In all, we collected investment data on a total of 1318 villages. In 351 of these villages, we collected such data twice, in ninety villages, at three points in time. The reliability of measurement ranged from 0.74 to 0.90, with an average value of 0.82, despite variations in methods, data collectors, and sources.

Operational Procedures

From an operational point of view, the major findings were that investment level is a palpable, measurable village characteristic; that there are large intervillage differences in this characteristic; and that these differences can be assessed reliably with a variety of approaches, to meet varying practical constraints. The method of choice is to

1. collect a maximum of data through on-site observations, based on structured checklists and a specified sampling procedure;

2. supplement these data with factual interviews of community leaders, to obtain information on indicators that cannot be observed by the data collectors directly; and

3. assign the task of data collection to resident field personnel, if available; to a central research or planning unit, if not.

The procedures developed for use by the Community Development Department and the Accelerated Rural Development Office were first-order applications of this approach in Thailand.

The calculation of a single, numerical index for each village was based on a normative procedure. Raw scores were converted to "stanines," in accordance with the distributional norms obtained for a large sample of villages.[10] The development of norms was carried out as a bootstrap process in Thailand: our eventual "norm group" consisted of 380 villages in three districts for which data had been collected as part of an ARD assessment in early 1973. A carefully selected, representative sample of a few hundred villages surveyed specifically for normative purposes would better have met the need, and this is the indicated approach for future applications.

Development of a Measure of Opportunity

The crux of the investment hypothesis, as earlier noted, was the utilization of available opportunities rather than the absolute level of investment per se. It was not so much the increase in public investments as the growth of an active, continuing posture of voluntary investments that we saw as the key development goal. To interpret a village's investment score from this point of view, it was necessary also to consider the realities of the available chances.

The opportunities for village investments include those that are manmade and those that are afforded by natural resources. In all probability, an adequate index of both could be obtained from district records and pertinent maps. But this was not attempted in Thailand.[11] Instead, a fairly crude index was developed for use in conjunction with the Investment Index. Data were assembled by the same team, from the same group of respondents.

The indicators that were used for this assessment are listed in Table 5.3. It will be seen that the measure was heavily biased toward manmade opportunities, and did not adequately reflect differences in the villages' natural resources. The reliability of the instrument ranged from 0.53 to 0.80 in thirteen studies, with an average value of 0.67.

Correlations between the measures of investment and opportunity in the same villages were consistently high, ranging from 0.52 to 0.73, with an average value of 0.62.[12] This is consistent with the conceptual

Table 5.3
Indicators for an Index of Village Opportunity

General adequacy of rice supply
Adequacy of village water supply
Nearness to all-weather road
Travel time to district town
Condition of connecting road
Level of government development funding
Highest class in village school
Distance to nearest seventh grade school
Number of economic facilities in village
Number of social facilities in village
Number of government training programs
Frequency of visits by government officials

formulation, but a more balanced index of opportunity would probably yield a somewhat lower figure. Because of the heavy emphasis on man-made opportunities in the index used, some of the amenities that were counted as present-day opportunities probably were the products of earlier village investments; and part of the high correlation obtained may reflect no more than the stability of the village's investment posture.

These measures of opportunity, coupled with the investment scores, provided two data points on each village that had not been available for development planning before. Their specific implications for resource allocation are discussed later in this chapter.

A third data point which also appears to be relevant to development planning is the factor of *village size*, measured as the number of house-holds. As a review of the investment indicators listed in Table 5.1 will show, we had attempted to control for the size of the village: seven of the indicators are expressed as ratios relative to the number of house-holds; the remainder are logically independent of size. But, despite these controls, a positive correlation between village size and invest-ment level was found in every sample of villages studied. This remark-ably consistent relationship is shown graphically in Figure 5.1. The linear coefficient of correlation for these data is 0.49; the curvilinear coefficient (eta) is 0.61. The correlation remains significant even when differences on the opportunity scale are factored out.

Apparently, village size operates as yet another type of opportunity factor. Villages with fewer than 100 households seem generally to lack the "critical mass" that an above-average level of investment activity requires.

The factor of village size is not a parameter that the development planner can readily manipulate. But it may be that fundamentally different development strategies must be formulated for the smaller villages, to which the approaches that prove effective in larger

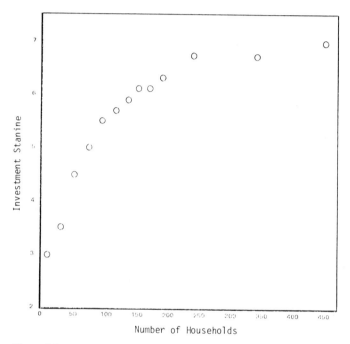

Figure 5.1
Village Size and Investment Behavior

communities may not apply. The effort that has been made in Thailand (and elsewhere) to link small communities to larger ones through an improved network of roads may be an especially productive strategy; its impact should be examined from this point of view.

Applications to Resource Allocation

Given data on village opportunities and investment levels, a number of rationales for resource allocation can be developed. The basis for these rationales is inherent in the following four (testable) propositions:

1. Villages high on both opportunity and investment are exemplars of the state of affairs that development programs should try to achieve. They will sustain a continuing, rapid pace of development with little or no government intervention.

2. Villages lower in opportunity than investment are prime targets for the large opportunity-creating projects that have been the bread-and-butter of technical assistance. They will be most aggressive in capitalizing on the new opportunities afforded by roads, irrigation systems, job opportunities, credit arrangements, and other "hard" inputs.

3. Villages lower in investment than opportunity are prime targets for the "softer" inputs that try to energize development efforts, such as training, organization, or information programs. In these villages, such programs can be exceptionally cost-effective, since the expensive step of opportunity-creation has already been completed.

4. Villages low on both opportunity and investment require a combination of opportunity-creating inputs and capability-creating inputs to help them capitalize on these new life-chances. If such inputs are not provided, these villages will fall further and further behind other communities, as a by-product of the development process.

The strategy of resource allocation that is formulated depends on the planner's objectives. The objective of creating a set of model communities to serve as vanguards of development in each district calls for one strategy. The objective of narrowing the gap among the villages of each district calls for an entirely different pattern of resource allocation. The goals must be specified by the planner; the investment and opportunity data suggest where and roughly how they can be achieved.

The selection of the specific projects that most effectively will implement a given development strategy requires additional judgments. When the strategy calls for the expansion of opportunity, these judgments are reasonably straightforward. Identifying the nature of the opportunities that a given village has the capacity to exploit calls mainly for technical judgments in such fields as agriculture or economics. When the strategy calls for the stimulation of investments in opportunities already available, these judgments are problematic. We made only the barest beginnings in the attempt to isolate the more subtle aspects of village life that motivate or inhibit active investment, and hold the key to productive intervention. This issue remains for future research.

Other Implications

The most direct implications of this research are for the design of development planning mechanisms in other countries. The specific indicators used in Thailand probably are not generalizable; the principles and methodological approaches almost certainly are. Their application and testing in a different setting are indicated next steps.

In addition to such applications of the total experience, four of the specific components of the research also merit further attention.

The first is the elaboration of the conceptual model, with special reference to the definition of investment behavior. In Thailand, we used an exceptionally broad definition, as earlier noted. We did not discriminate investment from "consumption," as economists use these terms, but considered all forms of modernizing behavior to be relevant village investments. For his dissertation research, Murray adopted a narrower focus. He limited investments to behaviors which: (1) are voluntary, (2) entail risk, and (3) are made for the express purpose of profit. He further differentiated investments made for personal profit from those that benefit the village as a whole, and argued that such individual and community investments have fundamentally different implications.[13] These constructs seem useful. Rationales based on a village profile of consumption behavior, individual investments, and community investments may provide a basis for crisper analyses of the complexities of the development process.

The second is the identification of the prerequisites to investment, which we had called "disposing conditions" in Thailand. Opportunity is one of these conditions; size appears to be a second. But much of the variance in investment behavior remains to be explained, especially among villages that are similar with respect to these variables and other physical characteristics. Establishing the nature of the other important determinants (such as, perhaps, the village leadership structure) could improve development planning significantly. The present state of the art is limited mainly to the creation of opportunity; a capability for stimulating investment in available opportunities would add a second, potent dimension.

The third is the extension of the approach to within-village variations. In Thailand, we worked exclusively with village aggregates to provide convenient administrative units for resource allocation. But the sizeable differences in investment behavior among households in the same village were readily apparent. In light of the growing emphasis on channeling aid to the poorer elements of the population, a household-based index of investment behavior would seem highly useful. Data on the opportunities and investments of the poorer families of the community, and of the barriers to these, should permit more precisely focused development inputs.

The fourth component is the application of all of these concepts and approaches to social development programs in the United States. Such fields as health, education, or housing afford many examples of variations in necessary investment behaviors among socioeconomic levels which are not fully explained by differences in access. An analysis of these variations from the above points of view may help to explain the general failure of remedial efforts and suggest more productive approaches. Conceivably, the ultimate benefits of the research on Thai rural communities could accrue to the American inner city.

NOTES

1. The U.S. Agency for International Development has adopted a standard format for project rationales, known as a "Logical Framework." This focuses on four successive stages (inputs, outputs, purpose, and goal) and on the assumptions that link them.

2. Activities continued over a six-year period, under the sponsorship first of the Advanced Research Projects Agency, then of the U.S. Agency for International Development.

3. Charles A. Murray, *Investment and Tithing in Thai Villages: A Behavioral Study of Rural Modernization* (Unpublished doctoral dissertation: Massachusetts Institute of Technology, 1974).

4. It is interesting that the English language contains no term that is the positive opposite of "anomie" or "alienation." The French word "engagement" comes close.

5. Second thoughts suggest that this initial formulation may have been overly broad. A somewhat more restrictive definition may have added precision, as noted in the concluding remarks to this chapter.

6. John D. Montgomery developed the theme in Montgomery and William Siffin, eds., *Approaches to Development: Politics, Administration and Change* (New York: McGraw-Hill, 1966), pp. 259-262; and in *Technology and Civic Life: Making and Implementing Development Decisions* (Cambridge: MIT Press, 1974), chapter 3.

7. Inherent in this proposition is also the impossibility of validating the investment hypothesis empirically, given the present state of the art. If active, continued investment is regarded as a near-ultimate indicator of life-quality, the validity of this hypothesis can only be validated against a criterion of life-quality that is more ultimate still. Such criteria have not yet been developed.

8. A more detailed account is given in R. E. Krug and S. M. Jung, *Systems for Evaluating the Impact of Rural Development Programs.* Final Project Report (Bangkok: American Institutes for Research, June 1974).

9. Murray, *Investment and Tithing.*

10. The stanine scale divides the range of scores into nine segments which are assigned integer values from 1 (low) to 9 (high). It assumes an underlying normal distribution; the segment size is one-half standard deviation, with the middle segment (Stanine 5) straddling the mean.

11. The needed developmental research was often compromised by the operational setting of the work. In the early stages, we lacked an official Thai counterpart organization, and for a time had no access to villages. When ARD assumed the sponsor role, research was constrained by the operational needs of this agency,

and by the AID emphasis on capability-building as the key project goal. Such constraints are to be expected in research of this kind; the real world is a reluctant laboratory.

12. Based on thirteen *concurrent* estimates (I and O collected at the same time) on a total sample of 1820 villages. Six *predictive* estimates (O collected a year before I) for 437 villages give nearly identical results.

13. Murray, *Investment and Tithing.*

6 VALUES IN INSTITUTIONAL PROCESSES
RALPH BRAIBANTI

You cannot step twice into the same river; fresh waters are ever flowing
in upon you.
Heraclitus, *Fragments*, 41, 42.
The subtlety of nature is greater many times over than the subtlety of
the senses and understanding.
Bacon, *Novum Organum,* Book I, Aphorism X.

Value Specification

In this volume there is implicit full or partial acceptance of the need for
determining values in a social system. Such value-identification has been
made more significant by three recent trends. First is the emphasis on
superordinate-subordinate state relations derivative in part from the
concept of dependence. Second, is the global demand (polycommunality)
by subnational cultural-linguistic-ethnic-religious groups for parity of
esteem. Third, is the movement toward indigenization of modes of
change.

   These idioms are interrelated. The assertion of subnational culture
must be based on root values which are predominantly indigenous. Notwithstanding certain terminological deficiencies, the term "indigenous"
is convenient. By it, I mean the use of human and material resources at
hand and the use of techniques compatible with the economy and culture, especially historical circumstances and psychic needs. The concept
of indigenization is the obverse of what has long been called *dependencia*
by Latin American economists. While the term in its initial use referred
to economic dependence, it more recently has been used to analyze cultural dependence as well.[1] A major idiom of contemporary international
development is the effort to eliminate both economic and cultural
dependence, while at the same time participate in global sharing of
technological advance. It is obvious that there can be no cultural independence without the identification of cultural roots, that is to say,
indigenization. In development economics, there is a perceptible movement toward the concept of indigenization, or cultural independence,

technology" which they arrive at by reconsidering labor-intensive as opposed to capital-intensive development strategies. Their use of this term is consistent with my definition of indigenization. The contribution of this strand of development economics to this analysis lies in the empirical validation of assumptions that labor-intensive methods and indigenous techniques can in some cases be cheaper and more productive than capital-intensive programs using exogenous techniques. Few yet subscribe to the revolutionary implications of E. F. Schumacher's collection of essays *Small Is Beautiful,*[2] even though it was he who first used the term "intermediate technology" as early as 1964.

There is also implicit recognition in this volume of the utility of the eight-part value construct first devised by Lasswell in 1950 and used herein as a generative as well as a unifying theme.[3] The eight values which can be referred to by the acronym PEWBSARD, are Power, Enlightenment, Wealth, well-Being, Skill, Affection, Respect, and rectituDe. The advantage of this construct is its potential for universal application, since these values are found in all societies. Their universal implementation is made exceedingly difficult by the four following constraints: 1. The specification or cultural manifestations of such universal values differ in various systems. Affection, respect, and justice have different specific meanings in Sweden and Saudi Arabia. The extreme emphasis on rehabilitation of criminal offenders in Sweden is hardly the same application of justice as the use of swift retribution practiced as Islamic justice in Saudi Arabai. Both systems subscribe to a concept of justice. Is one better than the other? Each must be judged in the context of the sphere for which the system is valid; this context includes religious values, way of life, and the crime rate which may be the consequence of the policy followed. Similarly the value of enlightenment to which all systems subscribe will be interpreted differently in Sweden and Saudi Arabia, the one with its freedom for explicit sexual information, the other which proscribes such freedom as ungodly and insists that enlightenment derives exclusively from the Holy *Qu'rān*.

2. The specific content of these universal values may also have a different sequence in priority of importance. This sequence as well as the content can be determined best by those living in the system and responsible for the lives of its citizens, though we assume that no system would be impervious to interpretation and trends in other systems.

3. Regnant values are rarely valid in the total society. Variations exist between various elites and the masses, between geographic regions, religions, ethnic and linguistic groups, urban and rural areas, and age groups.

4. The distinguishing between deeply held beliefs and what is merely the transitory consequence of economic or other technologically manipulatable circumstances is a national culture. This distinction is especially pertinent to Asian countries which have long been thought to have unique "Oriental" characteristics.[4] This was the consequence of an experientially limited frame of reference and comparmentalization of knowledge by culture areas. As we began to deal with "less developed" portions of society within otherwise advanced nations (Appalachia in the United States is one example) and with the newly formed national societies of Latin America and Africa, the expanded spheres of comparison modified our views about alleged uniqueness. An example may be illustrative. The probability that large clusters of personality traits are consequences of a culture of poverty with its syndrome of malnutrition, hopelessness, and fatalism, implies that culture transcends national-cultural areas. This was dramatically, although not intentionally, brought to our attention by the work of Oscar Lewis and Edward Banfield.[5] A reading of the description of the personality traits and of the structure of family relations and civic responsibility in the Mexican families described by Lewis and in the south Italian village described by Banfield is a rather shocking experience for a student of Asia. A change in place

and personal names reveals that the description fits many Asian villages and family structures. This suggests that certain personality traits and group behavior patterns develop in part as a consequence of the economic circumstances in which a particular group finds itself and not primarily because of any unique feature that is Oriental.

With the highly detailed kind of empirical research in plotting behavior patterns which has been done by anthropologists, and to a lesser extent by political scientists, this kind of hypothesis may be demonstrated more adequately in the course of the next few decades. If this turns out to be so, it will tend to destroy further the myth that particular behavior traits occur because of Asian, African, or other ethnocentric peculiarities. On the contrary, we may find that almost identical patterns occur in countries of different historical and religious backgrounds which seem to be at the same stage of economic and political development. This may also cause us to reevaluate the role of religious doctrine in the formation of behavior traits. In this respect both Lewis' and Banfield's works were illuminating because they upset stereotypes of religious and ethnic determinants of behavior. In southern Italy and in Mexico, we are not dealing with Buddhist, Confucian, or Muslim societies but with essentially Roman Catholic society and with an ethnic component which is almost totally different from that found in Asian countries. These observations distort the older concepts of the uniqueness of Oriental behavior and lead to a corollary related to value specification; some values may be less deeply embedded in a tissue of noneconomic culture than otherwise supposed.

It is at this point in value analysis that historical study plays a crucial role. It is history that most effectively reveals the time dimension of values in the system, illuminating the evolution of the value, the quality of the forces of formation (for example, fortuitous, scriptural, and so on), and thus helps reveal the value's primordial depth.[6] An example may be drawn from the political development of Japan. The decision, made during the Occupation, to extend the franchise to women was based on an assessment of the profundity of a value—namely the societal role of women. Historical analysis extended back three centuries would have revealed a value of female subordination, but if extended to the twelfth century and beyond, a different value, namely parity if not superordination of women would have been exposed.[7] Such historical analysis is essential as a method of extracting the intrinsic significance of a value. It is also essential to appraise the mythical strength of values as contrasted with real strength. Encrustations of myth especially in religious thought and in such social phenomena as the alleged idyllics of village life seriously distort the appraisal of value strength.

One of the earliest and most brilliant efforts to determine the specificities of cultures was the work of the philosopher, Northrop.[8] His aim was to determine the "inner normative order" or "living law" of each system, identify the points of congruence or equivalency, and base international relations (and, by extrapolation, human relations) on knowledge of such normative orders. His method was analysis of scriptures, art, and literary forms. Indeed, his interpretation of the aesthetic continuum as a component of Taoist painting and of Chinese calligraphy remains unique. But the difficulties were as formidable then as they are now. Even scriptural sources, however important, may be at variance with behavioral manifestations.

It is useful to catalog some of the sources which might be used in specifying values and suggest briefly some of the difficulties in each. The listing is obviously partial—suggestive rather than definitive—and the related difficulties are even more so.

1. Scriptural sources. The variety and scope of such sources and conflicting interpretations by sects. Authenticity, mythological encrustation, validation by new historical discoveries (for example, the Dead Sea Scrolls).

2. Juridical sources. Constitutions, and interpretations thereof by case law. Amenable to greater precision than scriptural sources, but subject to change both implicitly and explicitly reversible.

3. Statutes and administrative rules. The latter are rarely available in newly formed political systems. The former are good indicators of values currently held by lawmakers.

4. Political Party Manifestos. Here the distinction between pious platitudes and sincere reflections of felt values must be made.

5. Learned writings. Voluminous and amorphous, amenable to content analysis, but the quality of value reflection depends on writer.

6. Popular writings and commentary. Subject to serious distortion and bias even in technologically advanced systems.

7. Legislative debates. Sincerity versus stage acting remains difficult to assess.

8. Executive messages. The extent to which these truly reflect nationally espoused values is difficult to determine.

9. Ecclesiastical manifestos. Papal encyclicals and comparable statements by other churches. Here the extent of authoritarian, as against participatory, genesis is important.

The enormity, perhaps even impossibility, of submitting these sources at all levels of government to rigorous content analysis and then aggregating the result into a mosaic of the value system should be immediately obvious.

A new perspective for value analysis which combines phenomenology with philosophic insights is emerging. Firestone, analyzing the weaknesses in deriving indicators from survey research techniques, advocates that we "turn instead to the exploration of the long dormant, promising, but undoubtedly difficult task of analyzing the literature, film, art, songs, in general the imagery within the social communications of man. By examining the 'stuff of life,' these products of men in their natural habitats, we can approach more closely the goal of empirical theories of social change."[9] This is precisely the method used by the anthropologist Ruth Benedict nearly thirty years ago in specifying Japanese values for a nation then at war with Japan.[10] A subsequent UNESCO study using ethnographic methods more quantitatively oriented was no significant improvement in insight over the Benedict value analysis.[11] Also promising are the approaches of ethnoscience in anthropology and ethnomethodology in sociology.[12] In the former, the aim is to get inside the events as described by natives of a culture to see what kind of theory they use to organize these events. Linguistics, especially componential analysis, is especially useful here. Yet even this technique has its weakness in that it tends to equate talking about events with feelings about those events and does not allow for nonverbal manifestations of the native's organization of events. Psathas feels that ethnomethodology in sociology has a firmer phenomenological basis. It attempts to detail and order commonplace behavior to determine what is implicit or "felt" in men's minds. The emphasis can be nonverbal and the technique relies on the classificatory ordering of details of behavior.

Michael Polanyi's concepts of tacitness, indwelling, and emergence are especially illuminating in value specification.[13] They explicate the salience of the nonverbal, intuitive dimension of man's being, but no technique for specifying that dimension is given.

In sum, we can say of value specification that there is a significant movement away from quantitative listing and analysis of conventional written indicators as evidence of values. There is new perception of the importance of symbols, feeling, and intuition and a glimmer of techniques in psychology and phenomenology which can help in specifying and evaluating these tacit manifestations. Except for differences in methodological terminology, these new techniques are not dissimilar to those used by Northrop a quarter century earlier.

Process

The model proposed in this chapter can trace the process of the making of decisions in any specific institution, and can ultimately suggest the impact of structure and sector on that decision. Subsequently the manner in which both the process and the content of the decision reflect specified values of the system can also be determined. This can be done only if decision making within each institution is broken into phases or units which are common or nearly common for many institutions.

Sector and structure are inadequate and partial terms to describe institutional functions set in the context of process.[14] The reification of institution, sector, and structure rather than analysis of them in terms of process is an impediment to clear conceptualization. It is for analytical convenience only that institution, sector, and structure may be viewed as static. Their static aspect is momentary—only when the process they serve is halted, as to use Miller's metaphor—"when motion is frozen by a high-speed photograph."[15] Thus, structures, sectors, and institutions are undergoing change continually by the actions flowing through the process which they accommodate. Most of the changes are subtle and extended over a period of time; but a few are abrupt, radical, episodic, or catastrophic.

In the explication of process, the analysis of Lasswell is useful. No political scientist, with the possible exception of Merriam, has given as much attention to process as Lasswell. Following on this page and the next of this chapter is a reformulation and adaptation of his concept of process drawn from several sources.[16] Let us imagine an institution with component structure(s) and sectors suddenly "frozen as when motion is frozen by a high-speed photograph." This imagery enables us to understand what it is that these entities do when in motion and what makes them act. Even before the motion is unfrozen, the actors about to move are conditioned by various factors. The character of action ultimately taken on events is initially molded by the perspectives of the participants; such perspectives are predominantly subjective. When they are relatively stable among members of an institution they may be called myth, which "clarifies goals, provides a historical panorama of trends, formulates assumptions about conditioning factors, projects the future course of events, and fosters the invention and evaluation of policy."[17] The intensity with which myths are held is important, for such intensity will condition the effect of prescription on events, once motion is unfrozen. Little is known of the precise effect of perspectives on the autonomy of the mind of the participant to select responses to the flow of events.[18] Intensity may be associated with this autonomy. Of obvious salience are such factors as the social status, composition, preservice and inservice education, and isolation from society of the bureaucracy and its various cadres, levels, and groups. *Miranda* also constitute part of myth; *miranda* are basic symbols of sentiment and identification with things to be admired. The subjective perspectives of actors may eventually be determined from somatic events, but existing knowledge permits us only to infer the influence of such perspectives on events by such techniques as analysis of the content of communications which emerge from events.[19] The influence of prearena and arena perspectives on the administrative process is probably dependent on the relative autonomy of institutions. The hypothesis is ventured that the lesser the autonomy, the greater the influence of prearena perspectives. Correlatively, the lesser the autonomy the lesser the capacity of the institution to shape prearena perspectives in the mold of an institutional decision based on precedent and internal tradition.

Phases of the Decision Process

Once the structure has been unfrozen and actors begin to think and move, what do they act on? Here the central element in Lasswell's concept of process is the event—a transfer of energy in units of communication. As it flows through institutions, sectors, and structures, it is acted upon by participants; it becomes at those points an interaction which can be summarized as a sequence of communication and collaboration. Interactions can be designated by the use of three kinds of elementary subunits which can be combined into patterns of any degree of complexity: symbols, signs, and resources.

As an event moves processually towards a decision, it is acted upon by several influences. These we also can think of as phases of the decision-making process, if we remember that the "phases" are not fixed or linear. There is a circularity among the influences which may be operating concurrently. Indeed, their identification as influences or phases of process is for analytical convenience and ultimate comparability. To select and label these influences it seems economical and prudent to transfer a classificatory scheme from what may initially appear to be a body of knowledge irrelevant to the present effort. We refer here to the work of Lasswell and McDougal in their monumental efforts to advance a new theory for the interpretation of treaties and other international instruments.[20] Their work not only has been refined by application in many contexts, but it has been extensively commented upon by others and has been admiringly labeled as the Yale School and the New Haven school of international law. The essence of their theory is the use of context or total cultural configuration in interpreting treaties. While that has greatly influenced the present writer in other ways, it is another facet of the Lasswell-McDougal theory which has pertinence at this point. They view the social process globally and have divided the constitutive (social or policy-making) process into seven phases or classes of influence. These phases transcend the usual divisions of government (executive, legislative, judicial); indeed, they embrace all actions of the social process, such as communication, diplomacy, ideology. The seven phases appear to be an irreducible classification which has great expository potential.

We have taken these seven phases, conceived for another purpose, and reduced them in scope from a global to a smaller arena, viewing them, as it were, through the wrong end of a telescope. Since we agree that these seven phases (variously called functions and influences in Lasswell and McDougal's writings) appear to be universal in decision making in all spatial dimensions (global or local), we have applied them to decision making within particular institutions and to subinstitutions as well. This use of the seven phases was not the intent of the Lasswell-McDougal construct. Indeed, in that construct "administration" (which McDougal regards as an unfortunate concept foisted upon us by Weber) is merely a small portion—one of many strategies of one of the phases, application. There is no incompatibility between the original intent of the seven phases construct and its present application to a more restricted ambit. We agree that the accelerating interrelatedness of policymaking makes it global and that it involves the total social order. Yet the enormity of the task of tracing the flow of values and the interaction of institution, structure, and participants on a global scale is immediately apparent. Since there is literally no limit to the data to be used, its identification, control, and ordering are impossible; hence, the random use of data is one of the major criticisms directed against the globality of the construct. The application of the seven phases to specific institutions of a given social system allows for appraisal of that institution against whatever values that institution is presumed to reflect. Such appraisal also permits structural and intrainstitutional renovation based on the appraisal.

As an event moves processually towards a decision, its flow has been characterized by Lasswell and McDougal as being acted upon by seven classes of influences: (1) intelligence, (2) promotion, (3) prescription, (4) invocation, (5) application, (6) termination, and (7) appraisal. The intelligence phase is the obtaining and processing of information and relating it to the event. The phase characterized as promotion involves the persuasion of structural, sectoral, and institutional participants as to the direction of the decision to be made regarding the event. Prescription, which formulates expectations about a general norm of conduct and hence defines the role of the institution in relation to the event, can be of at least five types: (1) constitutive, which makes explicit how structure will operate; (2) supervisory, covering controversies regarding values involved; (3) regulatory, which deals with clientele affected who yet may require intervention to assure compliance; (4) enterprisory prescriptions, distinct from constitutive prescriptions, are administered by structures acting for all participants involved; or (5) corrective prescriptions which refer to corrective measures designed to redirect personal behavior. Any prescription of whatever type is analyzable into three components: (1) norms referring to the standard to be required, (2) contingencies to which the application of standards may be adjusted, and (3) sanctions which may be permissible to achieve and maintain conformity to these norms. Prescriptions are ascertainable from tradition, statutes, rules, doctrines, formula, myth, and *miranda,* as well as from the personality dispositions of the actors. Prescriptions are not fixed; they too begin to be modified once the motion is unfrozen. The invoking phase of the processing of events is the provisional determination that the concrete elements of the event conform to, or deviate from, the prescription.

Application is the final determination that the concrete event is to be decided upon in terms of prescriptions. The appraisal phase characterizes the decision made on the event in terms of precedent and effect on subsequent policy. This includes reporting, fiscal accountability, consistency with statutory or analogous intent and with national (or sub-national) goals and plans. The terminating phase puts an end to prescription and deals with expectations and unanticipated outcomes raised during the period when the prescription was in effect. The termination phase has not been given much attention in the United States,

Lasswell contends, but if "concern for human dignity and for the dignity of all advanced forms of life increases in coming years, it is probable that more attention will be given to obviating adverse effects of policy changes."[21] Such adjustment is the function of the termination phase.

Conspectus

We return now to a flux model which has been alluded to fleetingly elsewhere in this chapter. Our concern is to plot and possibly to prescribe the reconstruction of institutions in terms of the specified values of the particular system. Because the reconstruction is related only to values specified for the system we can claim that there is no ethnocentric bias in our model and that reconstruction is judged solely in terms of specified values. It is assumed that those values cannot be exclusively "indigenous" simply because no idea is really indigenous.[22] Rather there is a global diffusion and rediffusion of ideas and institutions, some of which, for a variety of reasons, effervesce at particular moments in history and in particular places. This global circulation is greatly influenced by the phenomenon of spiraling contextuality,[23] which is somewhat outside the arena of process. It is thus located because changing context affects participants on the edge of the arena (such as foreign advisors) and affects as well the intellectual and emotional postures of participants in the process itself.

The determination of the system's values remains a formidable task which must use every available technique including survey research, content analysis, artifactual analysis, and phenomenological techniques such as ethnoscience and especially ethnomethodology. Such syncretic technique rejects the notion of rationality and seeks a method for integrating the tacit, intuitive, emergent components of a culture with components allegedly rational. Insofar as the intuitive components have in the past played a more conspicuous role in Asian cultures, this feature of the model has special reference to the area on which this entire volume focuses. Moreover, this approach is consistent with concepts variously expressed by Bohr, Jung, Lasswell, Whitehead, Freud, Polanyi, and Northrop.[24] Here the problem, not yet alluded to, is a serious one. The intellectual and emotional consequence of a postindustrial culture premised on Cartesian thought has been a reconsideration and a perceptible rise in respect for tacit, intuitive components. Yet concurrently in Asia, we witness a rejection of the intuitive, tacit components in the interests of alleged scientific progress. Indeed the rejection is accelerated by agents of change from radiating societies—agents who are themselves unwitting purveyors of Cartesian thought. By specifying values from an indigenous base without conscious reference to the values outside that base, some kind of synchronic tempo between the conflicting paces of these intellectual modes may be achieved.

Our model can be used in any administrative entity. Having specified the values of the total system, we now seek to determine if those values are being diffused by the administrative process. We thus trace an event (defined, using Lasswell, as an exchange of energy). This event may be oral or a paper transaction which requires a decision or action. The event is then followed through seven phases of the decision-making process which have been reduced from the global scale as conceived by Lasswell and McDougal to a more restricted purpose here. These phases are not necessarily discrete; indeed they are likely to occur simultaneously or to overlap and to occur in varying sequences unlike the sequence in which they are listed. The flow of the event through this process is typically not linear; rather it is likely to oscillate. For expository as well as for operational purposes, however, we must think in terms of discrete phases. How are the agreed upon specifications of the PEWSBARD values treated in each phase? How do institution, structure, and sector affect the treatment of values in each phase? Our presumption is that if the values are adversely treated, that is, distorted, deflected, or negated rather than diffused, then reconstruction of institution, structure, or sector is indicated.

It is now appropriate to suggest some of the issues which may be examined in each phase. It must be emphasized that this is a skeletal list, suggestive rather than exhaustive.

1. Intelligence. The event has already been introduced or initiated. Information must now be sought bearing on the decision. What are the sources of intelligence and what are the perspectives of the suppliers? Does the intelligence include concern for future trends?

2. Promotion. What factors lead to promotion of preliminary resolution of the event? Are the factors of the prestige of the promoters internal to the organization? Do the promoters invoke a power base external to the agency? If so, this has an obvious effect on autonomy.

3. Prescription. This is the agreed upon decision resolving the event. Has it been stated with clarity? What has been the pattern of participation both internal and external to prescribing?

4. Invocation. Announcement or declaration of the prescription. This phase is relatively simple.

5. Application. The implementation of the decision at the cutting edge. This is an important but difficult phase to analyze.

6. Termination. Is the termination truly discontinuous, or is it merely a stage in transformation of goals and purposes? What are the manifold societal consequences of termination?

7. Appraisal. What have been the effects of the decision on the event? Could the effects have been changed by a different consideration of future trends in the intelligence phase? Has the total context in which the policy operated been considered?

While systematic analysis of value diffusion can and should lead to reconstruction of institutions, it must be kept in mind that the process here described is enmeshed in a tissue of constantly changing perceptions or context. These changing perceptions will be reflected in the specification of values which must be a perennnially recurring task. Further they will enter the arena of decision making accelerated by foreign aid and by communications technology. Both of the latter factors will mitigate against any system departing in too idiosyncratic a way from slowly evolving global norms. Yet systematic analysis of value diffusion specified deliberately from an indigenous rather than a global base will allow for maximum influence of characteristics distinctive to the particular culture. Therein lies the greatest hope for the preservation of the warmth and aesthetic comfort of individuality in the face of global standards of political design and individual behavior.

NOTES

1. See especially *International Development Studies (IDS) Bulletin* (Institute of Development Studies, University of Sussex, Brighton, England) 7 (April 1975).

2. E. F. Schumacher, *Small is Beautiful: Economics as if People Mattered* (London, 1973).

3. Like the seven phases of the decision process, the construct of eight values has been explicated in many contexts. See Lasswell's attempt to apply these eight values to his *Psychopathology and Politics* in the chapter, "Afterthoughts: Thirty Years Later," 1960 Viking Press edition (pp. 269-319). See also his "The Normative Impact of the Behavioral Sciences," *Ethics* 67 (1967): 1-42; Myres S. McDougal and H. D. Lasswell, "The Identification and Appraisal of Diverse Systems of Public Order," *American Journal of International Law* 53 (1959): 1-29; Other applications by Lasswell are: "A Note of 'Types' of Political Personality: Nuclear, Co-Relational, Developmental," *Journal of Social Issues* XXIV (1968): 81-91; "The Uses of Content Analysis Data in Studying Social Change," *Social Science Information* 87 (1968): 58-59; "The Prospects of a World University," in Tiselius and Nilsson, eds., *The Place of Value in a World of Facts, Nobel Symposium* 14 (Stockholm, 1971): 281-294; "International Lawyers and Scientists as Agents and Counter Agents of World Public Order," *Proceedings,* American Society of International Law (April, 1971): 366-376. The most extensive efforts to relate the specific content of the PEWSBARD value construct to particular societies were done for Vicos, Peru, and for the Northern Sudan. The former was a Cornell University project directed by Lasswell and Holmberg begun in 1952 and ending in 1961. Henry F. Dobyns, Paul L. Doughty, Harold D. Lasswell, eds., *Peasants, Power and Applied Social Change: Vicos as a Model* (Beverly Hills, London, 1971). The latter was a J.S.D. dissertation written at Yale under Lasswell's direction by a Sudanese scholar, Francis M. Deng, *Tradition and Modernization: A Challenge for Law Among the Dinks of the Sudan* (New Haven, 1971).

4. This myth has been effectively dissected in John M. Steadman, *The Myth of Asia* (New York, 1969).

5. The notion of a culture of poverty was introduced by Oscar Lewis in *The Children of Sanchez: Autobiography of a Mexican Family* (New York, 1961) and amplified in *The Scientific American* 215 (October, 1966): 19-25. Edward Banfield, *The Moral Basis of A Backward Society* (Glencoe, Ill., 1958).

6. The larger context of this problem is discussed in J. G. A. Pocock, "Time, Institutions and Action: An Essay on Traditions and Their Understanding," in Preston King and B. C. Parekh, eds., *Politics and Experience* (Cambridge, England, 1968), pp. 209-237.

7. On the social causes of the subordination of women from Fujiwara to Muromachi, see Sir George Sansom, *Japan: A Short Cultural History* (New York, 1943), p. 362.

8. F. S. C. Northrop. *The Taming of the Nations: A Study of the Cultural Bases of International Policy* (New York, 1952), esp. pp. 1-8. See also his earlier *The Meeting of East and West* (New York, 1946).

9. Joseph M. Firestone, "The Development of Social Indicators from Content Analysis of Social Documents," *Policy Sciences* 3 (1972): 249-263, quotation at 261.

10. Ruth Benedict, *The Chrysanthemum and the Sword* (Boston, 1946).

11. Jean Stoetzel, *Without the Chrysanthemum and the Sword* (New York, 1955).

12. George Psathas, "Ethnomethods and Phenomenology," *Social Research* 35 (Autumn 1968): 500-520. See also George Psathas, ed., *Phenomenological Sociology* (New York, 1973) and Maurice Natanson, ed., *Phenomenology and Social Sciences* (Evanston, Illinois, 1973). In the Natanson volumes, see especially in Vol. 2, Part VI, articles on "Phenomenology and Political Science" by H. Y. Jung, C. J. Friedrich, and J. G. Gunnell.

13. See Michael Polanyi, *The Tacit Dimension* (New York, 1966); W. A. Breytspraak, "Tacit Components of Social Inquiry: Reflections on Garfinkel, Polanyi, and Typologizing," *Soundings,* Fall 1972, pp. 312-334.

14. See definitions of institution, sector, and structure, in Ralph Braibanti, "External Inducement of Political-Administrative Development: An Institutional Strategy" in Ralph Braibanti, ed., *Political and Administrative Development* (Durham, N.C., 1969), pp. 3-107 and Ralph Braibanti, "Foreword–The Concept of Institutionality" in Robert S. Robins, *Political Institutionalization and the Integration of Elites* (Beverly Hills, Calif., 1976), pp. 1-10. In these works I define institutions as "patterns of recurring acts structured in a manner conditioning the behavior of members within the institutions, shaping a particular value or set of values and projecting values(s) in the social system in terms of attitudes or acts."

15. James G. Miller, "Living Systems: Basic Concepts," *Behavioral Science* 10 (1965): 193-237, esp. 209.

16. Application of the seven phases of decision making to a variety of contexts has been a central theme in Lasswell's writings: Lasswell and Kaplan, *Power and Society* (1950), pp. 192 ff.; *The Decision Process* (University of Maryland, College Park, 1956); *The Future of Political Science* (New York, 1964), pp. 43-89; "The Policy Sciences of Development," *World Politics* XVII (1965): 286-310; "Conflict and Leadership: The Process of Decision and the Nature of Authority," in A. V. S. De Reuck and Julie Knight, eds., Ciba Foundation Symposium on *Conflict in Society* (London, 1966); "Toward Continuing Appraisal of the Impact of Law on Society," *Rutgers Law Review* 21 (1967): 645-677; Lasswell and Richard Arens, "The Role of Sanction in Conflict Resolution," *The Journal of Conflict Resolution* XI (1967): 27-39; Lasswell and Myres S. McDougal, "Juris-

prudence in Policy-Oriented Perspective," *University of Florida Law Review* XIX (1966-67): 505; Myres S. McDougal, Lasswell, W. Michael Reisman, "The World Constitutive Process of Authoritative Decision," *Journal of Legal Education* 19 (1967): 253-300, 403-437; McDougal, Lasswell, Reisman, "Theories About International Law: Prologue to a Configurative Jurisprudence," *Virginia Journal of International Law* 8 (1968): 188-299; Lasswell and Allen D. Holmberg, "Toward A General Theory of Directed Value Accumulation and Institutional Development" in Braibanti, ed., *Political and Administrative Development*, pp. 354-399; "The Continuing Decision Seminar as a Technique of Instruction," *Policy Sciences* 2 (1971): 43-57.

17. Lasswell and Holmberg, "Toward a General Theory of Directed Value Accumulation . . .," cited in n. 16 above, p. 380.

18. For an illuminating discussion of this problem, see Joseph J. Spengler, "Theory, Ideology, Non-Economic Values and Politico-Economic Development," in Ralph Braibanti and Joseph J. Spengler, eds., *Tradition, Values, and Socio-Economic Development* (Durham, N.C.), pp. 1-56, esp. 41-43.

19. Harold D. Lasswell, "The Uses of Content Analysis Data in Studying Social Change," *Social Science Information* 87 (1968): 58-59.

20. See Myres S. McDougal, Harold D. Lasswell, and James C. Miller, *The Interpretation of Agreements and World Public Order. Principles of Content and Procedure* (New Haven and London, 1967); Gidon Gottlieb, "The Conceptual World of the Yale School of International Law," *World Politics* XXI (1968): 108-133; Sir Gerald Fitzmaurice, "*Vae Victis* or Woe to the Negotiators! Your Treaty or Our Interpretation of It?" *The American Journal of International Law* 65 (1971): 358-373; Richard A. Falk, "On Treaty Interpretation and the New Haven Approach: Achievements and Prospects," *Virginia Journal of International Law* 8 (1968): 323-356; Oran R. Young, "International Law and Social Science: The Contribution of Myres S. McDougal," *American Journal of International Law* 66 (1972): 60-77; Myres S. McDougal, "International Law and Social Science: A Mild Plea in Avoidance," ibid., 77-82; Harold D. Lasswell and Myres S. McDougal, "Criteria for a Theory About Law," *Southern California Law Review* 44 (1971): 362-394. Jerome Hall, "Methods of Sociological Research in Comparative Law," John N. Hazard and Wenceslas J. Wagner, eds., *Legal Thought in the United States of America Under Contemporary Pressures* (Brussels, 1970), pp. 149-169, esp. 158-165.

21. Lasswell, *The Future of Political Science,* cited in n.16, p. 80.

22. This is explored further in Ralph Braibanti, "Context, Cause and Change," in John H. Hallowell, ed., *The Future of Constitutional Democracy: Essays in Honor of R. Taylor Cole* (Durham, N.C., 1976).

23. The adjective spiraling is used deliberately to convey an important perception. By contextuality we mean a changing universe of referents which are perceived as having an associational, perhaps even a causal relationship with an event or a segment of knowledge. See "Context, Cause and Change," cited in n. 22 above.

24. For further analysis see Ralph Braibanti, "Conceptual Prerequisites for the Evolution of Asian Bureaucraftic Systems," in Inayatullah, ed., *Management Training for Development: The Asian Experience* (Kuala Lumpur, 1975), pp. 185-231.

7 DEVELOPMENT MALAYSIAN STYLE: EVALUATION OF GOALS AND INSTRUMENTS

M. SHANMUGHALINGAM

As a result of its strategic position on the narrowest passage along the sea route between India and China and the great trade routes between the West and the Far East, Malaysia has attracted the attention of foreign traders and travelers for many centuries. Chinese and Indian contacts began before the Christian era while the Portuguese and the Dutch occupied Malacca, a small Malaysian state on its west coast, during the sixteenth and seventeenth centuries respectively. However, the greatest impact on Malaysia in its recent past arose from the arrival of the British and the subsequent activities of the British colonial administration. The focus of this paper is on the government (especially the executive) as the dominant agent of change in the evolution of goals and instruments for socioeconomic development in Malaysia. Reference is made to value categories largely in terms of the Lasswellian PEWBSARD construct of Power, Enlightenment, Wealth, well-Being, Skill, Affection, Respect, and rectituDe, which are elaborated elsewhere in this volume.

The Colonial Legacy

The colonial legacy that is Malaysia's today is predominantly that of the British colonial era, the system of allocating values during the colonial administration, and certain spillover effects on the immediate post-colonial period. Starting with "direct" rule of the Straits Settlements of Penang (in 1786), Singapore, and Malacca, the British went on to administer "indirect rule" in the Malay peninsula following the Pangkor Treaty of 1874. Except for a brief interruption by the Japanese during World War II, British administration of Malaysian territory continued until August 1957.

The writer is grateful to Messrs. Chong Hon Nyan (Tan Sri), Malek Merican, R. V. Navaratnam, all of the Treasury, and Alladin Hashim, Wolfgang Kasper, John D. Montgomery, Stephen Chee, and Tawfik Tun Ismail, for their comments and advice. The views expressed here are the personal views of the writer and should not be taken as representing the views of the Treasury of the Government of Malaysia where the writer is attached.

Peninsular Malaysia, formerly known as Malaya (a federation of eleven states), obtained its independence from the British in that year. The former British colonies of Singapore, Sabah (formerly British North Borneo), and Sarawak joined Malaya to form the new federation of Malaysia[1] in September 1963. In August 1965 Singapore separated from Malaysia. Today, Malaysia is a federation of thirteen states with an ethnic breakdown of Malays (53 percent), Chinese (35 percent), and Indian (11 percent).

One of the principal consequences of the British colonial administration in Malaysia was the creation of what has been described as a dual economy. The modern economy of the plantations, the mines, and the commerce of the west coast contrasted starkly with the traditional subsistence economy of the east coast. The rubber and tin industries were, by and large, typical of colonial enclave investments which were geographically sited in the colonial territory but were, in substantive terms, an extension of the metropolitan economy. In this context, the colonial administration encouraged the shaping of wealth by foreign (largely British) investment, without any pressure for sharing this value with the rest of the population.

Even more serious than the dual economy was another consequence of British colonial rule in Malaysia, the growth of a plural society, defined as one comprising two or more ethnic or communal groups "living side by side but separately within the same political unit."[2]

The combination of the British colonial administration with British enterprise encouraged mass immigration of labor from China and India to fulfill the needs of low-wage labor for the enclave economy. The administration invested power in aid of wealth-shaping by British enterprise regardless of the social consequences. As a direct result of this policy, there was mass immigration of Chinese and Indians, concentrated between 1880 and 1930. Chinese and Indian laborers for Malaysia were recruited and organized on very different systems.

The chief importance of these systems was that they compelled employers to employ labour of one race only or to keep their Chinese, Indian and Malay labour forces separate: to deal with them separately, pay them in different ways, and provide different living conditions. Indian labour was normally paid directly; Chinese labour was paid by contractors, who were nominally and legally the employers. . . . Malays were normally employed on a casual basis, though regular employment increased considerably after World War II. They continued to live in Malay villages among their peasant neighbours. . . . the separation of the different races was aggravated by measures taken by the British Government to combat communist terrorism after 1948.[3]

The racial difference between the Malays, Chinese, and Indians was accentuated by differences of language, religion, customs, habits, and diet. As for the value structures of the Malay and Chinese communities, it has been asserted that they "do not agree on what is good in the sense of being most worthy of attainment in life."[4] It was believed that the Malays gave priority to rectitude, affection, and respect values, the Chinese emphasized wealth and skill values, and the Indians a mixture of both. Furthermore, the Malays and the non-Malays were physically separated to a considerable extent. Broadly speaking, the non-Malays were concentrated on the urbanized west coast, while the Malays were in the rural sector comprising the east coast and the north. The official census reports of 1931 and 1957 indicate the percentage of Malays in the urban areas as being 19.2 and 20.0 percent, respectively.

The pursuit of the colonial 'divide and rule' policies flourished in this context. The colonial administration concentrated on the shaping of power and wealth values without attempting to share these values with the rest of the population. In its emphasis on power and wealth goals the British colonial administration (unlike certain other colonial administrations) tried not to ruffle the system of sharing deference values in Malaysian society. With respect to religion, for instance, "The British discovered that Islam was a powerful factor in Malay Society and that cooperation with the Malays was impossible if Islam appeared to be threatened. The colonial authorities correctly assessed the role of Islam in the prewar years and attempted to avoid any policies that might disrupt Islam as a 'cultural gyroscope' for Malay society.[5]

The dual economy and the plural society were two of the most important results of British colonial administration in Malaysia. As Malaya approached independence, it was not only these two factors but also the interaction between them that became significant. The cultural, physical, educational, and occupational divisions between the Malays and the non-Malays was exacerbated by the widening economic gap between the indigenous Malays and the immigrant Chinese and Indians.

The activities in the enclave sector of the west coast stimulated peasant demand for imports, particularly of consumer goods. A new class of middlemen arose as the intermediary between the large foreign firms and the peasants, distributing imported articles and collecting the produce of the rural sector. It was not long before an oligopolist/oligopsonist, if not a monopolist/monopsonist, situation was created in many *kampongs* (villages) for the rural low income groups.

In 1955, two years before independence, the traditional (Malay) sector accounted for less than one quarter of the gross national product.[6] The census figures for 1947 and 1957 indicate that the Malay rural population increased by 368,000. Yet production in rural commodities in which Malays predominate showed a general decline during the 1950 to 1958 period.

The Household Budget Survey of 1957-1958 at the time of independence, showed that while the Malay rural household's average for all income groups was M$120, the Chinese urban household average for all income groups was more than twice as high at M$275. The mean income of Malay households was 68 percent of the national average.

With the political awakening which began in the early 1920s and developed momentum after the Japanese occupation, the Malays "became increasingly conscious of the adverse economic position of their community. And they realized that their participation in the process of development and modernization was characterized by a growing political and economic dependence."[7] It has been observed that "they used to be poor men in a poor country, and now they were poor men in a rich country."[8]

In August 1957 Malaysia obtained its independence. The road to independence was a smooth one. The Alliance, an intercommunal political organization representing the largest Malay, Chinese and Indian political parties won a spectacular majority of fifty-one out of fifty-two seats in 1955. Within two years, the leader of the Alliance, Tunku Abdul Rahman, led the country to independence as its first prime minister. The tunku held this post until September 1970 as the Alliance won comfortable majorities in the subsequent general elections of 1959 and 1964 and a majority in 1969.

Although it has sometimes been observed that bureaucracies in developing countries may tend to be weaker than those in developed countries, it is evident that the relative importance of the role of the bureaucracy will be greater in developing than in developed economics.[9] As for Malaysia, "nowhere in the world has the civil service gained as much prestige and esteem."[10] It has been observed that the British in Malaysia had absorbed the rulers and the aristocracy into the civil service, strengthened their position and privileges, and guaranteed their continuation and consolidation. Thus the British colonial administration sought to buttress the traditional shaping of deference values in the Malaysian polity. By investing power values for deference outcomes the British sought, in the long run, to strengthen their power base. "One is struck by the extent to which British colonialism and traditional rule share common traits."[11] The absorption of the rulers and the aristocracy into the government service made that service a place where two mutually reinforcing status systems met. Hence the prestige accorded to government service is enormous.

In spite of this, generally

The role of bureaucracies as determinants of social, political, and economic change has been subjected to relatively little systematic analysis. Broadly speaking, the tendency has been to view bureaucracies as dependent, rather than independent, social, political, and economic forces which condition the content, scope, and incidence of bureaucratic authority.[12]

The bureaucracy which Malaysia inherited from the British has been described as a "dual one" making use of "advanced processes of computerized statistical control but . . . also maintaining intact and undisturbed, office practices and procedures that were justly celebrated a hundred years ago, but belong today in a National Museum."[13] The Malaysian, 'modern bureaucratic machinery' in the late 1950s and early 1960s also has been described as being

superimposed on society that is itself schizophrenic, a society that in some sectors is decidedly modern while in others is much more characteristic of the traditional model. . . . When Malaya gained its independence in 1957 the country enjoyed the services of a highly sophisticated and unquestionably efficient bureaucratic apparatus.[14]

The decade of the 1960s has brought changes to the Malaysian environment in which both the political leadership and the bureaucracy have played important value-shaping and value-sharing roles.

The process of transition was considerably eased by the fact that the political leadership and the senior bureaucrats belonged to the same social groups. Both the former and the present prime ministers were former bureaucrats as were a number of cabinet ministers, chief ministers of and the sultans of some of the the states. The bureaucracy has been the chief source of recruitment for the cabinet and the party accounting for 40 to 50 percent of those holding the highest political offices in the country.[15] The investment of affection as loyalty served to ratify the power shaping functions of the political elite.

The Transition from Law and Order to Economic Development

With independence, the goals of the government shifted from the colonial administration's emphasis on the shaping of power and wealth to a new focus on the sharing of well-being, in particular, as well as wealth and skill values. The change in the goals of the government after independence have been described as follows:

1. There was a change from the emphasis on a balanced budget to an emphasis on an expanding economy.
2. There was a change from an unstated emphasis on urban development, or development for the modern sector, to a stated and actual emphasis on rural development or development largely for the uplift of the Malays in the traditional sector.
3. Social services, especially education, moved from a position of low priority to one of high priority, and were partially redefined as elements of investment rather than consumption.
4. There was an increased demand for, and finally the creation of, new organizations competent to plan for and stimulate the development of the economy.
5. There was a change in the character of protest from nationalism and communalism to communalism and class interest.[16]

As to the first point, it has been said of the balanced budget that "the requirements of balance may leave the government with fewer instruments than it has targets; and consequently may mean that objectives more important than balance must be ignored or that new instruments must be discovered."[17] And it is doubtful whether a strong case can be made for the last point. The character of protest in Malaysia has not, in fact, indicated any significant class interest. Ethnic divisions have been so strong that class interests are both inconspicuous and unarticulated. Ethnic divisions had been intensified during the Colonial period by the notion that the sharing of values involved a zero-sum game. The striking answer provided by the newly independent government to this constant-pie orientation was the development program that was launched after independence with the principal objective of wider sharing of well-being values. "Rural development . . . was basically to improve the rural sector so that better living conditions prevail."[18] The distinctive features of the development program in Malaysia immediately after independence were (1) the dramatic and new focus on rural development; and (2) the organizational technology and the new instruments used for promoting and reporting on the development program.

The rural development program was the government's response to centuries of neglect of the rural areas by the colonial administration in favor of infrastructure on the urbanized west coast where the enclave economy was based. A new Ministry of Rural Development was created in October 1959, shortly after the general elections. The new minister responsible was the deputy prime minister, the late Tun Razak.

The ethnic breakdown of the electorate for the elections were as shown in Table 7.1. Malays were in the majority in 66 out of 104 constituencies. More than 70 percent of the Malay population as compared to 17 percent of the non-Malays was in the rural areas. The delineation of electoral constituencies provided the rural sector with greater weightage than the urban sector. Malays have generally had a better turnout as voters on election day than non-Malays. The major opposition faced by the party in power was the fundamentalist Fan Malayan Islamic Party which was in aggressive and direct competition with the Alliance for the crucial rural Malay vote.

While the rural Malays and the agricultural small holders could be distracted by a colonial administration without much protest, in the newly independent situation they were in a position to demand that their claims be attended by whichever political party was in power. The result was that this hitherto neglected group was to be modernized by an unprecedented spurt of development projects, within a short period.

Table 7.1
The Ethnic Breakdown for the 1959 Malaysian Electorate

Ethnic Group	Voters (in thousands)	Percentage
Malay	1,217	56.8
Chinese	764	35.6
Indian	159	7.4
Other	4	0.2
	2,144	100

Rural development was very much the first item on the Alliance manifesto for the 1959 general elections.

While the new Ministry of Rural Development did not implement development projects by itself, the drive and prestige of the deputy prime minister enabled the ministry to stimulate rural development and in particular the construction of physical amenities and social overhead projects with spectacular success. Rural roads, telephone booths, health clinics, irrigation schemes, electricity supplies, and new schools mushroomed all over the countryside on a scale and at a speed which neither the bureaucracy nor the rural population could have imagined. During 1961-1970 no less than 3500 miles of new roads, of which 65 percent were rural roads, were constructed as compared to 472 miles constructed during the five year period from 1956 to 1960. Similarly, 289 secondary schools were constructed between 1961 and June 1963, whereas only sixty-five had been completed between 1956 and 1960. The 1961 to 1970 period produced no less than 917 midwife clinics compared to the mere twenty-six that had been constructed between 1956 and 1960. By the end of the decade, the rural sector accounted for more than three-quarters of the primary schools and about half the secondary schools in West Malaysia. In 1970, primary school enrollment was estimated at 90 percent.

The organizational technology that was behind this upsurge of development implementation was no less impressive. The now familiar "Operations Room technique" and the "Red Book" (Red for *R*ural *E*conomic *D*evelopment, and also as the antithesis of red tape!) were basic features of the operational style of Malaysia's rural development program as directed by Tun Razak. The operations rooms at federal, state, and district levels were designed to give development a systematic visibility which would illuminate delays or difficulties. A time schedule was drawn up for every project and entered on a wall chart which showed planned progress month by month. Subsequently, each month actual performance was also noted. Work on schedule was noted in black, that ahead of schedule in green, and that behind schedule in vivid red. Tun Razak personally attended 'briefings' at the National Operations Room in his ministry where every departmental head was required to attend fully prepared to deliver a detailed report on the progress of all projects executed by his agency. The same procedure was followed at the state and district levels with the state chief minister in the chair, but often with Tun Razak, a prodigious traveler, also present. The deputy prime minister thus obtained, at first hand, information on projects which might otherwise have escaped his attention in the federal capital.

The red books came in large volumes (two feet, six inches by three feet)—a size that was difficult to mislay. Each book contained a basic map of the district over which any number of map tracings could be placed. Tracings showed projects for land development, water supply, road, irrigation, and health. Each book provided, at a glance, an overall picture of a particular district's development projects.

The reporting system used in Malaysia has been described as one "whose simplicity and effectiveness would be hard to improve on."[19] It has been contrasted with the situation in Bangladesh (then East

Pakistan), where project directors had to provide ten to fifty different reports on a simple project. Some other neighboring countries have modeled their reporting and plan evaluation systems on the Malaysian pattern, equipped with wall maps, charts, audio visual aids, and other trappings. Few produced the results Tun Razak obtained, however; for without political commitment at the highest level, the technology was of marginal value.

A tangible measure of the newly independent government's commitment to development was the achievement of the Second Malaya Plan. Within a short span of time from 1960 to 1965, public sector development expenditure trebled, and public investment increased at an annual rate of no less than 24 percent, raising the public sector's share of gross capital formation from 23.5 percent to 42.3 percent.

Living standards increased as real consumption per capita rose 2.8 percent per year. During the same period, from 1961 to 1965, there were many tangible indications of this rise in living standards. In 1961, there were, on the average, eighty-two persons for each private motor vehicle and twenty-four for each wireless set, whereas in 1965 there were fifty-six persons per private motor vehicle and twenty-one per wireless set. Per capita annual domestic electric consumption increased from thirty-one to forty-four kilowatt hours, a rise of 42 percent.

The traditional system of budgetary allocation in Malaysia which was inherited from colonial times resembled "a poker game in which departments overestimate their requirements and the Treasury attempts to call their bluff."[20] It reflected excessive Treasury control coupled with inadequate reviews of substantive policy issues. The traditional line budgeting made a virtue of "saving" on expenditures by imposing detailed financial controls. Ministries and departments had to seek treasury approval before they could transfer funds from one "subhead" of expenditure to another within their total allocation. Treasury control of these transfers was a time-consuming process which lent itself to delay in the passage of minute sums rather than efficient financial management of major items of government expenditure. A study of this process revealed that in 1965, 90 percent of all virement requests were below M$10,000 (about US $4,000), and 95 percent were subsequently approved by the Treasury.

In 1969, the Treasury began the change from traditional budgeting to P.P.B.S. The system adopted by the Treasury of Program and Performance Budgeting was a modification of the Planning-Program-Budgeting System of the United States.[21] While the first two years included very small departments such as the Aborigines and Chemistry departments, by 1972 such heavyweights as the Education Ministry and the Royal Malaysia Police were among seventy-two agencies which had moved to the P.P.B. system.

The implementation of P.P.B.S. has brought the budget much closer to the Five Year Plan. The Treasury has changed its budgetary orientation from operation control to management control and begun consideration of the strategic planning aspects of budgeting.[22] It announced that it would relax further its financial control to enable heads of departments to implement development projects immediately and effectively.

These developments indicate how wealth values give way to other value commitments ranging from well-being to skill and respect.

The rural development program of the 1960s is perhaps best illustrated by the Federal Land Development Authority (Felda), which has made impressive progress in quantitative terms. By 1973, Felda had developed 565,000 acres and settled 28,000 families or 180,000 persons.

From an average of 24,000 acres of virgin land opened up each year during 1961-1965, it increased its rate to more than double in 1970, when 51,561 acres were developed. In 1964, it was heavily dependent on rubber, whose planted acreage amounted to 71,000 as opposed to 9000 acres of oil palm. By the end of 1972, there was a spectacular reversal as the oil palm acreage increased so sharply as to exceed that for rubber by more than 50,000 acres. Today, Malaysia is the source of more than 50 percent of the world's supply of palm oil.

Felda was also responsible for breaking the largely foreign estate monopoly of palm oil production. Oil palm has been traditionally an estate crop with an average production unit of 2,000 acres. As recently as 1964, the estates' total acreage was 181,000, while that of all other sources of palm oil production was not even one-tenth that figure. By 1976, however, Felda will be the largest single producer of palm oil, not only in Malaysia but also in the world.

While Felda was set up as an independent corporation to avoid government red tape in its initial years, it was not wholly successful in obtaining cooperation from some states and departments. Subsequently, the authority has worked more closely under the Ministry of Rural Development which was headed by the then deputy prime minister. The substantial investment by the latter of power, wealth and respect values gave Felda the necessary leverage for the speedy implementation of its programs.

Its famous Jengka scheme of 150,000 acres in Pahang was larger than all previous land schemes by the authority, since its establishment in 1956, put together. The 12,000 landless families that settled in Jengka were provided with an impressive array of physical facilities. The scheme provided for 270 miles of main roads and over 1000 miles of agricultural service roads; no less than fifty-six primary schools; over twenty secondary schools; and forty new water supply systems based on both surface and underground sources. Each village averaging 400 family units would contain a primary school, midwife clinic, community center, religious building, recreation field, health subcenter, and policy post. A full range of public services and utilities included sanitation systems, power, and telecommunications.

While the authority has undoubtedly been successful in the physical development of land, questions have been raised on two important aspects. Firstly, has the authority developed the settler and pursued a wider sharing of values while busily developing land? Secondly, has it made a substantial impact on the rural economy?

Felda was designed basically to promote the modernization of the neglected rural Malay community. In analyzing the Felda development model, one is struck by how closely it resembles the estate model used in the enclave economy. Working within the constraints of this model "the original commitment to a mixture of cultural and output goals gradually gave way to an almost exclusive commitment to output goals."[23] Since 1959, the authority has moved away from its early reliance on the traditional rural spirit of "gotong royong" (mutual self-help). More and more stages of development, clearing the jungle, burning, planting cover crop, and the main crop, bud-grafting and weeding had been passed on to contract labor, which was largely non-Malay. Thus the day when the settlers arrived on the scheme was deferred.

The selection of managers and field assistants, especially prior to 1964, had resulted in the inclusion of staff with a preponderance of estate backgrounds. Their competence, like that of Felda itself, was technical and economic. The problems of management at scheme level are aptly summarized in the lament of managers that their problems only began when the settlers arrived on the schemes.[24] In essence, "Felda scheme managers have behaved as if they were operating estates."[25]

The typical Malay *kampong* is a relatively homogeneous unit, while the fundamental unit of Malay peasant society approaches that of the extended family.[26] The extended family, which includes grandparents, uncles and aunts, and a host of relatives, serves the rational function of certain support in case of need. If A has been hurt by B, he does not strike back at B but reports the matter to the head of B's extended family (probably his grandfather, father, or elder uncle). The latter then settles the matter, usually to the satisfaction of A and B and their families. Yet, all these shaping and sharing of respect values has to be reformulated on Felda schemes. On the schemes, the majority of managers were below thirty years old, whereas some 74 percent of the settlers were above thirty.[27] The settlers came from villages where "age ranks high with religion and wealth as criteria for social status."[28] As a variation of the "Don't trust anyone over thirty" problem of the West, the managers' problems in these schemes was one of securing trust and respect[29] for "anyone below thirty!"

Another criticism relating to the economic impact of Felda has been that "land development and land settlement schemes are excellent devices, but the few thousands that benefit each year make up less than 10 percent of the total number that become landless every year.[30]

To absorb the annual increase in the labor force and merely maintain the existing absolute level of unemployment would require the development of new land of about 600,000 acres per year. During the decade of the 1960s, Felda was, in fact, developing 5 percent of that figure.

The achievements of economic policy during the 1960s may be examined under a few broad objectives, which the government followed in that period, namely: (1) economic growth (wealth, and in the long run power); (2) price stability (well-being); and (3) balance of payments equilibrium (power and respect in the short run).

Between 1960 and 1970, the GNP of Peninsular Malaysia[31] grew annually by about 6 percent. This growth rate was higher than planned and also higher than the 5 percent targets for development countries at the outset of the United Nations Development Decade. It is likely that the high degree of price level stability in the country would tend to understate Malaysia's real growth performance in comparison with more inflation-prone countries. By 1973, per capita GNP had reached M$1,360 (US$570), one of the highest in Asia. Malaysia's per capita product is surpassed in South and East Asia only by Japan and the city states of Hong Kong and Singapore.

During the 1950s and earlier, the economy witnessed spectacular fluctuations in the annual growth rate due to the instability of export demand, which accounts for more than one-third of the country's GNP. The economy has proved to be much more resilient to the adverse impact of external factors in more recent years. In 1958, a decrease in exports produced an absolute decrease in GNP. By 1971 and 1972, when exports declined for two consecutive years and when the price of rubber fell to its lowest level in more than twenty-five years, the economy was still able to register growth rates of 4.7 percent and 5.7 percent, respectively.

The growing resilience of the economy is the result of diversification in the economic structure away from the traditional reliance on a few commodities for export. Between 1960 and 1970, the share of exports in GNP went down from 39 to 33 percent. The share of agriculture in the gross domestic product has shrunk from 37 to 25 percent, while the share of manufacturing went up from 9 to 13 percent. The manufacturing sector has been growing at about twice the overall growth rate of the economy for the past twelve years. The share of agriculture would have shrunk more, were it not for the tremendous strides in modernization and efficiency made by the rubber industry in Malaysia. At the same time there has been substantial diversification into palm oil and timber as well as good progress in industrialization for import substitution, mostly in consumer goods. At present, Malaysia is the world's leading exporter of rubber, tin, tropical hardwoods, palm oil, and pepper.

A second important factor explaining the increased resilience of the economy is the transition in the role of the government as a participant in Malaysian development since independence. In the colonial and immediate postcolonial period, the operations of the public sector were frequently procyclical. For example, an absolute decrease in GDP in 1958 (-4.5%) was accompanied by a cut in public investment (-17.4%) and a GDP increase in 1960 of 11 percent by an increase in government investment of 29.6 percent, reflecting the policy of balancing the budget in every single year. Since 1969, the operations of the public sector have become consciously anticyclical. The export-led economic slowdown in 1970-1972 was countered by an increase in public sector investment of no less than 23.5 percent in 1971 and 40 percent in 1972. Government consumption was allowed to increase by 18.5 percent in 1971 and 14 percent in 1972. This partially offset the weakness in the export sector and the resulting weakness in private investment. Thus the public sector proved to be the principal stimulus to the economy in the last two years as it invested wealth and power values for respect, well-being, skill, and wealth outcomes.

During the 1960s, Malaysia's price stability was unsurpassed by that of any other country. The retail price index rose by less than 1 percent annually. The government's fiscal and monetary policies contributed in no small measure to the attainment of this record. It has maintained and further developed an orderly tax system, so that current expenditures could be met by current revenue and the bulk of development expenditures were financed by borrowing. The long-run growth of money supply was kept in line with GNP growth.

Throughout the past decade, Malaysia has maintained a sizable and regular trade surplus. This has ranged from the low level of M$275 million in the export recession year of 1964 to a high of M$1,481 million in the export boom year of 1969.

Malaysia is one of the few developing countries with a rather steady balance of payments surplus. Over the past decade Malaysia accumulated significant external balances. In 1972, total net reserves amounted to $2,930 million, that is more than eight months of retained imports.

The strong reserve position has boosted national and international confidence in the economy and insured the country against short-run speculative outflows of capital in the event of any unforeseen economic or political developments in Southeast Asia. An economy with substantial foreign trade would be hampered in the independent selection of policy options by inadequate reserve levels. Malaysia has not been forced to accept unfavorable "aid" terms for balance of payments reasons. However, there is no strong inhibition against a drawdown of foreign reserves to finance more rapid capital formation in the country, as and when sound economic projects are available.

Development in the 1960s—a Brief Critique

Development during the 1960s in Malaysia was characterized by a tremendous upsurge in physical construction of infrastructures, particularly for well-being, skill, and wealth outcomes in the rural areas. To a considerable extent this development of physical capital far preceded investment in human capital although "capital development depends upon human development."[32]

In the early 1960s government's political posture on development was centered on the amount of funds it had spent in its constituencies, especially in the rural sector, and increases in expenditure in the rural sector were chalked up as progress in rural development. Debates and questions from the opposition parties in Parliament were similarly centered on who the major "beneficiaries" of development expenditure were, and who were "left out." Subsequently, civil engineering feats in the construction of rural roads, bridges, schools, and health clinics were considered prime indicators of rural economic development.[33] Evaluations in the Ministry of National and Rural Development focused on programs in construction. This approach made short-run political sense as the results were more concrete and tangible and could be spread throughout the country within a short period. In the long run, however, "construction may become an end in itself if quantitative performance is emphasized to the exclusion of the qualitative."[34]

Meanwhile, unemployment had been increasing, particularly in the late 1960s. It is estimated to have risen to 8 percent of the labor force with urban unemployment at 10.2 percent and rural unemployment at about 6 percent. More than 80 percent of the unemployed were below thirty years of age. Malaysia's labor force grows at 3.2 percent per annum, one of the highest rates in the world.

Within sectors, as well as between sectors, economic growth seems to have involved non-Malays much more than Malays. Income in the modern urban sector where non-Malays predominate was three to four times as high as that in the traditional rural sector where Malays are concentrated.[35] Over the years as Malaysia's development requirements and the sociopolitical and cultural environment were changing, the reporting and feedback systems were virtually standing still. Stark evidence of the failure of feedback systems to change with their environment was provided on May 13, 1969. On that day immediately after the general elections there were racial riots in Kuala Lumpur. As Tun Razak stated, "On that day the very foundation of this nation was shaken."[36] The riots indicated deficiencies in the feedback of types "b" and "d" which resulted in an "f" type feedback (see Figure 7.1).

Since the first transition from colonial status to independence in 1957, Malaysia experienced a twelve-year period of political and economic stability. The racial riots of May 1969 which followed the general election results of 1969 seem to have spurred on a second transition. The period from May 1969 until today has witnessed many basic changes and also generated a reappraisal of the previous formula for national unity within both the political and economic spheres. Parliament was suspended in May 1969 and reconvened in February 1971.

While the events of May 1969 were followed by dramatic changes in the goals and instruments for development, some shifts had already begun to evolve. Felda, for instance, which had concentrated on wealth

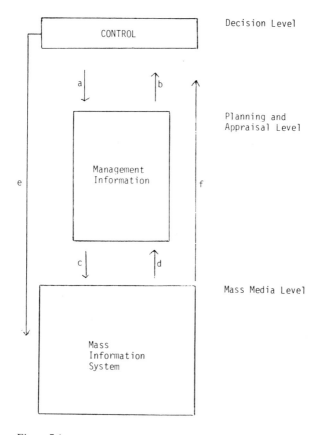

Figure 7.1
Single Feedback Model
Source: SEADAG Report on Development Administration Panel Seminar,
March 1972.

shaping through the early and mid-1960s, established a Settler Development Division in September 1967. The new division represented a significant reformulation of values affecting Felda's hitherto exclusively wealth-shaping focus. The new division highlighted enlightenment, respect, and affection value-sharing, paving the way for greater settler participation in decision making and in narrowing the communication gap between the authority and the settler. With a literacy level of 80 percent in Felda schemes, about 90 percent of the settler families subscribe to the monthly magazine with articles on topics ranging from community living to home economics. In contrast to the narrow approach of the early 1960s, which emphasized the engineering and other physical aspects of development projects, a broader 'systems' approach became evident in the late 1960s.

In December 1970, the Minister of Finance, Tun Tan Siew Sin, indicated in his 1971 Budget Address that the three broad objectives of the Second Malaysia Plan would be: (1) reducing unemployment; (2) raising the productivity and incomes of the "have-nots" of our society; and (3) achieving a higher rate of economic growth in order to be able to implement (1) and (2) more effectively.

In July 1971, the new prime minister, Tun Razak who succeeded Tunku Abdul Rahman in September 1970 presented the Second Malaysia Plan to Parliament. The Plan was the operational expression of the New Economic Policy (NEP) whose two prongs were: (1) the eradication of poverty irrespective of race; and (2) the restructuring of Malaysian society to correct economic imbalance, so as to eliminate the identification of race with economic function. Within a twenty-year target Malays were to manage and own 30 percent of the total commercial and industrial activities in all categories and scales of operation.

In the implementation of the Second Malaysia Plan and the New Economic Policy, a number of new instruments were established. The most significant of those were PERNAS, UDA, the SEDCs and RISDA. PERNAS (National Corporation), set up as a private company in November 1969, is to be one of the chief instruments for promoting the Malay industry and commercial community. Its main activities include equity participation, trading and distribution, insurance, construction, engineering, mining, realty, and manufacturing. In October 1971, it was authorized by the government as the sole agent for imports from the Peoples Republic of China. In addition to its capital subscribed to by the Treasury and the Central Bank it has been granted a loan of M$100 million under the Second Malaysia Plan.

The Urban Development Authority (UDA), launched in 1970 with wide terms of reference including urban renewal and development, is to be specifically responsible for assisting Malay businesses to operate in the main commercial areas. It has increased Malay visibility in the main commercial areas of the federal capital.

The State Economic Corporations (SEDCs) which have been established in all thirteen states are concerned with the creation of industrial estates and financial and infrastructure assistance to Malays in commercial, industrial, and real estate activities in general. The Rubber Industry Smallholders Development Authority (RISDA), set up in January 1973, is responsible for the modernization of the smallhold sector and for the reduction in the time lag between research findings and implementation by the smallholder sector. It has been observed that the move to create numerous public corporations doubtless marks a decisive reversal of the traditional laissez faire attitude."[37]

The Minister with Special Functions and Minister of Information, Tan Sri Ghazali Shafie, provided the rationale for the attempts to reformulate value outcomes for Malaysia's future, in particular by restructuring Malaysian society. Expressing concern with the identification of race with vocation he stated that "living in separate and 'safe' compartments did not and could never achieve for us an equilibrium. . . .

The urban or commercial community, and in the present context the Chinese, will certainly place economic values as the dominating value, while the Malay, who is compartmentalized in the agricultural sector, will objectify and place highly the expressive, respect of the cultural values."[38] The previous communal structure of society with static value-shaping and limited value-sharing which also "exhibits some features of a caste system, in that certain functions are performed by groups traditionally acknowledged to have ascriptive rights (and perhaps duties) to provide certain services, and are generally believed to have 'natural abilities' or skills—"communal pluralism" as opposed to "functional pluralism"[39] is no longer being defended or passively accepted.

The Second Malaysia Plan is to be guided by the principles of the national ideology, *Rukunegara*, proclaimed on 31st August 1970. The re-assertion of the deference values of affection, respect, and rectitude which had been submerged during the colonial period and in the 1960s are particularly significant in the declaration of *Rukunegara* which reads:

Our Nation, Malaysia, being dedicated to achieving a greater
unity of all her peoples:
to maintaining a *democratic* way of life;
to creating a *just* society in which the wealth of the nation
shall be equitably shared;
to ensuring a *liberal* approach to her rich and diverse cultural
traditions;
to building a *progressive* society which shall be
oriented to modern science and technology;
We, her peoples, pledge our united efforts to attain these
ends guided by these principles:
Belief in God
Loyalty to King and Country
Upholding the Constitution
Rule of Law
Good behavior and Morality.

A recent study based on very detailed interviews with 95 percent of the families involved (135) in a rural resettlement program in Selangor State over a two-year period confirms the current resurgence of respect values.[40] The resurgence of respect values is also indicated in instances such as the government's positions on signboards in shops and registered trade names on lorries. The deputy prime minister, Tun Dr. Ismail, indicated that there was no prohibition on the use of Chinese characters as printed on existing signboards. "However, in addition new signboards using the national language should be made." As for trade names on lorries, "registered trade names can be displayed with the proviso that the national language must be above any other language and that national language characters are more prominent than others.[41]

"As the functions of government multiply and its activities affect society in a direct and immediate sense, bureaucratic power begins to magnify, and bureaucracies move into a much more central role."[42] The functions of the Malaysia government have increased sharply since May 1969. It has set itself tasks which include the reformulation of values in the polity, the economy, and in Malaysian society.

As the major instrument for the shaping and sharing of values in Malaysia, the Malaysian bureaucracy itself will need to be modernized and better equipped to provide "leadership in the areas of decision making, policy formulation, program planning and review, control and management of the resources, program coordination and implementation." In 1969, training for the civil service as well as professional and nonprofessional officers in the bureaucracy was described as "pathetically inadequate."[43] In shaping and sharing the value outcomes of development, the bureaucracy in Malaysia has to contend with a situation where interest groups are divided along racial lines. In responding to the society and the context in which it operates it cannot afford to reflect passively the fragmentation between Malay and non-Malay, rural and urban, traditional and modern. The bureaucracy cannot expect merely to maintain the system but will be expected to act as agents of social change. The short-run problems of managing racial conflict and the long-run problems of racial integration could strain the bureaucracy and the national development program to an unprecedented degree.

It has been said that Malaysia "accomplished so much by attempting so little and administering it well."[44] In the past decade, the government's commitment to development and to reform as well as its pragmatic response to the problems of development were evident. The political leadership in the government has indicated in its recent policy statements that it is prepared to attempt much more than "a little" during the decade of the 1970s. The challenge of development for the Malaysian bureaucracy in this decade will be to administer this much greater attempt equally well.

In the economic arena the goals of the 1960s of growth with stability were overtaken by the now prime objectives of employment and income distribution. An analysis of budgetary expenditure in the 1960s shows that it helped to prevent a worsening of economic inequality. As for the Second Malaysia Plan and the New Economic Policy "the income distribution element inherent in the government's development program for 1971-1975 represents new dimensions of the budget's contribution to equalizing opportunities for all Malaysians. In addition, the measures taken to reduce the identification of race with vocation provide a source of mobility for those tied to traditionally low income occupations and should in the longer run lead to a socially more acceptable pattern of income distribution."[45]

Of the events of May 1969 and the past 1969 development phase it has been observed that

a leading Malay politician refers to the 'de eliticization' of Malaysia, and there is truth in the term, even if Western academics are always looking for the opposite as a sign of political progress. Malaysia, has always been, by Asian standards, an apolitical country. The stormy election campaign of 1969 which resulted in the riots was, in Malaysian terms, something of an aberration . . . So the present quiescence is not the quiet before the storm but the quiet which Malaysians prefer to any storm. At grass roots, Malaysian multiracialism prospers without violence mainly because Malaysians of different races do not talk too much about the many things that divide.[46]

Meanwhile a recent survey[47] of opinions among a sample of civil servants suggests that public participation has not been far behind the achievement of development targets.

Evaluation of Policy and of Targets:

Very successful	5.12
Successful	10.99
Moderately successful	45.67
Somewhat unsuccessful	5.64
Definitely unsuccessful	.79

Evaluation of Government's Achievement in Bringing about Public Participation:

Very successful	2.9
Successful	22.97
Moderately successful	51.57
Somewhat unsuccessful	17.85
Definitely unsuccessful	2.36

A preliminary attempt at gauging the value priorities during the three phases of development in Malaysia might be a useful way of summing up the changes.

During the colonial period, the administration operated in the context of a dual economy and a plural society which fitted in snugly with its *divide et impera* policy. The colonial ruling elite was concerned with growth in one sector, the enclave economy, and with the status quo in the other, the traditional economy. Thus, its concern with value priorities was for virtually opposite objectives—for significant change in the former and minimal change in the latter.

The enclave sector, as an extension of the metropolitan areas of Europe, carried with it the heavier values of the modern industrial sector of the West. In rough and simple terms it was the single-minded pursuit of wealth-shaping with minimal change in its environment ranging from the preservation of law and order to keeping its labor divided and cheap.

The traditional sector seemed to give priority to the value categories at the opposite end of the Lasswellian construct. Its value priorities of rectitude as religion and affection as unquestioning loyalty to their traditional leaders was convenient for the colonial administration. "The sultans were given greatly increased dignity and wealth but little real power."[48] The colonial administration was able to follow a policy of neglect towards the traditional sector that was far from benign. Various colonial administrators in postures ranging from condescension to cynicism encouraged the notion that well-being for the population in the traditional sector meant stagnation. "The Government has never desired to give to the children a smattering, or even a larger quantity, of knowledge which will not help them to more useful and happy lives than they now lead . . . the principal value of school attendance is to teach [them] habits of order, punctuality, and obedience."[49]

The colonial administration thus used the value priorities of rectitude, affection, and well-being to maintain its own power position.

With independence, value priorities were affected and rearranged in three major respects:

1. The sector whose value priorities were of crucial concern to the new administration was no longer the enclave economy but the very sector which had been neglected in the previous phase, namely the traditional rural sector.

2. Well-being was redefined from the paradoxical, if not cynical, interpretation of some colonial officials that the pursuit of happiness could best be achieved by stagnation. Instead, as set out in some detail earlier in this chapter, a massive rural development program was implemented. This program symbolized the independent government's interpretation of the value priority for well-being of its new power base, the traditional

rural sector. As befits an administrative elite, *quantitative* outcomes were pursued more vigorously than qualitative outcomes which tend to be identified with ideological elites.

3. While well-being was both in intensity and pervasiveness the priority, the value categories of skill and enlightenment might be interpreted as being the second priority, although with less intensity and extensiveness.

The priority given to well-being and the intensity with which it was sought can be understood from the aspirations visible in newly independent countries where the new power base has high expectations for its well-being shortly after independence. New administrations can be tardy in the delivery of these goods only at their own peril.

The priority for skill and enlightenment can be gauged from a number of indicators.[50] The major output indicator of education, literacy, defined as the ability to read and write in any language in Malaysia, increased from 51 percent in 1957 to 68 percent in 1970. The proportion of the population remaining in school in the six-to-eleven-year age group has increased from 80 percent in 1957 to 91 percent in 1973. The proportion in the twelve-to-fourteen-year age group leapt from 15 percent to 60 percent in the same period. The availability of opportunities for nonformal or informal education has increased rapidly with adult literacy classes and off-campus courses; there was a twelvefold increase in private candidates taking examinations for higher certificates. The government spends almost one-quarter of its operating budget on education. Expenditure on education was 4.7 percent of the GDP in 1970, whereas the international expectation[51] for a country with a per capita GNP of US$400 would be closer to half that level at 2.7 percent; for a country with a per capita GNP of US$800 it would only be 2.9 percent.

The number of major newspapers circulating daily has increased from sixty-one copies per 1,000 in 1960 to seventy-four copies in 1969. There has been even more significant expansion in the government-owned radio and television services. "In 1948, there were only three ancient radio transmitters of low power (one kilowatt shortwave and two ten-kilowatt mediumwave) operating from Kuala Lumpur, broadcasting limited airtimes and program fare."[52] Program hours for radio are now at the maximum of twenty-four hours per day with an estimated 92 percent of rural adults, as opposed to between 70 to 80 percent of urban adults now listening to the national radio. National television viewing has also been found to be very popular in the rural areas. Since its inception in 1964, the registration of TV sets has increased from 28,125 sets of 313,244 sets in 1973. Thus television ownership has increased dramatically from 1 set per 281 persons in 1964 to one per 31 in 1973. The provision of public telephone booths almost doubled between 1963 and 1973 with more than 60 percent of the booths in the rural areas. In 1970, 66.7 pieces of mail per capita were delivered as compared with only 25.7 in 1957.

The priority given to enlightenment and skill was manifest, not only in the above indicators, but in others which lend themselves to some rough international comparisons. One of the many examples of the conversion of skill to well-being is Felda's spectacular progress with palm oil production. In terms of Hirschman's "low latitude for poor performance," palm oil production represents a new skill of considerable significance for the traditional rural sector. The oil palm fruit pulp deteriorates rapidly after harvest and has to be processed within twenty-four hours. The rigid time schedule that this demands could provide an excellent intermediate skill for the traditional rural population before it is "clocked in" at factories and workshops.

Similarly, the adoption of budgetary reform by the Treasury and the government's achievements in terms of the 1960s objectives of steady growth, price stability, and external balance represent a considerable investment of skill and enlightenment.

These changes in value priorities and their redefinitions are, however, dwarfed by the *potential* of the developments in the third (post-1969) phase in Malaysian development.

The administrators[53] now are taking a more direct interest in the value orientations of key sectors of the population in order that persuasive strategies for development might be made even more effective. A striking example is the administrator's approach to the farmer and the latter's indication of value priorities in the traditional sector in two major rice growing areas—the Muda scheme and the Tanjong Karang rice bowl area.

The Muda irrigation scheme, one of the largest development projects undertaken by the government, was conceived in the midsixties as an engineering cum irrigation project with little coordination of agricultural extension and with even less regard for the value priorites of the more than 50,000 farm families in the 250,000 acre area. That seventy different long-term paddy varieties were grown in the area was just one of numerous problems posed at the onset. In the early stages the farmers were unconvinced of the sincerity and wisdom of government efforts to uplift (their) standards of living." In early 1970, the Muda Agricultural Development Authority (MADA), in the value priorities of the farmers and its concern for their redefined well-being, is summed up in the general manager's declaration that:

The emphasis is on people for agricultural development is about people, their well being and what they can become. The socio-economic well being of the participating farmers takes precedence over economic and physical targets, for these are useless if the actors are deprived from enjoying the benefits.[54]

MADA's organization includes a planning and evaluation unit with not only an economist but also a sociologist whose reports have covered the socioeconomic value system of the Muda rice farmers in developmental perspectives and the leadership pattern, activities, and behavior among leaders of farmers' associations. His study[55] on the commercial behavior of farmers in the Muda scheme expresses the administrators' great direct concern for the farmers' value priorities. The farmers' priority for the value categories of respect and rectitude as religion emerges as the most striking conclusion of the numerous surveys.

In one project the value priority for rectitude as religion and respect among the farmers was utilized to the hilt to promote a very successful rice double-cropping campaign.

Given the deep religious nature of the rural community agreement from the State government was obtained to have the Religious Department Assist. At the mosques, sermons conveyed the campaign message of employing supporting phrases from the Quran. In addition teams of senior officials and field staff prayed at different mosques each week, giving talks after prayers, stressing the important points given during the sermons. The religious aspect was further exploited by having special prayers and small feasts in the mosques at strategic times during the campaign. A special message campaign was launched in the form of personal letters. These letters were either from the District Officer or the Chief Minister. Such letters were sent to all traditional or informal leaders in the District.[56]

One of the major studies launched by the Malaysian Centre for Development Studies in 1973 was designed: (1) to study the value orientations of the rural communities in Peninsular Malaysia towards change, in the context of the government rural development efforts; (2) to examine the relationships between these values and development efforts of the government; and (3) to suggest alternative intervention programs for bringing about greater responsiveness to change.

Since the riots of May 1969, dramatic changes have occurred in the political context of executive action in promoting development. A series of coalition agreements between the ruling Alliance Party and leading opposition parties have created a striking degree of consensus in the political arena. In this context the administration would need to be even more sensitive to feedback from the masses.

The intensity and the priority given by citizens to respect values, which the administration had underestimated before May 1969, have now been not only recognized but also accepted. The development program has evolved to a new focus on state leadership and intervention in the pursuit of value outcomes aside from the traditional 'heavy' ones of power and wealth.

The restructuring of society which is one of the twin overall objectives of the Second Malaysia Plan involves acceptance, investment, and new commitment to development by citizens in the contextuality of a democracy and a mixed economy to a degree with few precedents in the history of development. The potential for conflicts between wealth and rectitude[57] value outcomes are but one of the many new dimensions of development that the administrator in Malaysia will face in the seventies.

The value priorities in the post-1969 phase differ from those of the colonial period and the sixties not only in definition and order but also in their scope. Well-being continues as a priority value category but has been redefined again as the quality of life. The annual economic report of the Treasury, for instance, devotes a whole chapter to the quality of life in Malaysia. In its pioneering chapter in 1973 the report evaluated critically the state of education, environmental quality, health, housing, income distribution, population, public safety, and the quality of working life.

The priority value categories in the post-1969 phase involve not only redefinitions and a broader spectrum but also greater interaction between the "rougher" urban values and the "milder" rural ones.

The value priorities of the bulk of the population in the post-1969 phase may be interpreted as respect and a redefined well-being through the investment of wealth and skill. The new goals of government go beyond the recognition of the population's value priorities and the harnessing of these priorities for the promotion of development through pervasive strategies. Whereas the colonial administration accepted and encouraged the plurality of values, nurturing some for change but freezing the rest into a sterile status quo, the independent government has identified the traumatic experience of 1969 as a crisis of values.

It now seeks through *Rukunegara* and the New Economic Policy over a prospective plan period of 20 years (1970-90) to cause the emergence of a new system of values and norms "which will synthesize and reorder the value systems in the culture of each group."[58]

The instruments that Malaysia requires for its new social and economic goals have been established. The goals of development involve radical changes in value priorities and outcomes. Both the administrator and the citizen now have set goals for each other unparalleled in the development and experience not only of Malaysia but of most of the developing world. Performance in relation to these ideals and goals during the seventies will be crucial to Malaysia's future.

NOTES

1. For purposes of standardization, the expression "Malaysia" is used through most of the text.

2. J. S. Furnivall, *Colonial Policy and Practice* (Cambridge: Cambridge University Press, 1948), p. 304.

3. T. H. Silcock, "Communal and Party Structure," in Silcock and Fisk, *The Political Economy of Independent Malaya,* pp. 8 and 9.

4. Shirle Gordon, "Social Implications of Communalism," *Intisari,* Vol. III, No. 2, p. 22.

5. Gordon P. Means, "The Role of Islam in the Political Development of Malaysia," *Comparative Politics,* January 1969, pp. 264-283.

6. I.B.R.D., *The Economic Development of Malaya* (Baltimore: Johns Hopkins University Press, 1955), p. 21.

7. R. K. Ratnam, *Communalism and the Political Process in Malaya* (Kuala Lumpur: University of Malaya Press, 1965), p. 13.

8. L. A. Mills, *Malaya: A Political and Economic Appraisal* (Minneapolis: University of Minnesota Press, 1958), p. 5.

9. Joseph J. Spengler, "Bureaucracy and Economic Development," in Loseph La Palombara, *Bureaucracy and Political Development* (Princeton, New Jersey: Princeton University Press, 1963), p. 232.

10. Syed Hussein Alatas, "The Grading of Occupational Prestige Amongst the Malays in Malaysia," in *Journal Malayan Branch Royal Asiatic Society,* Vol. 41, Part 1, 1968.

11. James C. Scott, *Political Ideology in Malaysia* (Kuala Lumpur: University of Malaya Press, 1968), p. 218.

12. Merle Fainsod, "Bureaucracy and Modernization: The Russian and Soviet Case," in La Palombara, *Bureaucracy,* p. 233.

13. John D. Montgomery and Milton J. Esman, *Development Administration in Malaysia* (Kuala Lumpur: Government Printer, 1966).

14. Robert O. Tilman, *Bureaucratic Transition in Malaya* (Durham, N.C.: Duke University Commonwealth-Studies Center, 1964), pp. 36, 63.

15. Robert O. Tilman, "Policy Formulation" in Wong Gungwu, ed., *Malaysia* (London: Pall Mall Press, 1964), p. 350.

16. Gayl D. Ness, *Bureaucracy and Rural Development in Malaysia* (Berkeley: University of California Press, 1967), pp. 89, 90. This book, which contains an excellent account of the operations of the rural development program in Malaysia, has been a major source of reference for this article.

17. Arthur Smithies, "The Balanced Budget," in *American Economic Review,* May 1960, pp. 301-309.

18. Rama Iyer, "The Securing of a National Commitment for Economic and Social Development," Report on 2nd Seminar on Development (Kuala Lumpur: Government of Malaysia, 1967), pp. 1-21.

19. Albert Waterson, *Development Planning, Lessons of Experience*, I.B.R.D. (Baltimore, Maryland: Johns Hopkins Press, 1965), pp. 358-362.

20. Montgomery and Esman, *Development Administration*.

21. See Milton J. Esman, *Administration and Development in Malaysia* (Ithaca: Cornell University Press, 1972) for a perceptive account of the problems and issues.

22. Robert N. Anthony, *Planning and Control Systems: A Framework for Analysis* (Boston, 1965), pp. 16-18.

23. Ness, *Bureaucracy*, p. 39.

24. This lament is comparable to that of the professor who stated that there would be no trouble on the campus if only there were no students on it!

25. Donald W. Fryer, "Some Aspects of the Malaysian Rural Development Program," in Robert Van Miel, ed., *Economic Factors in Southeast Asian Social Change* (Honolulu: University of Hawaii, 1968).

26. M. G. Swift, *Malay Peasant Society in Jelebu* (London: Athlone Press, 1965).

27. Felda, Social Survey (Kuala Lumpur; April 1971).

28. Alladin Hashim, *Land Development and the Settler—Some Social Aspects of Land Development* (mimeo) (July 1971), p. 14.

29. During a preliminary survey of settler attitudes and perceptions, it was observed that the older settlers consulted each other rather than the field assistants (who are generally even younger than the managers) when they encountered difficulties. Sim Wong Kooi, Personal communication.

30. Ungku Aziz, "Poverty and Rural Development in Malaysia," Inaugural Lecture as Professor of Economics at University of Malaya, September, 1963, Kuala Lumpur.

31. No reliable national accounts statistics are available for Malaysia as a whole before 1967. See The Treasury, Economic Report, 1972-1973 (Kuala Lumpur: Government of Malaysia, December, 1972), p. 37.

32. John D. Montgomery, *Foreign Aid in International Politics* (Englewood Cliffs, New Jersey: Prentice-Hall Inc., 1957), p. 37.

33. A leading Malaysian literary critic, Samad Ismail, has said of current Malaysian literature, for instance, that "rural development serves as a rich source of themes and subject matter for the writers. However they see the physical changes in the countryside mostly in terms of tractors and bulldozers, not impact on human values." *Straits Times*, April 7, 1973, p. 20.

34. Mavis Pathacheary, "The Operations Room in Malaysia as a Technique in Administrative Reforms," in HahnBeen Lee and Abelardo G. Samonte, eds., *Asia* (Manila: EROPA, 1970), p. 195.

35. Government of Malaysia, *Second Malaysia Plan 1971-1975* (Kuala Lumpur: 1971), p. 38.

36. National Operations Council, *The May 13 Tragedy* (Kuala Lumpur: Government of Malaysia, October, 1969).

37. Wolfgang Kasper, "Malaysia–A Case Study in Successful Development" (mimeo), 1973; paragraph 98.

38. Tan Sri Ghazali Shafie, Speech to the Senate, March 5, 1971.

39. Gordon P. Means, *Malaysian Politics* (New York: New York University Press, 1970), pp. 414-415.

40. K. P. Pataki, personal communication, and "Psychological Factors in a Rural Resettlement Program in Selangor State, Malaysia" (Draft mimeo), 1973.

41. *Straits Times,* February 19, 1973.

42. Fainsod, *Bureaucracy,* p. 233.

43. Malaysian Development Administration Unit and Staff Training Centre. *Training for Development in Malaysia,* Kuala Lumpur, November, 1969.

44. James F. Guyot, Review article in *Economic Development and Cultural Change,* Vol. 18, Number 3 (April 1970), p. 80.

45. The Treasury, *Economic Report 1972-73* (Kuala Lumpur: Government of Malaysia, December 1972), p. 43.

46. Harvey Stechwin in *Malaysia*: Financial Times Survey (London, 26 February, 1973).

47. Survey conducted by Mavis Futhucheary for draft Ph.D. dissertation, to be submitted to Manchester University, on "Bureaucracy, Politics and Development in West Malaysia."

48. Wilcock, "Communal and Party Structure," p. 11.

49. Frank Swettenham, *British Malaya* (London: George Allen and Unwin, Ltd., 1948).

50. Treasury, Economic Reports.

51. Based on H. B. Chenery, H. Elkington and C. Sims, "A Uniform Analysis Development Pattern," Development Report No. 148 (Harvard University Center for International Affairs, July 1970, mimeo.)

52. Dol Ramli, "The Uses of Mass Communication Media for Promoting Economic and Political Development," in *Development Forum,* Malaysian Centre for Development Studies (Kuala Lumpur, December 1968), p. 10.

53. Dubbed "an indispensable resource for the management of communal conflict," by Milton J. Esman, *Administration and Development,* p. 276.

54. Dato Mohd. Tamin Yeop, "The Role of MADA in Rural Development" (mimeo).

55. Afifuddin Haji Omar, "The Commercial Farming Behavior and Attitudes of Farmers in the Muda Scheme" (MADA, Kedah, February 1973).

56. Sulaiman Osman, "Approaches to Innovation and Change—Case Study," Fifth International Seminar on Development, January 4-13, 1970, Kuala Lumpur.

57. "They take their *adat* (custom) so seriously that they have a proverb which says *'Biar anak mati, jangan mati adat'* (Let the child perish, but not the *adat*). A contemporary call to reverse this proverb so that it reads . . . let the *adat* perish but not the child has not led to a conscious onslaught on the citadel of *adat*; rather the structure is being undermined by the impact of economic forces." Wan A Hamid, "Religion and Culture of the Modern Malay" in Wang Gungwu, ed., *Malaysia,* p. 180.

58. Tan Sri Ghazali Shafie, "Address to the Southeast Asia Study Group on Cultural Relations for the Future," June 17, 1971.

The conventional approach to the comparative analysis of social processes assumes that there is little difference in the relative importance attached to the various values[1] in different societies. The tendency has been to assign universally dominant importance to one or two values. The assumption was that human nature was similar throughout all human societies, in both space and time. The relative intensity with which various values are held by various societies has been assumed to be similar throughout the world.

This paper departs from such a universalistic assumption.[2] Its goal is to clarify the interaction between the traditional Korean value practices (which have assigned a dominant importance to affection and the legal techniques) and institutions imported from Europe (which are products of the Occidental emphasis on power and wealth). This interaction between the traditional Korean value practices and the imported legal system from Europe has been a subject of inquiry in the past.[3] The approach taken here will emphasize the variance in the relative position of values in these cultures.

Toynbee has pointed out that many societies have assigned the two values power and wealth the most important place in their social processes. The fact that Occidental man uses power and wealth as criteria by which to reckon human prosperity[4] clearly is visible even today. The nation-states, for example, are judged today internationally as advanced or underdeveloped by their power and wealth. The same is true in judging the worth of an individual.

I shall not go into the causes for such a cultural perspective here. Suffice it to say that as soon as the Occidental man began to perceive himself as well as other entities on the globe as the creatures of God, the Creator, the decision to separate the entities on the globe into human vs. nonhuman and subject vs. objects was inevitable. Once other human beings are perceived as objects separate and distinct from one-self, then the desire to dominate other human beings as objects becomes overwhelmingly important. But in an affective culture such as Korea, power as a value (which may be defined as "participation in the making of decisions") was less basic. Many Koreans have desired power and succeeded in pursuing it as the most important value; but pursuit of power was always considered inimical to the more basic value of affection.

A note of caution is in order. It is not intended here to ignore the fact that the exercise of power may rest on faiths, loyalties, habits, or apathies just as much as on violence and physical brutality. What is emphasized, however, is the fact that the threat of sanction is the essence of power, albeit sanctions may take nonviolent forms. The crucial point is that power cannot be defined in terms of decision making without sanctions and deprivations as well as effective control of interpersonal relations. To be sure, the control may be made effective by means other than violence or physical coercion; and sanctions, constraints, and deprivations may be directed against values other than physical safety and well-being. But one can hardly speak of deprivation, sanction, and constraint as conducive to altruism and other forms of positive affection of one against whom they are applied.

There is an inherent tendency in the exercise of power for sanctions and deprivations, no matter what form they may take, to become a dominant feature for the entire process. This tendency has been considered injurious to affection by Koreans. Koreans have endeavored to humanize the power process by insisting on the most nonviolent and noncoercive forms of exercise of power in every sector of the arena. Appeals to loyalties, faiths, and other forms of unegotistic affections were the least objectionable patterns of power practices. The more unobtrusive and tacit the appeals and the more affectionate the manner in which the appeals were made, the more acceptable the power practice.

In its haste to gain acceptance and standing as a member of the modern world community, Korea began to import the format for written prescriptions, institutional arrangements, and techniques of a legal system of Western Europe in the 1880s via Japan. Little concern was felt or expressed about the difference which existed in the modes of ranking the values in the order of their importance in Western Europe and Korea. The legal system of Korea was to be "modernized" by discarding the traditional authoritative decision process and substituting the Western European institutions and practices in its place. The difference in the pattern of value-ranking was a matter beyond any precise analyses at the time. Indeed, the difference is only vaguely felt even today. The reason for the failure of the imported system to function effectively in Korea is usually explained on the ground that the vestiges of the old value pattern are jeopardizing the imported system. The assumption is that the Korean value pattern has to be modernized as rapidly as possible by becoming European and that this course of events is inevitable historically.

The tendency has been to "muddle through." The professional participants in the process have been more interested in maximizing their interest by doing their best to preserve the purity of the imported system. The general populace simply structured their daily routine so as to stay away from the imported process as much as feasible. The imported system has become largely a plaything of the wealthy and the urbanized. This trend is projected to continue for the foreseeable future.

It is the objective of this writer to clarify the significance and ramifications of the difference in the pattern of value-ranking in Korea and Europe and the United States. This clarification is hoped to facilitate the formulation of strategies that would contribute to the realization of the goal of increased effectiveness of the modern legal system of Korea. Some accommodation on the part of the imported system to the indigenous value pattern seems both advisable and unavoidable. If zero-sum form of justice is unacceptable, a form of minimax justice has to be worked out. Less adversariness may render the adjudication process much more acceptable to the Korean masses.

Participants

Koreans are a group of Tungusic people inhabiting the Korean peninsula south of the Yalu and Tuman rivers who have shared the same language. Ethnically the Korean nation is said to be a composite of Ainus (Caucasoid people who inhabited the Far East in the paleolithic period), the Malay strain (dominant strain of the Japanese nation), and the Tungus who came from the north and the west into the Korean peninsula. Koreans have had a very homogeneous existence in terms of culture, life style, and world view. The world view of Koreans has been derived primarily from shamanism, which is shared by most of the ethnic groups who inhabit the Far East, Siberia, Mongolia, and Turkey.

Korea has enjoyed a unitary political existence as a nation-state with a monarchical form of government for over a millenium. Its political ideology has been primarily that of Confucianism, which came from China. But the Confucian state system as practiced in Korea has been a product of creative adaptation by the Koreans themselves.

The elites who had enjoyed the most favored value positions with respect to all values were known by the name of *yangban.* They were, as in China, a combination of literati and bureaucratic groups. An elite person who aspired to be a government official had to show a mastery of enlightenment, especially in the literary skills of the Confucian classics. Varying degrees of restriction in the sharing of the values for the non-elite was an important strategy by which the elite maximized its value position as a class. But the elite was also highly successful in its endeavor to inculcate a comprehensive system of authoritative symbols into the rank and file. The rank and file were participants in this community process of interaction in which affection was the dominant value, albeit the participation of the non-elite in the shaping and sharing of values was variously limited.

The groups that participated in the social process were linked by affection. Consanguineous ties were of paramount importance for a man's identity. The elite relied on lineage as the positive base value. Even the power arena revolved around lineage affiliations. These affection groups of premodern Korea had a very multiple significance which had little parallel in the extended families of premodern Europe. The factional competition for access to the power arena also revolved around lineage affiliation. From marriage to participation in the inner councils of decision making, affection via affiliation remained central in the life of an elite member.

Voluntary associations as known even in medieval Europe were not developed in traditional Korea. All such associations specialized to the other values than affection were openly suppressed as injurious to the integrity and the viability of affection groups. From power arenas to commercial markets, the propensity has been to analogize every pattern of interpersonal dynamics to the pattern of affective interaction. Private associations specialized to power were mercilessly suppressed as treasonous. Those specialized to wealth were discriminated against as cursed by moral depravity. The only nonaffection groups given legitimacy were those specialized to enlightenment. The rank and file were, of course, excluded from participation. These enlightenment associations of the elite gradually came to assume political significance as the provincial centers of power and even of wealth. There developed a mutual check-and-balance situation between those members of the elite who followed the bureaucratic career and those who remained outside the central arena as the enlightened opposition to those in power.

It is difficult to explain the role of an individual in the old Korea. The concept of an individual was a very amorphous one. It was not a totalitarian or collectivistic view. Nor was it anything analogous to modern individualism in America. In old Korea an individual was conceptualized as a part of the universe, and a part of the universe was represented in the individual. The individual was never conceptualized as an independent category, but as a mutually interpenetrating being with other human beings as well as with the material world. The individual was always viewed in the context of his affection network, never as separate from his blood relations. This is a difficult concept to grasp for persons with Western cultural perspectives. An example may be given to assist this understanding. A mother is said to feel on the death of her child as if a part of her died with her child. By the same token, when a parent dies, a child feels that a part of it dies with the parent also. The Koreans have tried to preserve this kind of affective interaction in their conceptualization of the role of an individual. Koreans conceptualized an individual within the context of all his spatial, temporal, verbal, and affective dimensions.

If we come to the modern period, especially the period after 1945, the participants in the social process we refer to are those now living in the Republic of Korea. Their territorial unit covers the area south of the 38th parallel, or subsequent to the end of the Korean war in 1953, the area south of the demilitarized zone. As the U.S. military government was established in the south, American advisors became important participants in the overall social process of South Korea. Japanese residents were repatriated, and Korea was spared an ethnic minority problem. The Republic of Korea was established in the summer of 1948. By mid-1949, when all U.S. military forces left, the domestic participants in the social process were Koreans exclusively, largely homogeneous in terms of national origin, language, lifestyle, and personality traits. In keeping with the trend throughout the globe, the Koreans decided to adopt parliamentary democracy as the basic constitutive process. But intensification of the Cold War confrontation with a separate communist regime in northern Korea produced a separate social process by Koreans committed to communist ideology.

In addition to the national government with its conventional separation of powers, the political parties have become important participants in the social process. Other private associations and pressure groups with similar organizing characteristics as their counterparts in European nation-states have also begun to participate in the social process. The premodern pattern of respect stratification was abandoned in favor of the more egalitarian pattern existing in other democratic communities. Universal education has replaced the monopolistic practices of the elite with respect to all of the values. Today, individuals are conceived as much more distinct and discrete categories.

Although formally the institutions of parliamentary democracy have been established as constitutive principles in South Korea, the actual practices of the participants in the new social process still contain elements of the old. The role of an individual is in many respects still as a prisoner of the traditional world view. The rules of the game for interaction among various associations are still in a confused state. In sum, affection still remains the dominant value in the contemporary social process of Korea.

Perspectives

As with human beings everywhere, Koreans posit the good life as their most valued goal. Koreans consider the greatest possible indulgence in affection as the most desirable state of human existence. Their desire is to be indulged with as many persons as possible. They are also aware that other values may be used as base values to maximize affection.

Therefore, Koreans are more likely to posit affection as the objective or the aim for which other values are to be used as base values. Of course, this does not mean that there are no Koreans who would place a higher priority on power and/or wealth than on affection. Inasmuch as affection is a deference value, however, it has a closer affinity with other deference values, such as respect and rectitude, than with welfare values such as wealth or well-being.

When we speak of the perspectives of Koreans as participants in the social process, their identities and expectations must be examined. Given a shamanistic world view in which "this-worldliness" prevails, Koreans never bestowed much recognition on the existence of a transcendental being (a deity or nation-state) with whom a man could exchange affection on an individual basis. The indulgence in affection is to take place with other human beings "in flesh and blood." Thus Koreans are, comparatively speaking, much less interested in their own ego identity as individuals than they are interested in their identity with the group in which affection is optimized. Koreans do not conceptualize even the affection group as an abstract entity, but identify themselves with human networks of affection which are concrete and this-worldly.

There are slight differences even in the metaphysical assumptions of Koreans and those held by more individualistic people. The temporal dimension is never understood as a unilinear phenomenon with a directional arrow, but rather as a rhythmic movement—yet not one in the form of a circle. Koreans avoid dividing the time dimension into segments of a straight line with clear distinctions as to past, present, and future. Even their language betrays this reluctance to segment the temporal dimension clearly. Moreover, clear separation is avoided between ego and non-ego and between ego and the nonhuman world. Koreans refuse to turn the material world around them into an object separate and distinct from their own egos. Even such an inanimate object as a piece of rock is never considered entirely separate from one's human self. Many European scholars have characterized such a mentality as primitive animism. But whatever the characterization, Koreans feel that even a piece of rock has some functional relations with the human ego even to the extent of believing that, when something is done to the rock, one's own ego can not entirely escape the repercussion. It does not mean that Koreans cannot distinguish intellectually between what is human and what is purely material. What Koreans are saying is that a man is biologically a part of the material world, and he has to be in a delicate balance with his material environment. Again, he thinks that he has a part of the material world in him just as a part of him is in the material world. A man without nature is not possible nor has nature any meaning without man.

Therefore, the expectations of Koreans regarding various phenomena are less segmented both in temporal and spatial dimensions. Koreans expect the rhythm of nature to continue in the future just as in the past and up to the present. Whatever is in harmony with the rhythm of nature is, therefore, desirable and good. On the other hand, whatever runs counter to the rhythm of nature is considered abnormal and evil. For example, it should be hot in the summer, and it should be cold in the winter, although Koreans will be the first to admit that hot summer and cold winter are not conducive to their personal comfort. Moreover, a man demonstrates his humanness by being able to maintain the network of intense affective commitments with other human beings, beginning with his own blood kin and continuing with those who are spatially proximate. If a man failed to retain humanness in his relations with other human beings or with the material world, the rhythm of nature would be upset to the point where man's well-being or even survival might be threatened.

The isolation of the cultural perspective of old Korea was shattered in the second half of the nineteenth century by the aggressive cultural perspectives of the Occident which were inflicted upon Korean culture.

This unwanted confrontation with domineering Occidental cultural perspectives was a painful and disastrous trauma for the Korean people. The occidental civilization, which reckoned human prosperity by the extent of domination wielded by the individual ego over the whole spectrum of non-egos, including the material world, was a sharp contradiction to the cultural perspectives of old Korea. To be sure, such aggressive cultural perspectives were not totally unfamiliar to Koreans. The northern nomads and the neighboring Japanese possessed a similar world view. But, historically, these nomads and Japanese had admitted the inferiority of their own cultural perspectives and accepted the more human and decent perspectives of Korea and China. The new cultural challenge posed by the modern Occident was an entirely different one.

This new civilization of the Occident insisted that human decency could exist only if man learned to isolate his ego and draw a clear distinction between his own ego and non-ego. This separation of non-ego from one's own ego was a prerequisite for establishing a dynamic dialectic tension between oneself and the material world as well as other human beings. Moreover, human prosperity was to increase in proportion to man's ability to dominate the whole spectrum of non-ego. The more power and wealth a society possessed the more civilized and prosperous that society was to become. This challenge was a severe trauma for Koreans. The result was, of course, a greatly damaged cultural identity and community perspective.

Koreans experienced, in addition to cultural trauma, political humiliation in the form of colonization by a neighboring power. The problem was not merely an intellectual debate as to the comparative superiority of one cultural orientation over the other but a very real problem of loss of political independence and ensuing colonization. Out of such an experience many Koreans have determined that they will never again succumb to the temptation of finding the meaning of life in the giving and receiving of affection. Instead, they are determined to pursue and secure for themselves a more aggressive and self-centered cultural perspective, one from which they would derive the energy to expand their national horizons and establish a more viable form of competitive life in the modern world. This, of course, does not necessarily mean that Koreans of today finally have succeeded in fully expunging from their minds the old cultural perspectives in favor of those of the modern Occident. The conflict between the two patterns of cultural perspectives still continues. This conflict has been a source of a great deal of emotional and psychological ambivalence. Indeed, there is a form of cultural schizophrenia. Many Koreans tend to move from one cultural perspective to another, depending on selfish convenience at a particular time. And yet, there is a dominant impulse to move in the direction of the modern Occidental world view and to suppress the vestiges of old cultural perspectives.

Institutions

Affection, respect, and rectitude have occupied a very high position in the order of preferred events in Korea. Among the other values, enlightenment and well-being have been next in importance. Enlightenment has been used as the base or the instrument by which the three values mentioned above were to be maximized. Well-being (safety, health, and comfort) was important because it was the fundamental requisite for the interchange of affection, respect, and rectitude. Among the remaining three values, power, wealth, and skill, wealth was most important, especially the material resources needed for sustenance. As for surplus wealth, the material resources accumulated above and beyond what was required for subsistence, an entirely different significance was attached to it. In the case of the remaining two values, power and skill, power was the most feared. The value of skill as a supporting element for wealth and well-being was given a positive valuation, while the variety of skill which tended to drive the possessor to seek isolation, individual initiative, innovation, selfish creativity, and so forth was given a negative valuation. In the following we shall review briefly the various institutions which were used by Koreans as a means to maximize or optimize preferred events in the past as well as at the present.

Affection
Affection is not meant here merely as the positive or "good" variety of interpersonal emotions. It includes not only such euphonic interpersonal emotions as love, loyalty, friendship, or intimacy, but also such "negative" ones as hate, anger, and even jealousy. What is involved here is the entire spectrum of interpersonal emotions from the most negative and destructive to the most positive and constructive. What matters is the intensity and the breadth of affection, not its ethical or moral quality.

As the primary social form in which affection is the dominant value, the family occupied the most important position as the institution within which one could optimize his values (desired events). Family in Korea, as in China, possessed a much wider significance than the extended family of the West. Koreans have used the term "family" interchangeably with "lineage." But the Korean concept of family has been even more inclusive in practice than the Chinese lineage. Koreans were much less oriented to patrilineality than the Chinese and, in practice, gave as much importance to the matrilineage as well as one's own in-laws. The importance of kinship through marriage was almost a unique feature in Korea in contrast to either China or Japan. Brotherhood and sisterhood created through marriage have been an important factor in Korean life generally, as well as in factional politics which reached a high point during the Yi dynasty (1392-1910 A.D.), for instance.

Among the various aspects of family affection, filial piety toward one's ancestors always has been most important. The term filial piety has been much misunderstood. It has been interpreted variously as a manifestation of authoritarianism or hierarchical orientation in Korean culture. But filial piety was simply a variety of family affection which was considered to be the most primary and basic.

Even in the power arena, when loyalty to the monarch and affection to one's family came into conflict, the Korean traditional polity gave preference and precedence to the latter. Indeed, one was considered not possible without the other. A filial son was considered to be a loyal subject to the king. Filial piety was such a basic virtue, it enabled its possessor to serve as a competent bureaucrat in the government. The authoritative symbols of the myths of old Korea have been so arranged as to mutually reinforce these two modes of identification. Family loyalty was given unqualified support by the prescriptions and political ideology of the state while the power symbols derived support from the family, or the familism, of the Korean people. Family was also given support by other value institutions such as rectitude, respect, and enlightenment.

Ancestor worship was given strong sanction and support by all the value institutions of old Korea. A detailed and correct knowledge of ritual was a single functional demonstration of one's achievement in enlightenment. Rectitude and respect institutions gave full support to ancestor worship. Indeed, it became the "religion" of old Korea, particularly of the elite. The written prescriptions of old Korea contained detailed procedures and formulas, especially for those rituals performed by the royal family.

This familism had a positive functional significance in old Korea. But from the modern perspective, it contains many negative elements; it tends to militate against achievement orientation. Since the demarcation of an ego boundary was strongly disapproved, individual initiative or creativity generated by the isolation of the ego was suppressed effectively.

The negative effect of familism on affective identification with groups other than the family needs a searching examination. The concept of devotion or dedication to such nonfamily entities as nation or state was developed very little in old Korea. Whatever affective identification with nonfamily institutions existed, was possible only when a strong analogy with family also was forthcoming. Koreans looked upon close identification with nonfamily associations as harmful to familism. Consequently, family loyalties tended to be transferred intact into other value situations. This was true in factional politics, in Confucian academies, and in the "familization of salvation" of the Buddhist religion. But this does not mean that Koreans in the past were not able to hold the concept of a nation or of a state. A nation was understood as an extended family. The precepts of kinship and brotherhood were the basis on which the concept of a nation was formulated. The king functioned as the head of this extended family, and the people were its members. The state was never conceptualized as a category separate and entirely distinct from the family. Just as egos overlapped partially with one another to make up a family, the state was composed of partially overlapping networks of families.

In the period subsequent to 1945, family has undergone a steady process of disintegration. Familism in the traditional sense has been condemned strongly by the new ideology of the modern power elite. More than the process of political westernization, the process of industrialization has been instrumental in undermining this tradition. The industrialization process demanded that the individual replace the family as the basic economic unit. The same ideal of the maximization of individual self-assertion which had prevailed in nineteenth-century Europe was now to prevail. In today's Korea each man is to be as independent as possible and to be his own master. The individualistic tendency which posits the freedom of an individual as the essence of humanness is now on the rise.

Rectitude

The religions of old Korea were secular, this-worldly, and familistic. It is customary to state that there were four religions in old Korea: Confucianism, Buddhism, Taoism, and shamanism.[5] History tells us that the first three came from China into the Korean peninsula around the fourth century. Shamanism is indigenous to Korea, although it has been subjected to various influences and pressures for syncretization. Buddhism, which originated in India, accepted a familistic orientation in order to render itself more amenable to the Chinese. The individualistic and other-worldly orientations had to be given up in favor of familism and a this-worldly orientation. It was this sinified Buddhism that was received by Koreans, which in addition, underwent a further process of syncretization by accepting various indigenous Korean totems and spirits.

The Taoism which came to Korea was a vulgar version of that teaching. Originally, Taoism had no ritual or organizational structure; but mostly out of reaction to Buddhism, it became much more organized and ritualized and within a short period, indistinguishable from shamanism.

Shamanism is a difficult religion to describe or explain. It may be more easily explicated by contrasting it with such a religion as Christianity. No transcendental supreme being or creator of the universe, including the earth, is posited by shamanism. A god who is guiding the historical destiny of the universe with a rational plan, called "providence," is lacking in shamanism.[6] It is a world view in which human existence finds meaning because of interpersonal affection. If Korea is an affective society, it is because of this world view. Shamanism refuses to assign a positive valuation to the isolation and separation of a man from his material environment or to an ego from other egos. It considers concordance with the rhythm of nature as the best measure of humanness and of meaningful life.

Shamanism is very much compatible with Confucianism. Indeed, Confucianism may be considered a philosophical and metaphysical systematization of the shamanic world view. It is also this-worldly and finds the meaning of human existence in the giving and receiving of affection. Koreans found Confucianism quite consonant with their indigenous shamanism, except that the former held more prestige because of its systematic and metaphysical content. Confucianism is a world view which defines virtue in terms of interpersonal relations and the quantity and intensity of the affection exchanged. A man is considered virtuous if he is capable of intense affective involvement with a large number of human beings. Man's affective commitment is to begin with man and end with man. A human being establishes primary affective relations with other human beings, never with an abstract entity such as a god. Interhuman relation is the only meaningful relation. A person's virtue and decency are to be judged by relationships with other people. There is no concept of salvation in Confucianism. Salvation which is to be had on an individual basis and at the time of death, as in Christianity, has no significance in Confucianism.

The importance of Confucianism in Korean history has been more as a comprehensive system of secular ideology than as a religion. It served as a political ideology in old Korea, especially during the Yi dynasty, when it successfully suppressed Buddhism. Although this political ideology was adopted by the elite as a means to maximize their value positions, they were compelled to gain mass acceptance for it primarily through persuasion and by setting personal examples. The elite of old Korea achieved a very high degree of success in permeating the entire system with this ideology. For a period of more than five centuries, this ideology, and the system justified by it, continued to survive despite the nearly fatal blows inflicted by foreign military invasions. The masses were persuaded by the ideology of Confucianism to accept the unfavorable distinctions of its system of social stratification, which favored the elite. The Yi dynasty was particularly successul in securing the psychological internalization of the Confucian pattern of authoritative symbols.

As far as institutionalization was concerned, Buddhism achieved its greater success much earlier in Korean history than Confucianism. From the beginning, it enjoyed the advantage of more colorful pageantry and richer ecclesiastical elaboration. In contrast, Confucianism had little pomp and color to make it attractive to the masses. Confucianism was a family religion without professional ecclesiastical structure or the proliferation of sanctuaries.

The institutions of rectitude in Korea have been very underdeveloped except in the case of Buddhism. Buddhism, however, had been subjected to systematic suppression and persecution during the five centuries of the Yi dynasty. Confucianism and shamanism offered little ecclesiastical elaboration. The secular nature of the process of rectitude is a dominant and distinguishing characteristic of the social process of Korea even today. In recent years Christianity has been a significant element in the rectitude process of Korea. The aggressive and monopolistic propensity of this newly imported religion has enabled it to propagate itself with rapidity and intensity.

In a period of rapid and confusing social change, the theology of Christianity offered spiritual comfort and a sense of security to the Korean masses. In a time of uncertainty and physical danger the otherworldly aspect of this "Westerners' religion," with its highly systematized doctrine and comprehensive organization, gained rapid acceptance by the common people of Korea. The promise of eternal life and the existence of an omnipotent God presented an alternative to ineffectual *mudangs* and *bonzes*. Its individualistic orientation found a responsive chord in the Korean mind. This was especially true for the lower strata of Korean society and for the masses living in the remote outlying provinces, where familism had been traditionally weak, during a period in which familism was being put to a severe test, and increasing self-concern and egotism were becoming more acceptable. The average Korean experienced a strong curiosity about the religion which had produced the very powerful and aggressive civilization of the modern Occident. At a time when the traditional Korean life style was being fatally demoralized and overwhelmed by a more aggressive civilization, Christianity appeared to offer an attractive alternative for Koreans, who were being subjected to political and cultural debacle and humiliation. Those Koreans who adopted Christianity as their religion often incorporated the shamanic and syncretic propensity of their subconscious psyche. It has been pointed out that many Korean Christians found it appropriate to accept other gods and spirits in addition to their Jehova. Jesus was, after all, a very capable shaman to many Koreans.

Some of the statistics (as of 1971)[7] are given for reference. Protestant Christianity had 13,000 churches with 3,200,000 members. Roman Catholicism had 393 churches with a membership of 780,000. There were 3721 Buddhist temples with 70,000 members. When compared with Christianity, Buddhism is not a membership-oriented religion; for Confucianism, the membership is even more difficult to record. The most prevalent indigenous religion, which is about one hundred years old, is called Ch'ŏndokyo. It is reported to have 110 places of worship with a membership of 636,000.

Christians are said to enjoy numerically superior representation among the modern elite of Korea. But the impact of Christian ethics on everyday life is difficult to ascertain. It may be surmised that Christians tend to be somewhat more individualistic and more conscious of Western preferences for freedom, equality, and the individualistic features of democracy. The dominant feature of the contemporary ethical and moral standards of Korea is their uncertainty and confusion. However, this may be said to be a mark of change and growth and not unique to Korea. But, in Korea, it is very intense, because the changes which are producing this confusion are themselves mainly the products of external pressures and impingements.

Enlightenment

Inasmuch as the ideologically acceptable strategy in every value situation has been indoctrination and persuasion, with a strong emphasis on legitimacy, the institutions specialized to enlightenment have been of great significance in Korea. The non-elite were excluded from the formal enlightenment process in old Korea. But even for the elite itself, the enlightenment process was at a low level of institutionalization. Their children began their study of the Confucian classics at home. In some cases, a teacher would use his own home as a place for several children to gather together to receive the beginning stages of literary instructions. Teachers were given no professional training or accreditation. Any person who had literary skills could offer his services as a teacher in his place of residence. There was rarely a schoolhouse or schoolroom as a separate architectural structure used exclusively for enlightenment instruction.

There gradually emerged a unified curriculum common throughout the country. This was found in textbooks. When a young man successfully completed the primary stages of instruction, he went on to concentrate on acquiring the faculties needed to win success at the state examination. Preparation for it usually was done in one's own home, without tutorial guidance from any established scholar, and took the form of memorizing the classics as well as other written Chinese Confucian texts. The examination tested a candidate on his ability to compose in literate Chinese a poem or an essay on such subjects as Confucian political ideology, economic doctrine, protocol and etiquette, ethics, and historical knowledge.

Those young people who preferred to pursue a purely literary career outside the bureaucracy usually gathered themselves around a distinguished scholar at one of many provincial academies. There they engaged in doctrinal discussions, scholarly arguments, and literary disputations. Confucianism was divided into several schools as the result of doctrinal disputes. Consequently, they were often "politicized" by the power process and frequently supplied ammunition to the factional politics that raged around the central power arena in the royal capital.

The highest institution of enlightenment was the state academy called Sŏnggyungwan in Seoul. It was on the same grounds as the state shrine where Confucius and his distinguished disciples were enshrined. Those who passed the first of the two levels of the state examination were recruited as the students of the academy. The academy was the highest institution of enlightenment, and as such it exerted a significant influence on the central power arena itself.

The power process itself was considered a form of enlightenment by Confucian political ideology; indeed, the whole power structure had an important educational overtone. In the formal government structure, there was an institution which served as the custodian of the correct propagation and interpretation of the Confucian classics as well as the highest level of literary skills. The Censorate performed the function of teaching the people the correct customs, manners, and morale. The king was considered the highest teacher and set a personal example for the people. The same thing was true on a diminishing scale for the bureaucratic hierarchy. Every bureaucrat was a teacher. The primary task of the provincial magistrate was to teach the people and govern by conviction, relying on the power of his virtuous example to persuade and teach his people. In view of the importance of the educational role of the government, and especially of the monarch, the Confucian instruction of the king was of paramount political importance. Not only during his tenure as the crown prince, but even after the coronation, the king was required to continue to receive private instruction in the Confucian classics with a heavy emphasis on history. A portion of every day was set aside for the lecture. It was one of the highest honors to be designated as the royal instructor. Such a position, of course, carried strong power inplications.

It is a distinctive feature of old Korea that the enlightenment process had a dominant rectitude significance. Even the power practices were garbed in enlightenment and rectitude symbols. Persuasion and appeal to the inner convictions of the masses were the legitimate strategies to be employed in the power arena. But in order to resort to such strategies it was necessary that the enlightenment process be fully utilized. Familism was supported through enlightenment; so were other institutional practices with regard to rectitude, power, and even skills. If specialization in wealth was looked upon with disfavor, such a perspective had to be inculcated and preferably internalized into every member of the polity.

In view of the extremely heavy emphasis on the ethical and moral content of the educational process in old Korea, the acquisition and refinement of skill were given less importance in the enlightenment process. Although knowledge was considered synonymous with virtue, knowledge in itself, without ethical and moral implications, was deemphasized. Since power had to be legitimized by rectitude, enlightenment which inculcated rectitude was the single decisive criterion by which the legitimacy of power (and the powerholder) was to be judged. Consequently, the power process constantly sought to strengthen enlightenment as a means to expand its legitimacy. The contents of the enlightenment process was, of course, tightly controlled by the power process so as to reinforce its legitimacy.

After 1945 the educational system of Korea was reorganized. Formal education started with kindergarten at the age of five followed by six years of primary school, three years of middle school, and another three years of high school, topped by four years of college. The curriculum was scarcely distinguishable from that found in Europe or America.

There has been a heavy emphasis on Western science and knowledge. Modern Koreans still have the conviction that enlightenment is the one surest means by which a man can guarantee for himself a favored position with regard to all values. Koreans have demonstrated a tremendous hunger and eagerness for education. There have been complaints that Koreans expend an abnormally high portion of their resources for education and the educational system is producing over-educated lumpen who are becoming the source of social and political instability and tension. Nevertheless, the educational system has been very efficient and productive.[8] The statistics (as of November 1971) show that 5,807,448 children were enrolled in primary schools, 1,529,541 in middle schools, 647,180 in high schools. There were approximately 200,000 students enrolled in colleges and universities.[9] The modern educational institutions of Korea have served as agents for the inculcation of the Western values of individualism and liberal democracy. These institutions have been instrumental in creating value confusion. They certainly have not contributed to the indoctrination of a specific authoritative ideology or a systematic myth as in the case of old Korea. These modern institutions are no longer the custodians of authoritative cultural standards.

Respect

The system of social stratification in old Korea was very rigid. Upward social mobility was almost nonexistent, although downward mobility was always possible. In time of great political and social upheavals a few members of the lower strata could make a temporary upward movement into a higher stratum. But such an aberration was always promptly rectified.

The system of social stratification in old Korea was primarily based upon the varying amount of rectitude or virtue a man was supposed to possess. This was the authoritative myth in old Korea. Superiority in enlightenment was a subsidiary qualification for membership in the elite stratum. Under the prevailing pattern of authoritative symbols, participation in the power arena was restricted to the members of the elite. Wealth was of little significance doctrinally, but in practice the elite enjoyed a favored wealth position as well. As the system persisted for half a millenium, power and wealth became the two vulgar indices by which membership in the highest stratum was to be demonstrated.

It is customary to enumerate five social strata or "classes" in old Korea. At the top was the *yangban* class. Of course, the royal family may be considered to have constituted a separate class, but the royal consorts were taken from the *yangban* class and it seems more appropriate to include the royal family as an upper portion of the elite stratum of the society. Below *yangban* were *jungins* who were the class of people who supplied the technical and administrative skills as petty officials and practical managers of the government affairs. The *jungin,* which literally meant "the middle people," were a very cohesive stratum with a rather ambivalent standing between the *yangban* and the common people. They intermarried only among themselves and were bound together by an informal nationwide network of kinship ties and common interest.

The third class was called *sangmin.* They were the "common people": farmers, peasants, craftsmen, artisans, merchants, and traders. There was an intraclass hierarchy in terms of respect. Farmers were given the highest amount of respect, secondly craftsmen, and lastly merchants. It was believed that farmers were engaged in an "honest" vocation, working with the rhythm of nature and producing the fruits commensurate with the amount of labor input. Craftsmen were considered to be creating genuinely productive values for society with their labor and skills. But merchants were considered to be engaged in a dishonest vocation because they took profit without adding any labor of their own to increase the intrinsic value of the merchandise they sold. It was said that merchants charged higher prices by simply transporting the same merchandise from one place to another. Moreover, the vocational specialization for profit making and the accumulation of wealth were considered dehumanizing by old Koreans.

At the bottom of the class system were the menial people called *ch'ŏnmin.* Included in this lowest class were butchers, slaves, shamans, prostitutes and other people engaged in entertainment for profit. There were two kinds of butchers, those who lived in a "butcher village" at some distance from urban centers and those who made up small groups that were constantly on the move, performing acrobatics and other entertainment for money; at the same time, they performed butchering chores and tanned leather. These people were a kind of Korean gypsy. They had come originally from the northern nomadic tribes. Although they were ethnically related to Koreans, their way of life was nonagricultural and nonsedentary. Thus, they were a roving minority among Koreans, and they defied the government's effort to settle them in one place to engage in farming. Owing to the differences in life style and cultural background, they remained an object of social discrimination and ostracism.

Slaves acquired the status by birth. If a person had a slave mother, he too became a slave. There were two kinds of slaves, one public and the other private. The public slaves were slaves attached to government offices and agencies. The private slaves were those held in the private possession of individuals. The origin of the slave caste in old Korea is not clear. Prisoners captured from invading northern barbarians were one source of slaves. Another source was the families and kin within a certain degree of consanguinity of a convicted felon. There were certain classes of criminal offenses for which the punishments included the enslavement of the kin.

It may appear strange that shamans were reduced to the lowest stratum of society in old Korea where shamanism was the most indigenous religion. This was the result of Confucian suppression of other forms of world view. In spite of systematic suppression, however, shamanism continued as a source of emotional comfort and a medium of group ecstasy during the five hundred years of the Confucian Yi dynasty. Inasmuch as shamans came to the house, the women of the *yangban* class found them to be of much comfort and solace, for the *yangban* women could not go outside the walls of their houses. The visits of shamans were socially acceptable and convenient. They performed seances which were supposed to cure diseases of both the body and the spirit. They prayed for sons, bureaucratic honor, and wealth, exorcised evils afflicting the family, divined the future, cleansed the house after the death of a family member, and sent the dead on to a comfortable and smooth journey to a new form of existence.

In old Korea, all the value institution processes were so coordinated as to render unqualified support to the orthodox class structure. The class structure was legitimized as an authoritative pattern of division of labor which was in full accord with the rhythm of nature. As such, it was an integral part of the world view as well as the political system. In fact, it stratified not only respect but all the values. As in other rigidly stratified systems the social stratification system was fully sanctioned by the power process. Any transgression by those belonging to lower strata against the exclusivity and integrity of the upper strata was most severely punished by the penal process. A term such as "offenses against the Natural Order" was used in labeling offenses which constituted "petty treason" in English common law. An offense committed by a social inferior against his social superior was punished much more severely than the same offense committed by a social superior against his inferior.

The rigid social stratification system that had existed during the Yi dynasty was abruptly destroyed by the colonization of Korea by Japan. The loss of political sovereignty also caused the downfall of the social elite. As far as the contemporary community process of Korea is concerned there is little formal system of social stratification. Stratification in terms of the amount of wealth enjoyed by a person is becoming the new modality. This change has meant the relative decline in the prestige enjoyed by those elite who are less munificently remunerated in monetary terms. Needless to say, this change has been the single most important cause for the alienation and embitterment of contemporary intellectuals. They are unhappy that a high level of achievement in the enlightenment process no longer automatically guarantees them the most favored respect position; they forget the fact that enlightenment is no longer restricted to the elite. Moreover, they are displeased that the nonmonetary rewards and compensation that had been given to specialists in enlightenment in old Korea are no longer forthcoming. This, of course, leads them to denounce the "callous materialism rampant today." In old Korea a high level of enlightenment also signified access to, and participation in, the power arena. Unfortunately what they see today is the so-called military-industrial complex, which dominates the power arena. It is unfortunate for the intellectuals that they usually have only contempt for the militarists and industrialists. The fact that the intellectuals themselves often are excluded from participation in the power arena because of a lack of modern technical expertise does not improve their estimation of these two classes of the modern elite.

The period subsequent to 1945 has continued to be marked with confused and rapid social mobility in both upward and downward directions. It is often said that common day-laborers in urban areas who engage in physical and menial labor today have the best genealogy in Korea. In other words, the rapid downward social mobility resulted in the degradation of the descendants of old *yangbans* down to the status of urban poor today. There have been many reasons for this. One important cause for this downward mobility has been the refusal of the *yangban* elite, in the beginning stages of Japanese colonization, to cooperate with, or accept, the operation of the colonial administration. The traditional *yangban* elite tried to be faithful to the Confucian commandment which enjoined them not to serve two masters. This meant that those *yangbans* who were conscientious in their adherence to the Confucian ideology refused to recognize the legitimacy of the Japanese rule. In extreme cases, they refused to send their children to the schools established and operated by the Japanese authorities. As a result, many *yangban* descendants were deprived of the educational opportunity to acquire modern knowledge and skills. Another example were the landholding *yangbans* who refused to register the titles to their lands with the colonial government under the colonial land registration law. The result was wholesale expropriation of *yangban* land by the colonial administration. In some instances the shrewd stewards of *yangbans* registered their masters' land under their own names, trusting that their masters would refuse registration. The resulting economic impoverishment contributed to the downward mobility of the descendants of loyal *yangbans*.

On the other hand, those who had fewer scruples in taking advantage of the social change and newly available educational opportunities under the colonial administration succeeded in moving upward in the social stratification system. Many of the new elite have come from non-*yangban* families. Modern Korea thus has become a highly mobile society socially. There is no set pattern of manners or speech which can be called distinctively elite. Despite this social mobility, however, no Korean likes to be reminded of his non-*yangban* background.

Well-being

Koreans were like any other human beings in their valuation of emotional and physical well-being. Their familism provided them with a sense of emotional security. For most Koreans, it also contributed to securing physical well-being through mutual aid. Where family failed, government stepped in. In cases of destitution, the government undertook the responsibility for providing free food and medical care. In old Korea destitution was synonymous with "familylessness." The traditional medicine was based on herbalism and acupuncture. Surgery was seldom employed; nor was pathological vivsection of the cadaver. There was no unified national licensing of medical practitioners. Every physician and acupuncturist held up his own reputation through his performance. Koreans shared the Chinese aversion against bloodshed of any kind; so that using knife or scalpel was disallowed. Even forensic medicine was based on the external symptoms and scars of the cadaver without any vivisection. The general appearance of lack of science notwithstanding, the traditional medicine of Korea had been a product of many thousands of years of experience and empirical observation.

The alleviation of suffering attendant upon misfortunes and disasters was the obligation primarily of the family. The family was in every sense a mutual aid organization. Well-being was a concern of the family. Government agencies provided grain storage and free medical care for the poor. The grain storage program was to collect and store grain during a bumper harvest and distribute it in time of famine. Natural disaster was viewed as a destruction of the rhythm of nature caused by inhumanness, especially on the part of the rulers. In other words, a natural disaster was thought to be a consequence of misgovernment. When it occurred, the first thing the elite had to do was to show proper signs of repentance and self-criticism by abstaining from singing, dancing, tasty food, and silk clothes. Then, an investigation was begun to discover any instance of flagrant misrule whereby some intense negative feelings and animosities against the entire community process might have been engendered. It was believed that by promptly correcting any instances of misgovernment the natural rhythm could be restored and the cause for destructive enmity on the part of those who had been unjustly oppressed would be removed.

Next to family and government, the neighborhood was an important unit for the well-being process in old Korea. Good neighborliness functioned without much institutionalization. But various patterned practices were so developed as to make the neighborhood a very effective and often indispensable institution of mutual aid and comport. In the farming neighborhood labor was exchanged on a reciprocal basis. When an intense labor effort was required, ten or fifteen households would form a loose labor cooperative and work the farm of one household at a time to cover all the households. Childbirth, weddings, funerals and mourning were all occasions for the neighborhood to chip in and help out. No one issued invitations or directives; all was done on the basis of mutuality. Over the decades, every family's mutuality ledger should balance out if that family were to remain decent in the eyes of the neighborhood.

In the modern period subsequent to 1945 a great deal of institutional philanthropy on an international scale has impinged upon Korea. The division of the country into two zones of occupation by the Soviet and the United States armies resulted in the displacement of many families and persons. The movement of these displaced persons in the form of refugees caused many international philanthropic agencies to take interest, and participate, in their relief. The United Nations refugee relief organizations and other institutions were very active in Korea. The Korean War of 1950 caused further deterioration in the well-being of all Koreans throughout the peninsula. Government programs and the relief work of international agencies contributed to the amelioration of the situation, but the war meant the destruction of many families. Many orphanages were established and run by foreign religious and philanthropic agencies. The traditional prohibition on the adoption of a child not belonging to one's own clan made the work of these agencies very difficult. The reason for such a prohibition was the traditional desire to protect the integrity of lineage—a manifestation of the strong familism that always had existed in old Korea. The births of many children born of foreign soldiers and Korean women gave rise to a heartbreaking problem. However, many of these interracial children were adopted by American and European families, and their number is steadily diminishing.

The general weakening of family structure has given rise to the problem of the well-being of the aged. So far old people's homes have not been in much demand in Korea. But as the size of families becomes smaller, in the direction of nuclear families, this will become a serious social problem for Korea. The war, as well as the rapid process of industrialization with crowded urban living conditions, has undermined continuously the extended family structure. The problem of well-being which has traditionally been the province and responsibility of family and lineage will increasingly have to be taken over by the government and other public and private institutions. The social security program of the government has not yet been well established in Korea.

Korea is still in the early stages of industrial revolution. The economic system as a whole has not been able to spare much resources for the purpose of greater equality in income distribution. The lack of material resources, capital, and technology has rendered economic development of Korea very difficult. The problem of social justice in terms of securing an economic minimum for every citizen will become increasingly difficult, especially for political and social reasons. Moreover, the definition of "economic minimum" itself continues to rise.

Skill

In old Korea skill, or opportunity to acquire and exercise capability in vocations, professions, or the arts, was divided conceptually into two categories. Those skills acquired, developed, and practiced for material gain and profit were given a low level of recognition. But the same skills if practiced for no material gain were given a high level of respect; for example, the literary skills of the *yangban,* calligraphy, brush painting, and other handicrafts practiced by the elite for personal enjoyment and "the cultivation of the self." It should be pointed out that the conventional notion that manual labor was given negative respect in old Korea is incorrect. It was the desire for material gain or fame that rendered manual labor ethically and socially demeaning. The apparent desire for fame and popular recognition was as fatal as the desire for material gain and profit.

In the case of various skills and crafts performed by the so-called lower-class people for livelihood, there were ethical as well as social gradations in terms of respectability. For agricultural skills the level of respect accorded was higher than others. For commercial skills the level of respect given was very low. The former dealt with the land and produced the least amount of artificial inflation of added values and the most acceptable personal perspectives as far as the dominant culture was concerned. Commercial skills, in the dominant preconception of old Korea, relied mainly on the ability to deceive others. Positive contribution rendered by commercial skills for the economic well-being of the nation was given little recognition by the dominant culture of old Korea.

Since skill groups generally corresponded with the system of social stratification, specialization for any particular skill was determined by birth and social status. In the case of the elite skill institutions were those specializing in enlightenment, such as the Confucian academies. In the case of the *jungin* group there were no formal institutions; for farmers there were no institutional groupings. The rural villages were the groups for the farmers, and as such the village was an organic entity, functioning both as a skill group as far as farming was concerned and an administrative district or unit as far as the power process was concerned. But the villages also had significance in terms of other values, such as well-being (village-wide cooperation and mutual aid) and wealth. Artisans and craftsmen were trained and organized by the government. They did not have any private associations similar to the guilds found in medieval Europe. Craftsmen and artisans worked for the government and were deprived of any direct access to the private sector. This did not mean that members of the elite in private capacity never had direct contact with the craftsmen and artisans. But such direct access or contact was limited to clandestine transactions which fluctuated according to the rapacity of the particular elite involved or the vicissitudes of the health and integrity of the authoritative doctrine.

Commercial activities also were controlled rigidly and supervised by the government. The government closely regulated both the quality and price of the merchandise sold by various stores and shops. If two stores were charging different prices for the same commodity with roughly the same quality, it imposed a penalty on such behavior. The antipathy built into the Confucian ideology manifested itself in the hostile attitude of the government toward the commercial activities by rigidly controlling and regulating all of them. The stores specializing in silk, fabric, cotton cloth, paper products, and fish products were given monopoly rights in return for meeting a certain portion of government revenue and consumption needs. There were few associations of tradesmen and merchants in old Korea. Although they had common interests to articulate through group action, they were not permitted to do so.

There was, however, a unique institution specializing in commerce, which was organized by peddlers on a national scale with the express approval of the government. These peddlers carried their wares on their backs or on their heads (women) and traveled extensively throughout the country. They took their merchandise to the homes of their customers. The female peddlers could go into the inner courtyard, where the women of the elite lived in segregation from the male members of the household, who inhabited the outer wing of the house. These peddlers were organized in provincial chapters which were further divided into smaller local subchapters. It is said that this national organization of peddlers was formed by the founder of the Yi dynasty who granted them a royal charter with monopolistic privileges in appreciation for their help in acting as the logistics supply network during times of military emergency. With a detailed and accurate knowledge of geography this organization did, in fact, play this role, for example, during the Japanese invasion of 1592. This royally chartered organization of peddlers was a unique feature in Korean history. Its membership was entitled to special privileges and protections. Every peddler had to belong to the organization in order to carry on his trade. On the other hand, membership protected a peddler from interference by the local government officials. The membership of the organization remained fiercely loyal to the monarchy and served as an effective intelligence network for the royal family. In the last decades of the dynasty, the organization was used by the conservative force within the elite to suppress by violence the reformist-constitutionalist movement in November 1898.

As in the case of other value institutions, the institutions related to skill competed with affection institutions and familism. Technical specialization and professional expertise were likely to encourage self-concern and individualism. Therefore, they were looked upon as detrimental to interpersonal decency. In a society where top priority was given to this virtue, the skill value was given only a very low level of respect. The desired virtue was to be attained by specializing in skills connected with written verbal symbols, without any interest in mercenary gain, rather than by cultivating technical and economic skills.

When we come to the contemporary period, subsequent to 1945, the situation has undergone a drastic change. The age of technology and of the technocrats has arrived in Korea. Such professions as medicine, business administration, and law are attracting the most intelligent and capable young minds. The field of engineering has become popular among young students as the most desirable field of specialization and vocation. This is a period of rapid industrialization and economic development in Korea. The technical knowledge and expertise in science and technology are in great demand. People are no longer bothered if a person is motivated by a desire for material gain in his pursuit of technical expertise.

There has been a tremendous proliferation of private associations related to the skill value. Many of these associations engage in transnational activities, participating in the exchange of intelligence concerning various fields of technology. Koreans increasingly are becoming members of international organizations as well as multinational corporations. Academic, technical, and professional certificates for various fields of technical expertise increasingly are gaining transnational credit and recognition, with the result that many Koreans go abroad to acquire technical expertise and return home to have their achievements in skills given full faith and credit. In terms of organizational influence, the medical and legal associations of Korea have come to enjoy the greatest amount of power and prestige. Economists, scientists, and engineers are not far behind.

Power

The fundamental distrust of power as a threat to human decency was a characteristic feature of Confucian political ideology. By making affection the dominant symbol in the institutionalized power process, Koreans attempted to humanize the power process. Such behaviors as open competition for power were condemned severely as "shameless." The development of a set of behavior norms specific to the power process was discouraged. Individual aggressiveness and the overt pursuit of popularity and influence were condemned as divisive and indecent.

The smaller the expectation of crisis and threat of violence in the power process the more "human" and decent it became. A variety of institutional mechanisms and devices were employed to ensure the decency and humanness of the power process. Remonstration of the monarch was institutionalized in the form of a special office. The verbatim record of every piece of communication that passed between the monarch and his subjects tended to restrain the absolutist tendency of the system. The royal lecture which reminded the monarch of the historical lessons concerning past tyrannies and despotic governments was another agency by which the greatest possible amount of decency and humanness was to be preserved in the system.

It has frequently been pointed out that this refusal to draw a clear distinction between the affection and power processes was the reason why old Korea failed to develop dynamic and effective power institutions. Old Korea never became a militarily powerful and wealthy nation. It never was able to expand its territory by military conquest. On the contrary, Korea was always a target of devastating invasions by its predatory neighbors. But it cannot be denied that the power process of old Korea was a more human and decent one than that of other monarchies of the time. The ideal of humanness and interpersonal decency in the power process was to a large extent realized in old Korea.

During the period subsequent to 1945, the parliamentary democratic institutional structure was imported from the west. This imported system has undergone a painful process of trial and error during the past quarter century. The division of the country, the destructive war of 1950, and the side effects of rapid industrialization have all conspired to make the experiment in liberal democracy a very painful and difficult process for the Korean people. The fact that there are two systems based on different ideologies, competing against and confronting each other, on the Korean peninsula has added a further negative dimension to the experiment. Koreans have not yet fully accepted as legitimate the aggressive individualistic norms of the power process, and this has rendered the democratic experiment very dubious of success. Liberal democracy is based upon the premise that humanity must be first atomized into self-sufficient, self-disciplining, and discrete egos before these atomized egos can be brought together for mutual interaction. This premise has not been fully grasped and indoctrinated into the Korean mind. The carry-over of the traditional perspective, which had endeavored to inject as much of affection into the power process as possible, still continues. The result has been a confusion in the cultural norms concerning the power process. In other words, the two sets of different rules have been mingled together to create confusion. Instead of proceeding on the basis of rational individualism, Koreans are still likely to proceed on the basis of interpersonal feeling and a particularistic notion of decency and affection. The notion of abstract rational legality has not yet gained full acceptance by the people as legitimate. Nor has the traditional valuation of affection as the legitimate measure of humanness and decency retained its full vitality. The result is that neither set of cultural norms has allowed the power process to develop a full degree of legitimacy in Korea.

Wealth

Wealth was the most mistrusted value in old Korea. It was considered injurious to affection, interpersonal decency, and humanness. Institutions related to wealth have been discussed above in the section dealing with those related to skill. Wealth had been such a despised form of vocation that even today a negative attitude toward it survives to a large extent. This has given rise to confusion and ambivalence. With the overwhelming impact of industrialization and the desire for economic progress the people are confused as to whether they can pursue wealth openly and still retain the respect of the community. This confusion has contributed to the painful delay in establishing community norms of behavior with regard to the wealth process. Certainly there has been no general acceptance of the capitalistic ethics developed in Europe; nor has Korea's own system of capitalistic ethics been developed. There is still considerable fluctuation between the two extremes of condemning and approving wealth as a respectable value in Korea. The spectacle of a son of a rich businessman suing his own father for money still offends the Korean sensitivity. The fact that wealth usually undermines interpersonal affection in favor of selfishness is demonstrated anew every day in Korea.

Korea's commitment to the private enterprise system of economy has put the wealth process of Korea in close contact with the rest of the world and made the Korean economy susceptible to external economic influences. These external economic influences have affected the whole gamut of the community process of interaction. Koreans have been compelled to establish various institutions related to wealth which are functionally and formally similar to those developed in the West. Multinational corporations, joint investment ventures, long-term loans, and capital funds borrowed from international financial agencies have all affected the development of wealth institutions in modern Korea. The impact of the development of such institutions has been to undermine steadily the old pattern in which the affection value held the predominant position in all value institution processes. But the resistance put up by the old pattern of value priorities is also very strong. It appears that the transitional period in which the confusion and conflict between the new and the old ways of ranking the values in order of importance will continue for some time in Korea.

Policy Recommendations

Even in the modern Occident from where Korea imported its modern legal system, technical legal doctrines always have played a very important role. Terminological definition and doctrinal analysis of technical rules often have been considered the most important element of judicial decision making and legal scholarship. In the case of modern Korea the emphasis on technical rules and theoretical doctrines has been especially pronounced in view of the fact that its legal system is an import from abroad rather than an outgrowth of its own legal culture. Linguistic translation and logical comprehension of the imported prescriptions alone were a very difficult and vexing task for an average Korean jurist. It is not hard to understand the difficulty a Korean law student encounters in his endeavor to assimilate a stupendously large quantity of written materials in the field of law continuously produced in Continental Europe and the United States. It is small wonder that emphasis on definition and written prescriptions usually have taken up most of the intellectual and temporal resources of Korean students of law. Under these circumstances a greater clarity is needed in the consideration of the preferred goals of the community and the policy choices which may best facilitate the realization of those goals. Instead of the mechanical manipulation of imported legal doctrines, Korean lawyers ought to concentrate on the functional consideration of policy alternatives by which the overriding goal of human dignity may best be attained.

Nowhere has the technical-doctrinal approach to law been more sterile than in modern Korea. Without clarifying the concept of human dignity as the paramount goal within the particular context of community perspectives of modern Korea, Korean lawyers simply have engaged in the mechanical application of the imported written prescriptions. The result has been the alienation of the legal system from the community process of interaction. The masses are simply structuring their daily life in such a way as to have as little connection as possible with the legal process. In the case of the judicial process this tendency has been most pronounced. The judicial system has become a plaything of the urbanized and the affluent. Of course, the criminal aspect, the adjudicative process, has had a more general impact on the masses. But this dominant impingement of the criminal process on the masses only has reinforced the aversion of the masses to the legal process as a whole.

A democratic shaping and sharing of all values and the promotion of human dignity have been posited and accepted as the preferred goals of the Korean constitutional system. "Indigenization" of the imported legal system has been proposed as a means to facilitate the achievement of this objective. Others have proposed the speediest possible Westernization of the Korean culture as the most effective means to achieve legal development and the modernization of Korean law. The objective, however, is not the preservation or the extirpation of the traditional legal culture but the establishment of a democratic mechanism by which the shaping and sharing of all values may be maximized in the direction of greater human dignity. In order for the modern legal system of Korea to perform this function, it must secure rapport with, and the support of, the community perspectives of authority. Sentimental affinity with the modern legal system imported from the West is lacking not only in the case of the masses but in the case of the majority of the elite also. Although it is not impossible for political prescriptions (supported by the threat of severe sanctions) to be an effective and sometimes creative agent for causing change in community perspectives, they are more difficult to change than customarily supposed. Therefore, it appears necessary for the imported legal system to make adjustments to the community perspectives of authority in order to become more relevant and effective in the cultural setting of Korea.

By way of recapitulation, the following are the salient features of the community perspectives of authority prevailing in Korea:

1. Nonindividualistic Perception of the Ego and the Self. In interpersonal relations the thoughts, feelings, and circumstances of those

affected are always taken into consideration. The particular circumstances to be affected by the application of a particular rule are emphasized. Conceptualization of the individual as an abstract category or unit is strongly discouraged. There is a strong reluctance to perceive an ego or a self as an independent autonomous unit with clear boundaries separating it from other egos or selves. An ego always is conceived in its relations with other egos, with a portion of it overlapping partially with other egos. In everyday linguistic usage the first person singular pronoun "I" is not only never written in a capital letter, but very rarely used. Rather, a form of the first person plural is used. But even this pronoun is different from the English "we" in the sense that it is not a collection of discrete and independent "Is," but an amorphous collection of overlapping and interpenetrating egos. In the case of possessive pronouns, the tendency to avoid their use becomes extremely clear and strong. Moreover, in ordinary conversations not only the speaker as a subject is dropped altogether in the form of a pronoun but the addressee also is completely omitted from the speech. The desire again is to avoid the demarcation of a clear boundary between the speaker's ego and the addressee's ego. The underlying impetus is the non-isolation of egos, the maximization of interpersonal affection.

2. Aversion to Interest Definition. From property interest to political interest on the most inclusive and abstract scale, the propensity is to avoid a clear definition of interest in interpersonal relations. Definition of interest not only promotes egotism and selfishness, but it increases the probability of conflict between two or more egos. The basic orientation is not to adjust or balance interests once defined, but to avoid the definition of interests in the first place for fear that such definition might increase the probability of interpersonal conflict. Although under the impact of Westernization and industrialization the reluctance to define interests precisely is diminishing, the practice of Cheyenne

Indians of killing a horse when a dispute develops as to its ownership may be illustrative of the Korean perspective.[10]

3. Antipathy against Competition and Conflict. Competition in which there must be a winner and a loser in a clearly defined fashion was discouraged in old Korea. The same reluctance continues to this day. Even in the case of the state examinations, in which not all applicants could pass, the wariness and caution were evident. A man might engage in a competition of literary skills, but Koreans were always careful that there were to be no clear-cut winners and losers. Except among the military and the young, competition was to be avoided as much as possible in order not to harm interpersonal affection. Conflict was to be avoided, not to be resolved rationally or successfully. The best means of resolving conflict was to bring the parties to the conflict to agree that there was no conflict and only a misunderstanding that there was one. A successful provincial magistrate was not one who displayed wisdom in judging disputes but one who succeeded in securing the condition where there would be no conflict or, with disputants who insisted that there was one, that it be resolved by the magistrate. Conflict resolution process was not meticulously formalized. The adversary system of securing justice was never developed in Korea. It was simply too warlike and crisis laden to be acceptable. It was too much of a threat to interpersonal affection to be acceptable by the Korean society. The goal was not the discovery of the truth. The goal was the maximization of interpersonal affection.

4. Hostility to Zero-Sum Decision Making. A decision in which the outcome had to be in zero-sum terms has always evoked hostility from the community. A decision in which the outcome was to be in terms of the minimax principle was much more in consonance with the Korean community perspectives of authority. The idea that if one side had to gain everything while the other side had to lose everything was treated with suspicion and distrust by Koreans.

Consequently, a decision which culminated in a zero-sum outcome was never welcomed by Koreans. In human affairs Koreans always believed that right and wrong more or less coexisted in equal measure in every interpersonal relation. A person never monopolized only the right or the wrong.

The following may serve to summarize the recommendations:

1. The modern legal process should be encouraged to lose its foreignness or strangeness.

2. The judicial process should be directed toward informality and personalization.

3. Conciliation and mediation rather than adjudication should be emphasized.

4. The outcome of the judicial decision process should be in minimax terms. Justice should be particularistic and situational rather than universalistic.

5. The legal process as a whole should be accessible to the most indigent and powerless masses.

6. Affective spontaneity and a high level of personalization should be the dominant feature of the legal process of Korea.

NOTES

1. The term "value" is used here as defined by Professors Harold Lasswell and Myres McDougal. Harold D. Lasswell and Abraham Kaplan, *Power and Society* (New Haven: Yale University Press, 1950). Myres S. McDougal, "International Law, Power, and Policy," in 82 *Recueil des Cours* 137 (Hague Academy of International Law, 1953).

2. Lasswell also denies such a universalistic assumption. Lasswell and Kaplan, *Power and Society,* p. 56. Harold D. Lasswell, *Power and Personality* (New York: W. W. Norton & Company Inc., 1948), p. 16.

3. For example, Pyong-choon Hahm, *The Korean Political Tradition and Law* (Seoul: Hollym, 1967).

4. Arnold J. Toynbee, *A Study of History* (London: Oxford University Press, 1969), vol. 5, p. 16.

5. Pyong-choon Hahm, "Religion and Law in Korea," *Kroeber Anthropological Society Papers,* vol. 41 (Fall 1969), pp. 8-53.

6. Toynbee, *A Study of History,* vol. 9, p. 40.

7. *Haptong Yon'gam 1972* (Haptong Yearbook for 1972) (Seoul: Haptong T'ongsinsa, 1972), p. 269.

8. The National Census of 1966 shows that 8.9 percent of the total population (29,159,640) were illiterate (2,605,443 who were above the age of 12). *1966 Population Census Report of Korea* (Seoul: Economic Planning Board, Republic of Korea, 1969): 18. The report submitted by the Ministry of Education to the National Assembly in October 1972 states that 95.7 percent of primary-school-age children are enrolled and attending primary schools.

9. *Haptong Yon'gam 1972,* pp. 265-267.

10. Karl Llewellyn and E. Adamson Hoebel, *The Cheyenne Way* (Norman, Oklahoma: University of Oklahoma Press, 1961), pp. 224-225.

9 RESPONSIVE BEHAVIOR AND POPULAR
DECISION MAKING: THE PROMISE OF MODELS
GARRY D. BREWER

Overview

This paper presents the reader with the barest outlines of one potentially important methodological device for the understanding and management of contexts as complex and rich as those found in most development settings. Formal model building is a useful tool whose various limitations need to be as well understood as do its many commendable strengths.

Summary discussions of why models are important, of how models are commonly built, and of what general problems impede their full development and utilization are presented in succeeding sections. This is not a thorough technical discussion; it is meant as a straightforward introduction for the interested layman.

This paper is concerned fundamentally with development and change.[1] The subject matter is rich in its complexity and diversity; so too are the concepts and methods used to organize, understand, and manage that substance.

Clearly, no one will ever make an exhaustive, much less definitive, list of all aspects of any particular context that are or will be important for the study of development and change. The same may be said about the intellectual concepts and methodological procedures used to understand and manage these contexts. The crucial, constraining importance of the research or operational question is not to be underestimated in this regard.

Any research problem—and by extension, any operational problem—demands formulation in precise enough terms that an appropriate investigation may be undertaken. Typically, research problems in this area are not clarified adequately, a contention attested to by the aimlessness and lack of cumulation of much of the literature concerned with development. Difficulties in matching research questions with appropriate intellectual concepts or research techniques are seldom clearly articulated. As Abraham Kaplan remarked, researchers, whose sunk cost in intellectual capital may be considerable, become accustomed to certain techniques to the exclusion of others.[2]

It is rare to find that the research question, well understood and defined, has determined what method is to be employed. Indeed, just the reverse appears to occur routinely.

Many social scientists feel uncomfortable using and learning about sophisticated, often quantitative, methodologies. Such is even more true with those having direct operational responsibilities. Cowed by the jargon and blinded by the technical brilliance of methodological virtuosity, many of the uninitiated simply give up trying to understand what the elegant models and pristine numbers actually mean. This is as unfortunate for all concerned as it is unnecessary.

One of the main purposes of this paper is to point out several features of an interesting method. However, one must be concerned to keep substance in the forefront, where it rightfully belongs.

The Problem-Solving Approach

Objective: To Be Contextual and Problem-Oriented

In the following discussion Harold Lasswell's general recommendation to be both contextual and problem-oriented is explicitly adopted.[3]

Most research on development issues suffers from a distinct lack of contextuality and from insufficient attention to the policy-relevant questions posed by responsible decision makers. Both of these undesirable characteristics are at least partially attributable to the significant complexity of most development matters and to the frequent fragmentation and dismemberment of such matters by specialists who are discipline- rather than problem-oriented.

To be contextual means taking a view of the whole system, considering the interrelationships of the constituent parts to the whole in such a way that the entire system's past, present, and future are illustrated in important and meaningful ways.

To be problem-oriented means identifying the actual operational problems in a given system context, both those reported by active participants and those that individuals—because of parochial interests, limited perspectives, or both—are unaware of. Such problem or question identification is enhanced by the exercise of several distinct but interrelated intellectual tasks including the clarification of the relevant goals in a given context, the description of past trends and sequences, the clear explanation of structural features conditioning those trends, the projection of likely futures in light of the specific sets of goals, trends, and conditions found to be operating in a context, and finally, the creation and explication of plausible, feasible, and desirable alternatives for a given setting.

A central challenge facing policy science is to create conceptual and procedural apparatus that will free individual scholars to think more productively in terms that are both contextual and problem-oriented. By conceptual apparatus we mean generalized principles for perceiving and orienting oneself with respect to a given empirical context; and by procedural apparatus, we mean a variety of methodological techniques for illuminating and managing in full and useful ways the data produced in a context. Formal models, the topic at hand, are one such procedural apparatus. If the phenomena comprising development were simple and the symbolic environment less rich, the challenge would not be of high priority. Such is not the case, however, and we are best served by getting on with the task at hand.

The so-called intellectual orientations are nothing more than crude conceptual devices that enable us to organize and integrate the work of individual specialists. They are crude, but they are important—particularly if we are to understand many of the current problems facing those interested in the general area of development.

Impediment: Specialized Conceptual Apparatus

Using the five intellectual tasks facilitates detailing several common difficulties evident in current research and practice in the development substantive area. If we are to understand better the rationale for using procedures such as formal models, we must first understand the operating conceptual apparatus.[4]

Goals: The Pursuit of Comprehensive, Aggregate Results   For example, much goals-related work suffers because "value or normative" specialists have allowed themselves to be separated from specific empirical, referential context.[5] As a result, their work characteristically contributes little to our understanding of either empirical behavior or the associated underlying structure responsible for that behavior.[6]

One aspect of the everyday world classified by goals specialists is the issue of uncertainty and the value trade-offs associated with decision making. In J. Roland Pennock's perceptive article, "Political Development, Political Systems, and Political Goods,"[7] one is given an indication of what trade-offs in the present and future degree of associative freedoms one must be prepared to endure to achieve given levels of political stability, foreign capital formation, and increased welfare. Unfortunately, this awareness that goals are a truly contextual enterprise and that the goals intellectual task has coequal status with the other four tasks is neither pervasive nor well established among normative specialists. Goals-related works are usually not tied to any specific context and, therefore, contribute little to our understanding of either empirical behavior or the underlying structure responsible for it. Without such a basis, it is quite difficult to use such work for projective, policy, historical, or scientific purposes.

Trends: The Study of Recent and More Remote Events   The purpose of much historical work is to detail the behavior of individual systems. Characteristically the work is rich and descriptive and takes the element of time directly into account.[8] Trend or historical specialists, however, frequently overload themselves with minutiae to the extent that the temporal elements underlying their analyses are obscured. This tendency is particularly regrettable because the concepts of development and change are explicitly time dependent. A corollary problem that stems from a preoccupation with detail is the nongenerality of such historical work.[9] Overattention to specific behavioral patterns often occurs at the expense of any consideration being given to the general underlying features responsible for that behavior.

Other characteristic weaknesses of the approach are that historical work is seldom predictive. It rarely is concerned with how alternative developmental sequences to the single one being described might have been realized, and is only as an aberrancy—as in the case of Marxian historians—concerned with the ideological or normative content and implications of the description. In short, by selecting narrowly from the whole available symbolic array, trend specialists have allowed themselves to become insufficiently contextual.

What one might reasonably expect from trend specialists are robust descriptive narratives featuring the elaboration of specific details of a given context as it unfolds over time. If the work is particularly well done, it may even be possible to tease out of the verbal representation weakly explanatory and tentative causal relationships, a point to which we turn subsequently.

Conditions: The Identification of Interrelated Factors   Whole and part come into the direct consideration of scientific specialists dedicated to the discovery and measurement of the underlying structural features of a context. This concern for determining structural characteristics by rigorously measuring behavioral data is important but may be quite diversionary if the other four intellectual tasks are not explicitly taken into account.

Scientific or condition specialists frequently demonstrate two unproductive intellectual patterns. Often in haste to measure, they overlook the research or analytic question, with the result that simple numbers replace complex good sense.[10] At another extreme, data are eschewed entirely in the interests of formal, theoretical elegance.[11] Neither style of behavior, pursued in isolation, has ever had very much to recommend it if one's purposes are serious and operational.

The condition's intellectual task is important because of its concern for rigorous measurement and its general desire to clarify the underlying structures responsible for the behavior in a context. An area of great potential contribution is in the specification of alternative structural interpretations, the development of multiple theoretical, scientific explanations of contextual behavior.[12]

Projections: The Unfolding of Events   Projection is rarely done by development specialists, and the main methodological techniques actually employed are so esoteric that scholars who know how to forecast are separated from both the substantive problems and other specialist colleagues. Representative techniques include extrapolation, model building—or its variants, gaming and simulation—and the collection of expert opinion and judgment.[13] Ideally, although extremely rare in practice, all of these techniques could be combined to best advantage.

Fundamental difficulties in accounting for "great men," revolutions, technological breakthroughs, and natural disasters, while making the projection task hazardous, do not diminish its importance. The raw ingredients needed for productive projective efforts are clear: quality data on important trends, some understanding of how these data are interrelated, and finally systematic methods and procedures by which nonquantified, but expert opinion, may be brought to bear on what is implied by the extrapolated trends.[14]

Alternatives: The Creation and Selection of Purposive Interventions
Creating and selecting alternatives, the invention and implementation of
collective public choices, require that one have a sense of a context's
history, of how important elements are interrelated, of what key deci-
sionmakers' goals are, of what societal objectives collectively are and
might become, and of where the considered system is generally heading
should no policy interventions occur. Unfortunately, responsible policymakers seldom are so comprehensively informed. In fact, intuition,
unformed by analysis, and incrementalism, untempered by longer term
considerations, dominate as key modes of public policymaking in
nearly all societies.

Specific strengths of the intellectual task are that it forces one to
account for an assortment of operating goals that must exist in any
context; it focuses attention on the need for the evaluation of the past
performance of public officials–if we do not know who was successful
for what reasons in the past, how can we select those capable of making
reasonable choices in the future? And it forces one to confront the
goals' tradeoff issue–how much of one goal needs to be sacrificed to
obtain another? At what costs? To whose account?[15]

A Basic Idea A major argument presented so far is that the complexity
of most subject matter confronting scholars and operators in the development setting causes fragmentation as a result of their specialized
intellectual training and interests in the former case and as a result of
inherent limitations of information processing in the latter case. To
counteract these undesirable tendencies, a contextual and problem-
oriented approach is advocated, primarily for its consciousness-inducing
and potentially integrative aspects.

Model building is at best a technical procedure that captures many
desirable features that are best characterized as both contextual and

problem-oriented. For that reason alone it is at least a procedural option worth additional consideration.

The Model Building Process

Undoubtedly other terms might be applied to the four-phase process that characterizes a model's "life"; however, for our present purposes, it is useful to distinguish between intention, specification, control, and validation.[16]

Intention, Specification, Control and Validation

Intention   The intention phase of model building involves figuring out who wants the model, what he wants specifically, what his purposes are, and what research questions might guide the overall effort. It is elementary but nonetheless distressing to see, for example, how many entrepreneurs are ready, willing, and able to sell formal, often computer based, models without regard to an individual policymaker's unique problems or the specific context in which the problems are located. The intention phase cannot be stressed enough. It helps define what is to be included and excluded in an analysis and gives one an a priori sense of what an answer might look like should if drop out of the anlysis at some point.

Specification   This is more difficult and concerns developing one's preliminary notions of intention sufficiently to begin formalizing a model by working out the important structural details of the context. Most development work has not moved beyond the specification phase.[17] Seldom does one pass beyond merely identifying important elements in a context; assembling these pieces usefully or productively is even more problematic.

Control   This phase involves ordering and managing one's data. Discussions of social indicators are preliminary exercises in the control phase, and, one might speculate, these have not progressed any farther than they have because they have been divorced from explicit considerations of intention: who wants what sorts of indicators for what purposes?[18] Identification and specification imply the need for data control; actually putting data into order allows their reuse for other purposes or in other specified relationships. Control is a functional area that scarcely has been developed with respect to most development scholarship. The creation of economic indicators is an occasional exception to this. Control receives little attention unless one's models do not work, in which case attention is expended trying to figure out why there are so many holes in the data, and why data are of such poor quality. Inevitably it turns out that one has not paid early enough attention to the control aspects of the process.

Validation   This is really the last thing that one should do, and, given all prior problems, it may be that validation never actually gets done. Perhaps the process terminates after passing through intention, specification, and slight control. To specify a problem may be sufficient to understand and manage that problem. If one progresses to the point of identifying the important elements in the context, defining them to some extent, and making a few measurements of them, that may be quite enough. It may be unnecessary to force formalization to exact many of the practical and intellectual payoffs. Validation may be misleading to the extent that it diverts scarce attention away from prior issues of intention, specification, and control.[19] This view is somewhat heretical and probably not shared by many technicians; but then the issue is more pragmatic than technical.

A Pragmatic View   Richard Bellman, who is a distinguished mathematician among other things, made a cogent observation on understanding a context by collecting bits and pieces of information from various perspectives. Bellman's argument is persuasive. With some information about the structure of a system and some information observed about inputs, outputs, and internal behavior over time, he claims, one must deduce all missing information concerning structure, inputs, and outputs.[20] One never finishes. The context may be changing, and one remains sensitive to those changes. A central idea is that there is never a "final" model. One must never be satisfied just with data or theory, and certainly depending extensively on one's intuitive feelings about a context is inadequate. Both data and theory, of course, matter, but the real job is their integration, a decided strength of the model building technique.

While the trick Bellman characterizes appears uncomplicated, it is not easily accomplished. The comment is particularly appropriate with respect to making some theoretical sense of contexts as complex as those encountered in the development setting.

The Formal Representation of a System

Presented in this section are a concise statement of a formal system and then an easy-to-follow, step-by-step illustration of how one simple social process has been specified and represented. The promise of this procedural apparatus will be clarified in the process.

A Formal Statement[21]

A model may be described in terms of a formal system conceived of as a state vector X_t and a set of relationships G:[22]

$$X_t \equiv \begin{bmatrix} x_{1,t} \\ x_{2,t} \\ \cdot \\ \cdot \\ \cdot \\ x_{n,t} \end{bmatrix} \qquad (4.1)$$

$$X_t = G(x_t, x_{t-1}, \ldots)$$

The state vector is merely the set of variables and parameters needed to describe the state of the system at any point in time. The relationships G are hypotheses about processes, inferred from the observation of real world systems, describing how the components change as a function of each other through time. (x_t is included on the right side of the equation because one component $x_{i,t}$ may be a function of some other component $x_{j,t}$ within the same time period.)

The structure of a class of systems (for example, countries in a region) is the set of variables X_t and the set of relationships G. Together they constitute a theory, a temporary commitment to, and representation of, the phenomena of importance in the system. A model of any one of the systems is the general structure with the magnitudes of the variables and parameters specified to represent the particular context. The behavior of the model is the set of time series of the $x_{i,t}$ (the individual components of X_t) which are produced as the model generates successive state descriptions.

A Simpler View

A simple illustration of a social process that has been formally modeled demonstrates some of the concepts and ideas that allow one to move from verbal representations of a social context to increasingly more rigorous formulations.[23]

Paul A. Samuelson's early work on the multiplier and accelerator analysis is our point of departure.[24] The technical terms, multiplier and accelerator, could be discouraging; however, the article is a simple and elegant formalization of several macroeconomic concepts summarized in four simple equations. Obviously lacking the robustness of the Keynesian theory from which it was derived, the formulation is precise, understandable, logical, and hence satisfies our present needs.

Define:
Gross national product at a point in
time is composed of consumption, investment,
and government expenditures.

Hypothesize:
Some portion of GNP is consumed in
subsequent time periods.

Hypothesize:
Some portion of marginal changes in
consumption is invested (if the change
is positive) or disinvested (if negative).

Hypothesize:
Government expenditures stay at about
the same percent of last year's GNP
from period to period.

Figure 9.1
An Illustrative Example–A Verbal Flow Chart

Flow Charts   The general problem is to describe gross national product
in terms of other relationships. At this level the simplest logic of the
process by which GNP is generated is broken down into manageable
parts, and some boundaries are established for the total context (see Figure 9.1). In this example, one deals with the entities, gross national product, consumption, investment, and government expenditures. No other
factors are explicitly considered, which is not to say that other factors
do not matter. Many other considerations are subsumed within the
gross entities selected and depicted in the flow chart; however, those selected are determined to be of primary analytic and theoretical concern.

    We shall start with a verbal representation of the context. Words are but one way to represent these ideas, and we consider others. Verbally, GNP is made up of consumption, investment, and government expenditures. Following Samuelson, we ignore foreign investment. A second idea is that consumption is somehow related to GNP, perhaps proportionately. A third notion is that investment is sensitive to fluctuations in consumption. For example, if consumption in one year increases over the prior year, more investments will be induced. Increased private investment will follow increased consumption, and the converse. Theoretically and realistically, people generally are not as eager to invest their money in a downward trend as in an upward trend. Finally the government either always expends the same amount, which is how Samuelson did the original analysis, or the government expends some proportion of the GNP, a richer although still overly simple way of conceiving of the problem and the way it is done here.

English, or almost any spoken language, can represent processes; and the spoken language is forgivingly imprecise. To represent something in English is virtually to predetermine vagueness. One can "gray over," blur details, and leave undefined exact relationships. For example, what does "in some proportion" mean? What is "proportion"? "Insensitive," what does that mean? A notional idea of plausibility is transmitted by these terms without having to demand much precision. A beauty of English is that it is capable of capturing the richness of a process without enforcing great precision. Anyone who builds models should try to flow chart them using verbal concepts.

Within the flow chart are one definitional tautology and three behavioral-theoretical hypotheses about the interrelationships of entities. To the extent that the whole is logically consistent, to the extent that the individual components contain, as tentatively stated relationships, all entities of primary interest, and to the extent that intercomponent relationships are logically and theoretically plausible, one may proceed with more formal statements of the context.

$$Y_t = C_t + I_t + G_t \tag{4.2}$$

$$C_{t+1} = aY_t \tag{4.3}$$

$$I_{t+1} = \beta(C_{t+1} - C_t) + I_t \tag{4.4}$$

$$G_{t+1} = \gamma Y_t \tag{4.5}$$

Where,

Y_t = gross national product* at time t

C_t = consumption expenditures at time t

I_t = investment expenditures at time t

G_t = government expenditures at time t

a = proportion of gross national product at time t that is consumed

β = proportion of difference in consumption between time t+1 and time t that is invested

γ = proportion of gross national product that at time t is expended by the government

*All units constant currency.

Figure 9.2
An Illustrative Example—Mathematical Notation

At this point, however, it may be that many of the verbally stated relationships are not logically consistent. It also may be that empirical evidence to support or refute the formulated relationships is not available. It may be that the whole context has logical gaps not easily bridged by known theory and new measurement and testing. Alternative possibilities include forsaking the verbal formulation because it has neither scientific utility nor meaning, or retaining the formulation until additional information is developed. Should one elect the latter option, it would be foolish and unnecessarily expensive to force the verbal flow chart into more rigorous notation until the logical, theoretical, and data problems are resolved.

Mathematical Notation   Words are rich in their variety of meaning but frequently vague when used for logical reasoning; mathematics is exact in its logic but usually understresses meaning. If one is willing to accept the loss of verbal variety in the interests of rigorous logical specification, a mathematically stated version of the verbal flow chart might be constructed. An example is reproduced in Figure 9.2.[25] Gone are the vague, albeit useful, qualifiers, "some," "a portion," "about," and so forth; they are replaced by hard statements of cause and effect. Gross national product at a specific point in time is equal to the sum of consumption, investment, and government expenditures at that point; consumption at a specific point in time equals a fixed percentage of gross national product from the prior, discrete point in time, and so forth. No other options, no other meanings, no other interpretations satisfy the exact conditions described by relationships (4.2) through (4.5).

A notion of the timing of things, the flow of things, comes across too, when we move from the verbal flow chart to its mathematical representation. Getting this far is commendable because elements often cannot be identified or measured. What does "consumption" mean? Can we measure it? What determines it? In fact, major breakthroughs in economics were the conceptualization of GNP and then its crudest measurement. If one is able to progress this far, and sometimes it is possible, then at least there are the beginnings of the identification of what goes with what—a major step.

Besides producing more rigorous descriptions of the context, mathematical representation enables a model builder to perform some essential "bookkeeping" chores. Checking for dimensionality and for logical completeness are two important tasks rarely carried out for social science models.

Dimensionality refers to the units of measurement assigned a model's entities. In the illustrative example, all the variables are measured in monetary terms, for example, dollars—more specifically, dollars defined in accordance with a standard accounting convention like "market" or "constant" currency. The parameters (α, β, γ) are all dimensionless or pure numbers. As a model becomes more complicated, one easily loses sight of the need to balance units, to assure dimensionality. And any equations that represent a system must be dimensionally homogeneous. The operation of the system cannot violate the requirement of dimensional homogeneity for the describing equations. This is a fact of enormous importance, for apples cannot equal oranges no matter how elegant the relationship.

Consistency checking refers to several logical operations routinely carried out where mathematical notation is a common currency. One simple example might be illustrated by reversing the order of the relationships (4.3) and (4.4) from the sequence presented in Figure 9.2. A value for C_{t+1} must be calculated before a value for I_{t+1} may be determined; I_{t+1} depends upon or is a function of C_{t+1}. Consistency and dimension checking must be carried out as a regular technical matter of course. To the extent that they are ignored, one must be alerted to possible errors in formulation.

Representation by Code   A final form of representation might be in a computer code. The computer cannot read the information in Figure 9.2, and one must put this into machine-readable form to process it.

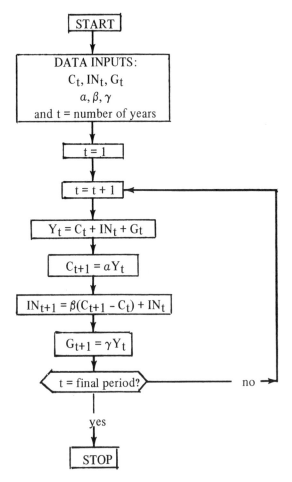

Figure 9.3
An Illustrative Example—Ready for Coding

MAIN 1   SOURCE STATEMENT

```
C      ILLUSTRATIVE REFERENCE
       INTEGER T,TT,FY
       REAL IN
       DIMENSION Y(50), C(50), IN(50), G(50)
C      INPUT
       READ(5,1)C(1),IN(1),G(1),ALPHA,BETA,GAMMA,FY
    1  FORMAT(3F10.0,3F10.3,8X,I2)
C      DO LOOP
       T= 1
       DO 50 T= 1,FY
       TT=T+1
       Y(T)=C(T)+IN(T)+G(T)
       C(TT)=ALPHA*Y(T)
       IN(TT)=BETA*(C(TT)-C(T))+IN(T)
       G(TT)=GAMMA*Y(T)
   50  CONTINUE
       WRITE(6,98) ALPHA,BETA,GAMMA, FY
   98  FORMAT(1H1,'INITIAL CONDITIONS'//5X,'ALPHA',F7.3,'  BETA',F7.3,
      1'   GAMMA',F7.3/5X,'NUMBER OF PERIODS=',I4)
       WRITE(6,99)
   99  FORMAT(1H4,'ILLUSTRATIVE EXAMPLE'//5X,'OUTPUTS'/2X,'YR.'4X,'Y(T)',
      16X'C(T)  '5X'IN(T)'6X'G(T)')
       WRITE(6,100)(T,Y(T),C(T),IN(T),G(T),T=1,FY)
  100  FORMAT(1H0,I3,4F10.0)
       STOP
       END
```

Figure 9.4

An Illustrative Example–FORTRAN Code

Table 9.1
Outputs from Illustrative Example

Initial Conditions
ALPHA 0.800   BETA 0.500   GAMMA 0.150
NUMBER OF PERIODS = 20

Illustrative Example
Outputs

YR.	Y(T)	C(T)	IN(T)	G(T)
1	900.	700.	100.	100.
2	965.	720.	110.	135.
3	1053.	772.	136.	145.
4	1171.	842.	171.	158.
5	1331.	937.	218.	176.
6	1547.	1065.	282.	200.
7	1838.	1238.	369.	232.
8	2232.	1471.	485.	276.
9	2763.	1788.	643.	335.
10	3480.	2211.	855.	414.
11	4448.	2784.	1142.	522.
12	5755.	3559.	1529.	667.
13	7520.	4804.	2052.	863.
14	9902.	6016.	2758.	1128.

There is a subtle problem at this juncture. Respecification of a mathematical formulation into a computer code involves additional losses of meaning and content. A computer code or language is based on its own logical assumptions and relationships. Just as verbal languages differ in form, content, and possible meanings, so, too, do computer languages.[26] Our simple illustration suggests some of these distinctions. In Figure 9.3, the mathematical notation has been translated into a form ready for computer coding. For such simple cases, the translation is easily made; for more complicated cases, each having multiple plausible possibilities for processing, achieving the best correspondence between the mathematical and computer formulations requires considerable skill.

A coded example program is presented in Figure 9.4, and outputs from that program are shown in Table 9.1.

Operations with the Model   To recall earlier points made about the alternatives' intellectual task helps to make the connection between models and policy. Model building forces one to be explicitly aware of a given space-time configuration; it makes one formulate, however crudely at the beginning, the interrelationships among important elements identified according to someone's intentions or purposes. It provides a construct that can be scrutinized, replicated, revised, and at some point validated. It also provides a device which may be operated to examine the consequences of predetermined changes in the modeled context. This operation may take several forms, and one of the best known is sensitivity analysis.

Sensitivity analysis helps to determine the effects of systematic changes in a model. The technique involves varying a model's initial values to determine what systematic outcomes result. Inputs that can be varied include initial conditions and parameters; alternative structural specifications may also be analyzed in this fashion.

Relative impacts of these known changes are then compared with the reference runs, or time series generated by the model that best fits the observed historical data from which it was constructed. Because the process is essentially unbounded, that is to say, there is a very large number of individual changes that might be made to a given formulation, one must have some means to guide the selection of such changes. The importance of the research and operational "Question" must be stressed once again at this point. The "Question" is one valuable means to inform the researcher-model builder on ways to reduce the analytic policy space. It is critical because the implications of each unique combination of relationships, initial conditions, and parameters must be traced out individually.

Operating the model through techniques such as sensitivity analysis may provide a way around man's information processing limitations, a point of some consequence to operational personnel. It may allow decision makers to examine many more alternatives than would be possible unaided, and it allows them to do this at relatively low societal cost. The selection from among all plausible alternatives remains, of course, a man-dependent function even though their prior exploration is a machine-dependent one.

Some Observations and Caveats

While one can take a simple idea, initially grossly represented, through increasingly precise steps until attaining a rigorous description of it, many important elements in a context may be lost in the process. Besides the loss of richness, one can oversimplify and assume away enormous amounts of detail. After all this example describes a national economy in but four equations.

A number of general, summary warnings must be considered carefully and often before embarking on a large-scale model building enterprise. We next consider several of these matters.

The Source of Ideas

Where does one get the words to begin representing a context? Often the raw ideas can be gleaned from case studies. A good historical case study may be worth its weight in gold to a model builder if done correctly and well. Scientific pretentions seldom obscure real factual detail. From a decent case study one gets some ideas of precedence, order, and importance. What comes before what and what is truly relevant in a context? For example, in a model-based study of the Philippines and Turkey, great quantities of historical literature were carefully read and thus contributed to more formal representations of those two developing contexts. Theoretical literature is sometimes helpful. One may glean some crude hypotheses for subsequent specification, for instance. Demographic theory suggests what might be causing people to move from rural to urban areas, as well as what might be inhibiting the process, the "push-pull" phenomenon. Economic theory often provides useful points of departure for formal modeling. Political theory occasionally offers valuable insights.

One takes a bit of this and a bit of that (in Bellman's quaint way of phrasing it) and tries to put it all together. For the simple model presented in our work *Organized Complexity*, we worked nearly two years doing this kind of reading, thinking, and sorting out of possible elements and relationships. Once through this phase of the initial specification, it took about six months to formalize the model. Assembling the pieces shows one what is not known, for example, what preliminary investigations and data searches are required. For instance, we uncovered a number of problems and identified several large holes in our information by making verbal summaries and flow charts. Important processes were not connected, relationships did not make sense, sequences were not logical, and interconnections were not clear. To answer these specific problems, whose importance had been stressed during the initial specification phase of the model-building process, we had to find out if anyone had thought or written about them; we consulted anthropology, studies of religion, geography, and many other specialized works that we probably would not have considered had we not had to fill in the blanks in the flow chart.

On Precision

Precision is a very sophisticated matter. One must know how tentative and fuzzy things really are as opposed to how precise these same things appear to be when put into a formal model. One must be sensitive to think explicitly about the complexity of the world while building and manipulating simple, precise, and caricatured representations of that world.

Demographic processes are usually very nice, because they are generally data rich and relatively easy to understand. One can represent many demographic processes in short order merely by working with a good description of what appears to be going on in the context and with some good data of that phenomenon. Here is a class of events that often lends itself to precise representation. Political processes, on the other hand, are generally more troublesome. Just to understand what is going on is difficult enough because key concepts are seldom sharply or consistently presented. In this case, one must be considerably more wary of falsely precise representations.

Random and unique events often confound one's efforts to be rigorous. In any given context there will be certain elements that simply cannot be managed analytically. Trying to ignore them or to assume them away may lead to the most serious difficulties. One needs to be sensitive to the importance of specific exogenous and stochastic events. How does one account for Magsaysay's fatal plane crash in a political model of the Philippines for the period encompassing the period just before, during, and after the event? Sharp societal discontinuities such as economic depressions and revolutions are also extremely hard to anticipate and represent in a formal model. This observation leads one to consider a related point.

In much formal model building there is a conservative bias and assumption that past trends and sequences will persist into the future. This usually implicit assumption makes model building an increasingly chancy proposition and renders results increasingly less precise and reliable as time series are projected into the future.[28] This is not to say that modeling is simply not worth doing, obviously not. At the very least it is worth doing because it enables us to collect many disparate bits of information that are important and to assemble them in one place sufficiently well that some integration and control occurs. But one needs to be sensitive. Many technically competent people are not sensitive to the richness of real events, just like the "great men" of history, and obviously these things count.[29]

Modeling is only one kind of tool with certain well known strengths and deficiencies; however, let us not be so naive as to think that it is the only tool available.

Some Final Thoughts

The following are brief, summary statements of some general pertinence to anyone interested in either using or building models for policy or research purposes. The main reason for listing them is to remind the reader that model building, whatever its many considerable virtues, is not a panacea. It is but one additional tool to be used in the difficult tasks of understanding and managing a development context.

A model costs something in terms of a considerable number of important factors that must, in the formalization process, be omitted, assumed, guessed at, or measured with great difficulty and little certainty.

Events often are in such a state of flux that no one could possibly describe a present situation well enough to specify a model in detail; and, even if possible, contexts routinely change in less time than it takes to build a model of them.

Discontinuous events (war, coups d'etats, disasters, "great men") do in fact play important roles in many developing societies, and these are inherently difficult to model formally.

Few nations produce the data necessary to support large-scale model-building enterprises.

Many important policy contingencies cannot be anticipated, implying that one only occasionally will be able to second guess important events sufficiently well to have an appropriate model standing by.

Decisions are routinely made with short or no lead time, thereby reducing the potential applicability of a model-building strategy considerably.

Model building is an expensive process as measured in the time, technical talent, and computational equipment required; unfortunately, most developing countries are not overly blessed with any of these necessary ingredients.

Many, if not most, of these general comments are to varying degrees correct and will apply to specific model building undertakings. However, recall that model building is but one of a wide variety of problem-solving techniques that, when taken together, begin to approximate a truly problem-oriented and contextual strategy for the understanding and management of rich and complex development settings.

NOTES

1. For a thorough review of many of these matters, one must recommend Samuel P. Huntington's excellent essay, "The Change to Change," *Comparative Politics,* Vol. 3, No. 3 (April 1971), pp. 283-322.

2. See notes on the "methodological hammer" in Kaplan, *The Conduct of Inquiry* (San Francisco: Chandler, 1964).

3. The point is often made in Lasswell's writings and teachings. His *A Pre-View of Policy Sciences* (New York: Elsevier, 1971) contains a recent, concise statement.

4. A much fuller treatment of these five intellectual tasks, including detailed bibliographies, discussions of what each has to offer the study of development, and representative examples is contained in Garry D. Brewer and Ronald D. Brunner, eds., *Political Development and Change: A Policy Approach* (New York: The Free Press, 1974).

5. Abraham Kaplan has characteristically addressed these issues squarely in his *American Ethics and Public Policy* (New York: Oxford University Press, 1963), p. 94 and elsewhere.

6. Gibson Winter, a rare exception to the characteristic case laid out here, has sensed this problem and tried to redress it. See his *Elements for a Social Ethic: Scientific Perspectives on Social Processes* (New York: Macmillan, 1966), p. 215 ff.

7. *World Politics,* Vol. 18 (April 1966).

8. Eric Nordlinger, "Political Development: Time Sequences and Rates of Change," *World Politics,* Vol. 20 (April 1968), pp. 494-520, has captured the essence of this point.

9. It is disturbing to see with what tenacity many historians hold to this unproductive view. Hans Meyerhoff, *The Philosophy of History in Our Time: An Anthology* (Garden City, New York: Doubleday, 1959), p. 19f has articulated the extreme view on this issue.

10. R. J. Rummel, "Dimensions of Conflict Behavior Within and Between Nations," *General Systems* (1963 Yearbook), has demonstrated the problem in one way; and Irma Adelman and Cynthia Taft Morris, "An Econometric Model of Change in Underdeveloped Countries," *American Economic Review* (December 1968), pp. 1184-1218, have done it rather differently, but without much more success.

11. Albert O. Hirschman's "The Search for Paradigms as a Hindrance to Understanding," *World Politics,* Vol. 24 (April 1970), is an excellent statement of the problem.

12. One rare example is contained in Robert P. Bush and Frederick Mosteller, "A Comparison of Eight Models," in Paul Lazarsfeld and Neil W. Henry, eds., *Readings in Mathematical Social Sciences* (Chicago: Science Research Associates, 1966), pp. 335-349.

13. Projections work in the development area is scarce. Frank T. Klingberg, "The Historical Alteration of Moods in American Foreign Policy," *World Politics* (January 1952); and idem, "Predicting the Termination of War," *Journal of Conflict Resolution* (June 1966), provide two, not very well known examples of this sort of work. The National Bureau of Economic Research has been responsible for much of the economic projection activity in this country over the last forty-five years; see NBER, *Long Range Economic Projection—Studies in Income and Wealth* (Princeton: Princeton University Press, 1954), for one notable example.

14. The Delphi method of expert opinion pooling and assessment is one such technique that has been tried in a number of contexts, including several developmental ones. See Olaf Helmer, *Analysis of the Future: The Delphi Method* (Santa Monica: The Rand Corporation, P-3704, October 1967), for a more complete treatment of the technique.

15. See John E. Koehler, "Economic Policymaking with Little Information and Few Instruments: The Process of Macro-Control in Mexico," in Brewer and Brunner, eds., *A Policy Approach,* for one solid example.

16. These concepts have not yet been widely employed, but they have proved to be useful to detail the "life" of a model as it progresses through the general process. See Martin Shubik and Garry D. Brewer, *Models, Simulations, and Games—A Survey* (Santa Monica: The Rand Corporation, R-1060-ARPA/RC, June 1972), for one such application.

17. James M. Beshers, *Population Processes in Social Systems* (New York: The Free Press, 1967), has spoken well about this matter.

18. Bertram Gross, *The State of the Nation* (London: Tavistock, 1966), is a general summary of the status of the indicators movement ca. 1965. The problems cited have not essentially been resolved.

19. Two excellent statements of the technical details involved in validation of formal models are contained in Thomas H. Naylor and J. M. Finger, "Verification of Computer Simulation Models," *Management Science* 14, No. 2 (October 1967): B-92 through B-101; and Richard L. Van Horn, "Validation of Simulation Results," *Management Science* 17, No. 5 (January 1971): 247-257.

20. Richard Bellman, *Mathematical Aspects of a Theory of Systems* (Santa Monica: The Rand Corporation, P-3032, 1965), p. 3.

21. Much of the argument in this section is developed more fully in Ronald D. Brunner and Garry D. Brewer, "Policy and the Study of the Future: Given Complexity, Trends or Processes?" in Brewer and Brunner, eds., *A Policy Approach.* My debt to my good colleague Ronald D. Brunner is inestimable.

22. The vector notation is introduced in Richard Bellman and Robert Kalaba, *Dynamic Programming and Modern Control Theory* (New York: Academic Press, 1965), p. 5.

23. A related illustration has been carried out in the context of urban models in Garry D. Brewer, *Politicians, Bureaucrats, and the Consultant: A Critique of Urban Problem Solving* (New York: Basic Books, 1973). The use of formal models has reached an important stage as evidenced by the considerable activity that is going on in a wide range of substantive areas.

24. Paul A. Samuelson, "Interactions between the Multiplier and the Principle of Acceleration," *Review of Economic Statistics* 21 (1939): 75-78.

25. The model is represented in difference equation form. See Samuel Goldberg, *Introduction to Difference Equations* (New York: Wiley Science Editions, 1961), for a very readable primer on the technique.

26. Howard S. Krasnow and Reino Merikallio, "The Past, Present, and Future of General Simulation Languages," *Management Science* 11 (November 1964): 236-268, have an excellent summary discussion of this matter.

27. Ronald D. Brunner and Garry D. Brewer, *Organized Complexity: Empirical Theories of Political Development* (New York: The Free Press, 1971). In this work, my colleague Brunner and I attempted to work through some of the limitations of theory and practice in development scholarship. Departing from Daniel Lerner's theory of modernization, presented in his *The Passing of Traditional Society* (New York: The Free Press, 1964), we explored a simple model of modernization and mass politics developed for the Turkish and Philippine settings, compared this with current empirical investigations, and concluded that much current work suffers unnecessarily from the fragmentation and specialization noted throughout this paper.

28. See Garry D. Brewer, "Analysis of Complex Systems: An Experiment and Its Implications for Policymaking," in Todd R. LaPorte, ed., *Organized Social Complexity: Challenge to Politics and Policy* (Princeton: Princeton University Press, 1974), for a full investigation into the issues of precision and the length of time of one's forecast, model size,, and accuracy, and the problems of information overload and management in an operational setting. Issued under the same title and available from (Santa Monica: The Rand Corporation, P-4951, January 1973).

29. Jay Forrester, *Urban Dynamics* (Cambridge: MIT Press, 1969), and several closely related works by Forrester and his associates are not to be recommended on just these grounds alone. This kind of work maximizes technical virtuosity to the nearly total exclusion of both data and theory, and hence represents yet another variety of vacuous overspecialization.

10 THE CONTINUING REVISION OF CONCEPTUAL AND OPERATIONAL MAPS

HAROLD D. LASSWELL

The Emphasis on Feedback

A distinctive modern development in the formation and execution of policy is the systematic use of feedback. Decision makers have always been affected to some extent by current evidence of the success or failure of their programs. Today the search for information is deliberate, and it is systematically incorporated into the decision process.

Incoming information is adapted to the intelligence and appraisal components of a decision process, and in turn all other components may be affected (promotion, prescription, invocation, application, termination). In the strictest sense, feedback is part of the appraisal function. It is the gathering and processing of information required to assess the degree to which policies have been put into effect and to assign provisional responsibility for the result.

Part of policy formation is planning to obtain the data required for appraisal. Arrangements must be made in advance if observers are to be stationed at the most advantageous positions, and if the most informative records are to be kept. As new records are fed into the system it becomes evident what revisions ought to be introduced. In addition to changed operating procedures it often is evident that conceptual maps or models require modification, whether they refer to goals, trends, conditions, projections, or alternatives. Information relating to appraisal refers to events internal to decision and to the impacts of decision.

The Internal Process of Decision

The act of appraisal starts with descriptions of trend, since appraisals are concerned with events that begin with policy commitments. The question is whether or not post-commitment events conform to the goals and objectives of policy. On the basis of trend information it is possible to impute responsibility for subsequent events to officials or structures. The head of an administrative agency is formally responsible for conformity or deviation. Since realistic analysis must go beyond that imputed to effective responsibility, it must discover the degree to which official actions have contributed to success or stood in the way.

Causal questions require scientific models that refer to two sets of conditioning factors: intradecisional and extradecisional. Competent investigation may show, for instance, that although an agency must bear imputed responsibility for a shortfall in housing starts, the legislature or the Ministry of Finance failed to supply the money necessary to achieve the policy goal. Such factors are intradecisional.

Analysis of trends may warrant the formulation of a scientific model asserting that the formal path of policy agreement and execution is smooth if the following conditions are met: (1) key legislative, bureaucratic and military figures come to an informal understanding in support of particular decisions and of the allocation of authority and control in the decision process itself; and (2) the essential conditions for policy execution are present in both the natural and social environments.

An appropriate scientific model outlines both informal and formal routines, confirms these interdeterminative conditions in relevant past situations, projects the routines into the future, examines the degree of confirmation in current feedback data, revises the model accordingly, and implies an amended projection of the future.

Recent feedback results may show that flood damage has been less than anticipated. Since the drainage system has been altered, it is reasonable to assume that intensities of demand for improvement will drop off. The fundamental scientific model remains unchanged if it postulated that intensities of demand vary directly with elite perceptions of vulnerability. Reduced threat of flood implies diminished elite demand.

Decision Impact

Possibly the improved drainage system can be explained as an impact of past decisions in the context (defined to include the natural as well as the social configuration). The explanatory model of decision impact—evolved from past cases—may assert that impacts are high: (1) if elite elements support particular decisions and structures of decision; (2) if the elite have or can obtain the technical facilities required to give effect to decisions; and (3) if the non-elite are supportive or acquiescent.

Current feedback may confirm the explanatory model and also provide data about the realization of goals and objectives that suggests the wisdom of reordering priorities and resource allocations. In view of the degree to which the danger of flooding has been reduced by the new system of drainage, it can be proposed that other objectives receive higher priority and larger resource allocations. Moreover, it may be organizationally efficient to disband the task force assembled to put through the drainage program and either transfer or eliminate personnel.

The salient generalization for our purposes is that feedback may be used: (1) to change the immediate policies and structures of a decision process; (2) to add to or modify the description of trends in the immediate or in larger contexts; (3) to revise explanatory models that account for interdeterminative routines in the immediate arena (or in a wider set of arenas); (4) to alter the projections relating to the local and to more inclusive contexts; (5) to re-evaluate the priorities among goals and objectives in the immediate or in more comprehensive settings. We are asserting that current feedback potentially contributes to a configuration that covers particular policy contexts and theoretical models specific to the five intellectual tasks and to the basic conceptual map of social process.

The Emphasis on Specification

If theoretical models are to be related to particular contexts and revised in the light of fresh information, abstract terms must receive specific meanings. The conceptual map of social process refers to participants who seek to optimize values (preferred outcomes) through institutions interacting with resources. Specifiers of participants and resources are relatively easy to select. Values and institutions are double reference categories in that a short, inclusive list of value terms facilitates the making of comparisons across boundaries in time and space. To use an approximate parallel, the value terms are like the cross-hairs in the sights of some rifles and photographic apparatus. The location of any detail can be perceived in reference to them, and comparable details in other situations can be described by using the hairs as a frame of reference. Any context can be compared with any other by classifying the total flow of interaction according to the fixed list of value terms, and by keeping general definitions constant. The list of "institutions" (and of institutional practices) can be extended indefinitely.

A step towards highly specific indicators is the introduction of definitions to guide the interpretation of values and institutions. These definitions stand between the most general statements and the most particular indicators. The relevant procedures may be exemplified in part by reproducing a table of definitions originally prepared for the SEADAG Development Administration Panel (January 1972) with the assistance of Professors Montgomery, Lerner and Braibanti (though they are not to be held accountable for the final result). The brief definitions and examples are intended to suggest how a short list of value-institution categories in a conceptual map can be employed to provide a frame of reference for more detailed definitions and for progressively more particular specifications of each item. (Types of indicators will be considered later.)

Fundamental to the conception of development is the investment of values in ways that directly embody the goals of development or are perceived as compatible with them. It is worth reiterating that analyses of a process called development must be made from explicit observational standpoints. A corollary is that more than one analysis can be made of the same national, transnational, or subnational situation.

We postulate that the overriding "goals for the investment of values" are compatible with, and instrumental of, the progressive realization of human dignity as outlined in the Universal Declaration of Human Rights (and cognate documents of an authoritative character). The left hand column of table 10.1 refers to the values to be invested. The right hand columns list the values for which the investments are made. (The latter are "scope" values; the former are the "base" values employed as means.) The presentation assumes that a designated value is the principal, though not the exclusive, target of investment. Obviously each value can serve as a base for all values, including itself. The brief ex—amples are given to stimulate the reader to think of equivalent details in the context most appropriate to his own problem.

The examples are positive rather than negative, and in practice must be augmented to include disinvestment as well as investment. A further limitation is that organized and unorganized activities are not treated separately, although for many purposes it is important to distinguish between the two. (For instance, quality of life may be defined as a profile of individual experiences.)

We note further that the "goals of development administration" are understood as Professor John Montgomery has defined them for us. It is clear that a satisfactory formulation must specify the changes in individual behavior with sufficient definiteness (and tentativeness) to guide administrative judgment in planning programs and appraising results.

Behavioral indicators of such changes would include evidence of acceptance of those norm standards (or prescriptions) required by modernization which must be incorporated into the perspectives and operations of individuals acting in their various roles and also as total persons. The specifications include the roles specialized to value "shaping" and "sharing" in the various sectors.

In the *power* sector, for instance, officials are among the shapers, and the ordinary citizen is principally a sharer (even though everyone performs both types of function in varying degrees). In the *enlighten-ment* sector the shapers include scientific observers and "gossip special-ists" while the sharers are less active audience members. Producers are the *wealth* shapers; consumers are sharers. *Well-being* shapers are physi-cians and medicine men; sharers include patients. The shapers of *skill* acquire proficiency; the sharers of skill performances enjoy the activity and its fruits. The shapers of *affection* outcomes include those who form families; they usually receive affection. The *respect* shapers in-clude ceremonial and high status figures who guide the conferring of recognition. *Rectitude* shapers—such as priests—guide the formation and application of the criteria of responsible conduct; sharers are objects of evaluation. In general, the shapers of any value outcome are relatively specialized in the activity or status involved. The sharers are less special-ized and do not "cumulate." Any value can be treated as a base for fuller realization of the same or another value.

Further, the formulation must specify that the norms are held with sufficient intensity to result in the investment of time, labor and capital (or more generally of all values).

To invest is to engage in value shaping by employing values as bases to obtain further value accumulation, rather than to enjoy them. The following are brief examples:

Power is invested in modernizing if an official risks his position to introduce a new administrative procedure. *Enlightenment* is invested if scientific knowledge is used to foster innovation in communications, for instance, rather than allowed to "go to waste" in the role of a traditional gentleman-scholar. *Wealth* investment includes all outlays to improve the technology of production. *Well-being* is invested when physical safety is imperiled in improving the care of the ill. *Skill* is invested when artistic capability is used to make modern buildings appealing. *Affection* is invested when friendships are cultivated in order to assist a modernization program, or old friends and relatives are drawn in. *Respect* is invested when an honored name is given to endorse an innovating project. *Rectitude* is invested when a religious or moral leader influences his followers to cooperate in modernizing projects.

Note further that development in a context usually postulate continuation of the context-wide decision process in a given situation. Hence the formulation of development goals includes effective norms of conflict avoidance and resolution (as Professor Hahm put it) by the use of practices that keep the body politic intact.

Other indicators of modernizing behavior may be formulated to include the toleration of peaceful supersession of the context-wide decision process (often to avoid or put an end to severe conflict).

In some cases goals may be formulated to tolerate coercive division of the area.

Further, the context-boundaries may be kept intact, while coercive means of conflict resolution are used for revolutionary and modernizing change.

It is worth emphasizing that all PEWBSARD sectors have "arena equivalents" in the arena in which the inclusive power decisions are made for the sector. Organizations are often relatively specialized to one or another sector, and have internal arenas (and also interact in arenas with other organizations). The following are examples of associations other than power with arena equivalents: societies of research scientists, agricultural cooperatives, medicare associations, teachers' organizations, mothers' associations, heroes of war and labor, and temple or shrine organizations.

Table 10.1
The Investment of Values

Values Invested	For Which Values							
	P	E	W	B	S	A	R	D
P Power	1	9	17	25	33	41	49	57
E Enlightenment	2	10	18	26	34	42	50	58
W Wealth	3	11	19	27	35	43	51	59
B well-Being	4	12	20	28	36	44	52	60
S Skill	5	13	21	29	37	45	53	61
A Affection	6	14	22	30	38	46	54	62
R Respect	7	15	23	31	39	47	55	63
D rectituDe	8	16	24	32	40	48	56	64

Investment for Power

1   P for P   continual broadening of participation in important decisions (nurturing a durably wide decision process)

2   E for P   campaigns to clarify the "nation-building" advantages of modernization

3   W for P   use of resources to induce and reward enlarged participation in decision processes (for example, offers of expenditure on request of hitherto isolated villages)

4   B for P   physical fitness exercises as a public service (preparedness drills with modern tactics and instruments)

5   S for P   training in skills of political action for hitherto passive elements in population (keeping records, drafting applications, and so forth)

6   A for P   mobilizing of popular figures to widen participation in politics and government

7   R for P   mobilizing high ranking figures to widen scope of political action

8   D for P   reinforcement of political action by ethical and religious figures

Investment for Enlightenment

9   P for E   political campaigns to organize support for scientific research (for example, in agriculture)

10   E for E   research work on a cumulative program of investigation

11   W for E   investment in enlarging capability for public information (for example, transistor radios)

12   B for E   improvement of health and protective services for those engaged in research (for example, hazardous expeditions)

Table 10.1 (continued)

13	S for E	training in the operation of mass media facilities
14	A for E	encourage love of modern higher learning by personal interest (by cultivation of friendship with promising students)
15	R for E	encourage recognition of importance of new scientific knowledge by traditional men of knowledge (by recruiting traditional ritualists for scientific demonstrations)
16	D for E	cultivate ethics of enlightenment (no unacknowledged source of knowledge)

Investment for Wealth

17	P for W	forced savings and resource allocation
18	E for W	research for industrial development
19	W for W	capital allocations for roads and other basic facilities
20	B for W	mass health programs in industrial plants to cut down absenteeism and turnover
21	S for W	training of labor force in occupational skills
22	A for W	enlistment of positive cooperation of family enterprises
23	R for W	select economic change agents from respected groups
24	D for W	mobilize religious sanctions for economic innovation (including technical changes on temple lands)

Investment for Well-being

25	P for B	regulations adopted and applied for public health
26	E for B	clarify modern conception of disease and some basic implications for hygiene
27	W for B	investments in health facilities
28	B for B	age group recruitment to build health for later years (for example, infant and child care; programs with pupils and students)
29	S for B	encourage supplementation of traditional by modern skills of health care and accident prevention (for example, retrain midwives)
30	A for B	love of family utilized to motivate modern programs; love of body versus disregard or self-damage (encourage home sanitary precautions and early recognition and referral of a problem)
31	R for B	fitness achievement as basis for recognition (granting awards to individuals and groups)
32	D for B	emphasizing ethical and religious basis for modern health programs (adapt traditional shrines and temples)

Table 10.1 (continued)

Investment for Skill

33	P for S	government sanctions used to provide educational opportunities in village, and so on
34	E for S	research on skill needs of emerging polity and spread of understanding
35	W for S	provide resources for skill acquisition as a form of self-expression (for example, in the arts)
36	B for S	enhancement of environmental conditions for acquisition and exercise of skills
37	S for S	improving technique for teaching the skills required by modern technique (teacher training, for example)
38	A for S	transfer fraternal spirit (identity) of traditional crafts to adaptation and innovation of modern skills
39	R for S	increase recognition for excellence in new methods (for example, awards overcoming any barriers of social discrimination by using respected figures and occasions)
40	D for S	theological or ethical encouragement of responsible behavior in acquiring and utilizing skill for worthy purposes (dissemination of "work ethic")

Investment for Affection

41	P for A	public authorities encourage congenial relations by prompt intervention or avoidance of abrasive conflicts that grow out of modernization (that is, rapid follow-up of complaints, mediation)
42	E for A	research and dissemination of results of examining some traditional (or modern) practices of expressing affection (for example, continuing in extended family domiciles or in independent family units)
43	W for A	develop facilities to provide affection re-enforcement for those who engage in modernization or are affected by it (clubs for strangers, child care centers for working parents, care of orphans, clubs for old persons with superannuated skills)
44	B for A	practices about care of body and mind that show concern for lover, friends, and neighbors (personal hygiene)
45	S for A	disseminate arts of love and friendship that produce no harmful consequences
46	A for A	cultivation of friendly approach as a hostility prevention and reduction measure (selection of friendly agents, training in approaches interpreted as friendly)
47	R for A	equalize affection relations by razing barriers of discrimination (multiply cross-group occasions)
48	D for A	ethical and religious reinforcement of new norms in choosing objects of love and strategies of expressing love (for example, approval of contraception by cult leaders)

Table 10.1 (continued)

Investment for Respect

49	P for R	selection of modernizing agents of change in power positions (changing elite composition)
50	E for R	clarify and justify new respect relationships for modernizing agents (campaigns to explain how reduction of old social barriers allows more members of the community to win recognition for display of latent qualities)
51	W for R	use of resources to transpose or reformulate respect for modernization (memorial parks, buildings, monuments for modernizers)
52	B for R	dramatic and remarkable cures arouse admiration of modern medicine
53	S for R	arouse respect by demonstrations of excellence in skills of self-expression (new art form exhibits—music, painting, and so forth)
54	A for R	family expressions of affection for those who achieve respected modernizing ideas (reconciliation of temporary alienations)
55	R for R	enlargement and specification of new respect symbols (older respect leaders participate in recognition of modernizing role by crossing old barriers)
56	D for R	ethical and religious reinforcement of respect for those who live up to obligations related to new technique (mentions in obituaries or equivalents)

Investment for Rectitude

57	P for D	sanctioning and correction of deviation from modernizing norms (anti-corruption, anti-nepotism)
58	E for D	campaigns to clarify advantages of modernizing codes of personal and group conduct (asserted to expedite nation building)
59	W for D	use of resources on behalf of distributive justice (voluntary redistribution of land as moral and pious act)
60	B for D	use of health and recreational activities explicitly linked to modernizing norms (girl guides movement)
61	S for D	use of modernized rituals (recitation from memory Sun Yat-sen's Three Principles—or an equivalent; new instruments employed in ceremonies)
62	A for D	family encourages modern careers as ancestral obligation (permits child to leave home for distant school)
63	R for D	doctrinal reinterpretation of norms of right conduct to sanction modernization (factions or cults propagating new obligations to master the new)
64	D for D	introduction and exemplification of new standard codes for civil servants

---

One important goal of development administration, then, is the generation of opportunities for the behavioral modernization of individuals and organizations, and the creation of an environment favorable to affirmative response to those opportunities.

Principles of Content and Procedure

The definitions carry us toward choosing detailed specifications that employ numbers, tables, graphs, maps, equations, and the like. These selections have the fundamental purpose of organizing the focus of attention of decision makers. Two sets of guiding principles are in point. Principles of content refer to manifest meaning; principles of procedure deal with the ordering of content for deliberative purposes. The value categories are defined as relevant content when they are distinguished according to goal, trend, condition, projection, or alternative.

The five problem-solving tasks (goal, trend, condition, projection, alternative) provide an agenda for ordering the focus of attention. They can be most effectively applied in "spirals," that is, by returning time and again to all five tasks. New detail and novel relationships emerge continually.

A basic principle of procedure emphasizes the differences in perceptual style that distinguish decision makers from one another. As a rule style differences are the result of previous exposure to distinctive environments of culture, class, interest, personality, or level of crisis. Those who have been socialized in a peasant culture, for instance, are less dependent than urbanites on print. The same observation applies to members of the lower urban classes. Presumably engineers (a well-educated interest group) are quick perceivers of numbers and equations. In many societies personality and cultural factors combine to evolve a highly verbal and imaginative group of poets, story tellers, and oratorical leaders.

The significance of contrasting perceptual styles for decision is apparent. Unless relevant message content is made available in several styles, degrees of effective participation will be adversely affected; unless a clarifying order of presentation is followed, judgment will be less realistic than the participants are capable of making.

The contextual principle is a fundamental guide to the strategists of decision management. The contextual principle affirms that every problem is considered most advantageously when the entire social process is kept in view. A comprehensive and continually updated map of the relevant social process is essential.

Procedures are required that bring the pertinent contours of the context to the notice of all participants, and do so in ways that facilitate the formation of the most realistic judgment of which they are capable.

A generalized agenda for the consideration of a problem under "no crisis" conditions may be phrased as follows:

1. Examine alternative formulations of the problem in terms of the discrepancies between goals and current or prospective states of affairs; consider proposed solutions according to probable impact on the social context, and the benefits, burdens and risks of acceptance (including continuation of present policy); devise and execute strategies of positive or negative commitment;

2. At each step bring to the focus of attention of each audience-participant a comprehensible and vivid presentation of the relevant context; subsequently modify presentations to include pertinent detail on matters perceived as crucial.

The agenda proposes substantially the same sequence for all audience-participants, ranging from persons having the most inclusive to those with the most fragmented view, and from participants having the most to the least expert contribution to make to the decision process. It might be assumed that experienced leaders in a body politic would have an overview of the situation so inclusive and realistic that little effort need be expended to present an updated map of the whole. Such assumptions are partly false, since change is unceasing. It is also true that some social contexts are traditionally neglected, including regions and centers that are extremely remote or nearby.

Part of the strategy of decision calls for the use of presentation techniques that mobilize interest without doing violence to the available or probable facts. For instance, exhibits may be presented in a "policy room" (a war room) that identify emerging problems in every value-institution sector. The following are brief reminders:

P (voting continues low)

E (remote peasantry increasingly bored with official broadcasts)

W (more seed grain consumed)

B ("filth diseases" resurgent)

S (teachers residing less often in community during scholastic year)

A (family quarrels increasing)

R (public edifices more defaced and run down)

D (monks again attacking technical innovations)

A timing problem is when to introduce what degree of detail in the local centers; and how to involve unofficial local organizations in contributing to their own "map and chart rooms" (decision seminar, social planetarium).

Principles of content and procedure apply to every official or unofficial arena. One strategic aim is line-drawing between what is included in or excluded from attention, whether the arena is specialized to intelligence (planning), promotion (campaigns), prescription (legislating), invocation (policing), application (most administrative operations), termination (land compensation boards), or appraisal (inquiries into efficiency).

In conventional court procedure in our society, for instance, the positive function (of inclusion) is expedited by such procedures as:

(1) presenting at the start a clear statement of the conflicting claims to be disposed of by the decision maker; (2) providing for a preview of the modes of justification of the conflicting claims; (3) providing for a decision maker who is deemed to be competent and impartial (jury selection); (4) arranging for skilled counsel for the disadvantaged; (5) making pertinent data available to all concerned; (6) permitting independent inquiries to decision makers; and (7) isolation from competing objects of attention.

The arrangements to exclude negative matters from attention are usually most prominent in discussions of decision process. These procedures include: (1) exclusion of "irrelevant and immaterial" matter as evidence; (2) prohibitions on inflammatory statements likely to arouse passions that interfere with good judgment; and (3) protection from pressures on decision makers or other participants in the performance of their duties.

The Balancing of Verbal and Nonverbal Presentations

With regard to the presentations intended to reach the attention of decision makers, a tactical question is how to achieve an optimum balance of the verbal and the nonverbal. Since perceptual style differs, it is to be assumed that effective modes of presentation differ from one another. The results of laboratory research are suggestive. They are, however, of limited transferability to decision arenas, since the arenas are concerned with social practices, and laboratory work is principally focused on variables. The variables are arranged in complex patterns to constitute a practice, and we know that the role of a patterned whole cannot be adequately predicted by observing the behavior of parts. Practices interact with practices; that is, those who participate in practice x^1 are continually engaged in an explicit or implicit process of evaluating x^1 in reference to x^2 (et al.) as a net contribution to the value position of the participants.

The strategy of search for more satisfactory knowledge about presentation includes: (1) selection of a time period (and assets other than time) in which presentations can be prepared at varying levels of cost (in money and other values); (2) selection of the decision makers in specified arenas who are to be exposed to presentations; (3) the choice of the criteria to be applied to impacts internal or external to policy processes. Several sequences of inquiry may be followed: (a) The time period and the available assets for preparatory activities may be varied while (2) and (3) are held as constant as possible; (b) the attributes of decision makers and arenas may be systematically changed while (1) and (3) are constant; (c) appraisals may be shifted, while (1) and (2) are varied.

Although the research strategy outlined above is well-known, it is important to recognize that the actual procedures of investigation are more likely to resemble a prototype or an intervention than an experiment. Prototypes or interventions are located in real world situations and compare institutional practices with one another.

Combinations of words and non-words can be classified and varied in many ways. A working classification is as follows: (1) abstract terms and definitions, (2) verbally described cases, (3) charts (and tables) with little emphasis on cases, (4) charts (and tables) oriented in reference to cases, (5) mathematical models, (6) static pictures, (7) moving pictures (with/without color), (8) scale models, (9) dramatic representations involving individual and group interactions more fully than in (7). A program of investigation may be planned to bring diverging groups to the same level of comprehension, if possible, by skillful management of presentation patterns.

Quantitative Specification

The preceding discussion has underlined the importance of making conceptual maps sufficiently specific to aid policy formation and execution. The significant characteristic of a usable map is the provision of a comprehensive image in which the principal contours of the social context are explicit. The contours draw attention to value-institution sectors and to the features most pertinent to goals, trends, conditions, projections, and alternatives. We have glanced at the use of definitions and of principles of content and procedure as means of arranging the focus of attention in ways that best facilitate the task of decision.

We have had little to say about the choice of quantifiable specifiers, of indices amenable to measurement. References have been made in passing to quantified information. No direct stress has been put on the systematic search for social indicators of sufficient measurability or comprehensiveness to guide the preparation of an exhaustive counterpart of a conceptual map in a selected text.

Deferred discussion does not imply that measurement is unimportant. On the contrary, as will be demonstrated, our concern with measurement is substantial. The problem, as usual in the study or management of human affairs, is how to prevent the abuse of an instrument of enormous potential relevance.

For instance, one should not expect to find complete measures of the fundamental terms employed in a conceptual map. The function of conceptual terms is to provide the observer-participant with a guide to his focus of attention, enabling him to become oriented towards the details of any given situation and to perceive likeness and difference in reference to other contexts. The indicators are cross-cultural to a limited degree (as between literate and nonliterate societies, for instance). Index-instability is a consequence of the shiftability of contexts through time, which implies that today's index is open to revision, since it is a detail, and details change in relation to the whole.

Aggregate measures are especially open to abuse unless their limitations are continually emphasized. The GNP is a case in point. Policymakers and technical experts alike have too often assumed that the gross national product provided figures in terms of which goals could be validly formulated and achievements appraised. GNP computations have not, however, routinely included resource depletion nor the side-effects of industrial accidents and disease, or of declining national unity resulting from most favorable treatment of one region over another, or of one linguistic and cultural minority over another. Even in the absence of satisfactory indicators it is obviously important to deal with such questions systematically and by explicit estimates of magnitude. With adequate procedures in the decision process, these matters can be kept continually at the focus of attention and judgment.

When supplemented by other forms of social accounting and where appropriately subaggregated, the GNP can be less misleading in the future than it has been in the past. The subaggregation can be according to value categories, selected institutions, participants, or other salient categories. The pluralization of development goals presumably will be stimulated by modes of social accounting designed in order to subordinate money units to other units, and to give prominence to multiple values.

The "Quality of Life" slogan signifies a noteworthy change in the perspectives of many leaders (and many of the led) in the contemporary world. It reflects cumulative disenchantment with the disruptive consequences of economic development when interpreted as the science-based technology of highly capitalized industry. An alternative conception of Balanced or Selective development seems to be making its way in some countries of "advanced" or "advancing" technology. The quality of life has gained meaning in reaction against the continuing miseries of many as these deprivations have been dramatized in the phase that Daniel Lerner has made distinctively his own, "the revolution of rising frustrations."

The affirmative implications are that priority is given to investment in middle-sized industrial units that maintain their anchorage in village and town complexes. A new emphasis on cultural creativity encourages the linkage between the new and enlarging world and the rich legacies of expression in all the arts. Expressive development requires spontaneity and joy in the creative act in the double role of artist and audience.

We do not ignore the challenge of seeing how far it is possible to go in evolving measurable indicators that may be applied, if desired, to samples of every human interaction. Specific indicators may be chosen from among the primary elements of an act (or interaction). Four classes of events constitute the elements: (1) symbols, or subjective events; (2) signs, or somatic or environmental resources specialized to communication (words, gestures, print); (3) deeds, or nonsign behaviors with no direct involvement of the resource environment; (4) nonsign resources and resource manipulations (ploughing).

Whether an act is classed as a value or a practice it can be described as a pattern composed of the four primary elements. These arrangements are the style of an act, whether individual or collective. An example is machine voting in our society. The symbols are the subjective events involved in planning to go to the polls and giving support to Democrats or Republicans. Signs are the movements and the environing resources specific to communication (sounds, printouts). Deeds are nonsign movements (walking to and from the booth). The resources are the nonsign features of the environment (the balloting machines).

Indicators of resources, deeds, and signs can be observed directly and recorded. The symbols (when they are the subjective events of other persons) are not. For many purposes, however, we are accustomed to interpret the messages transmitted by signs as satisfactory indicators of intentions and interpretations. The referents of a sign are meanings or references. The implication is that simple indicators of one element are often sufficient for descriptive purposes. All four elements are of possible relevance as components of a composite indicator.

Consider what is involved in measuring outcome events, which are the culminating interactions among participants in social process. Most generally, we perceive that an act is describable according to direction and intensity. Direction is the potential completion of the act, classified according to the identity of participants and their value demands. Intensity is stress toward completion (including the completions).

If every interaction were spelled out by the participants it would communicate directions, their identities and demands (in value-institution terms). Act intensities would be communicated in statements, such as declarations of determination, and exemplified in deeds and resource manipulations. (Individual pairs or macroaggregates may be the interactors.)

A spelled-out interaction between A and B includes the following: A's statements of direction ("I am a member of the elite of x negotiating with another elite member of x"; "I am demanding value 1(wealth) in the institutional form of a transfer of land"; "I am offering value 2(power) in the institutional form of an ambassadorial appointment").

B's statement of direction ("I am a member of the elite of x negotiating with another elite member of x"; "I am demanding value 2(power) in the institutional form of an ambassadorial appointment"; "I am offering value 1(wealth) in the institutional form of a transfer of land").

A's statement of intensity ("I am determined to obtain an enlarged landed property at once").

B's statement of intensity ("I am determined to get an ambassadorial appointment").

A's exemplification of intensity (A is spending hours persuading B; A has arranged the appointment).

B's exemplification of intensity (B is spending hours persuading A; B has arranged the transfer).

The procedures of content analysis can be used to measure the identity statements of A and B. A single assertion during the time period of the interaction may be enough to establish identity. Intensity measures per time interval include frequency counts of evocative words. For measuring deeds, the hours of time interacting or preparing for negotiation may suffice. Land resources may be described in terms of relative size (for example, in the top twenty) or treated as a hypothetical sale summarized in money units. The ambassadorship may be described according to the number of equivalent appointments available in the political structure (the top ten). Weights may be assigned to statements of determination, deeds and resources.

A suggestive approach to exchange categories and exchange ratios (prices) is to describe all (or a sample) of the outcomes in which A and B are engaged with one another during a given period in a relevant social context; or to describe all the interactions of A, B, and of other participants with all the others.

The example given above does not exhaust the categories relevant to the transaction mentioned. Microanalysis may demonstrate that values other than wealth and power were at stake even though these two were most prominently in the minds of A and B. By obtaining an enlarged estate the wealth position of A was increased; also his respect position. Respect changes are measurable by interviews (questionnaires) in which respondents rank themselves and others as socially equal to, or below "my" position. Perhaps the respect position of B was also enhanced in the transaction. The prestige units that were given and received were the "potential evaluations by the social environment" in degrees of standing (status).

Further analysis may indicate that A's rectitude position was improved in the transaction with B, because the property included a holy place and A became its revered protector. If it is desired to be more explicit about rectitude, proper investigation may show that the sacred places of the country may be ranked in order of holiness. Once again, B indulged A in rectitude by transferring to him the means of eliciting the appropriate predisposition from the social environment. B may have lost some of his former rectitude status in the transaction.

Additional analysis of our largely hypothetical case may show that B sought the appointment from A, in large part, as a means of perfecting his expert knowledge of the foreign country to which he was accredited and improving his skills in a foreign tongue as well as in the art of diplomacy. In quantitative terms B may now have the possibility of becoming one of the top national figures with expert knowledge of foreign countries. He could be ranked in terms of enlightenment and skill (as seen by professionals).

Offsetting these advantages, B may have added risks to his personal safety and health (well-being) in a degree that can be estimated from casualty figures. Interviewing, content analysis, and participant observation techniques may show that B suffered a value deprivation in political terms that may offset the power potential of the appointment. Ambassadors are often viewed as of doubtful loyalty to the nation. (Intensive study of B and his colleagues may show that the opposite is actually the case.)

Studies of transactions within a value-institution sector may expose the complex and changing ratios that differentiate one pattern of pre-outcome, outcome, and post-outcome interactions from another. Transactions that include two or more sectors enlarge enormously the possibilities of comprehending how a developing society works. Pricing, bartering, and mutualism can be seen in appropriate perspective as partially satisfactory institutional practices by which all values are continually shaped and shared in a changing map of social process. Outcomes involve degree of competition and conflict.

The updated map of the world community, or of its component territorial and pluralized groupings, may answer the traditional question: Who gets what when and how? The participants ultimately to be compared to one another in reference to all values include the assisting and the assisted nations, the elite, mid-elite, and rank and file of each nation, the geographical regions of each country, the varying centers and regions of population density, the groups of varying language and culture, and of biological characteristics. By distinguishing between value and institution, it is feasible to appraise the role of institutions as value shapers and sharers for the few or the many and to maintain an exploratory perspective toward all the ideological and technological complexes functioning in the world community.

INDEX